AF342151

THE
FERRY

a drive-through history 1850 – 2010

Published by:
Ferry Publications, PO Box 33, Ramsey, Isle of Man IM99 4LP
Tel: +44 (0) 1624 898445   Fax: +44 (0) 1624 898449
E-mail: ferrypubs@manx.net   Website: www.ferrypubs.co.uk

Bruce Peter & Philip Dawson
Edited by Trevor Barrett

Editor's Foreword

This new abridged edition of the original 'encyclopedic' work of the same title by Bruce Peter and Philip Dawson, which was published by Ferry Publications in November 2010, is intended for more general rather than academic and research readership and aims to reach all those with any interest in the development of sea transport, and particularly ferries.

Although it economises on some of the more technical and often complex aspects of ferry design and innovations, as it does on the corporate politics and upheavals of ferry owners and operators, it includes reference to every ferry described by Peter and Dawson in the original work, albeit here in terms often more biased towards passenger and vehicle facilities, and to the travel experience itself, than to the nitty gritty of design, construction, layout and operation.

So whatever your interest in this increasingly crucial, competitive and fascinating aspect of global seaborne transport, this new shorter edition of The Ferry is intended to take it onboard. Ferries, operators, architects, designers, ports, routes, services and even disasters are all here – from the pioneering Leviathan of 1850 to the giant ro-pax ships of today.

Produced and designed by Ferry Publications trading as Lily Publications Ltd

PO Box 33, Ramsey, Isle of Man, British Isles, IM99 4LP

Tel: +44 (0) 1624 898446   Fax: +44 (0) 1624 898449

www.ferrypubs.co.uk   EMail: info@lilypublications.co.uk

Printed and bound by Gomer Press Ltd., Wales, UK +44 (0) 1559 362371 © Lily Publications June 2011

All rights reserved. No part of this book or any of the photographs may be reproduced or transmitted in any form or by any means, electronic or mechanical, including photocopying, recording or by any means of information storage and retrieval system without written permission from the publisher, save only for brief extracts which may be used solely for the purpose of review.

Contents

CHAPTER ONE

The Cinderella Myth

Generally speaking, ferries are perceived as the Cinderellas of passenger shipping – unglamorous working vessels whose regular comings and goings pass without comment and whose increasingly vital contribution is rarely acknowledged. Yet dispensing with the roles that these vessels perform would have an immediate impact on our everyday lives.

Most of Britain's trade is with EU countries and many of the commodities we buy arrive by ferry or container ship. If you tallied up the capacity in lane metres of ferries docking at British ports within a 24-hour period, you'd come up with a figure almost equivalent to a queue of traffic stretching bumper to bumper from London to Sheffield.

Thus there can be no doubting that ferries are essential elements of our 21st-century integrated transport logistics systems. Ferries are also ingenious examples of floating technology and amongst the most complex and sophisticated of modern ships. Only a ferry typically combines into one effective and cohesive whole the roles of passenger liner, cruise ship, cargo vessel, car carrier and (sometimes) ice-breaker.

The creation of a new ferry from drawing board to reality is a challenging and highly technical process which takes years and involves the skills of naval architects, designers and engineers. There are many factors to consider, from the number of passengers and vehicles to be carried to the national and international safety regulations and conventions with which the new ship must comply in order to be registered.

Unlike aircraft, which are more or less generic, the majority of ferries are tailored to suit particular roles, to serve specific ports and to operate mainly in certain sea conditions. So other key factors coming into the equation at the earliest concept stages include the required operating speed, how often the vessel will be bunkered and provisioned, and – in terms of helping to determine the ships's overall dimensions – the navigating constraints of the waterways, harbours, quays and linkspans she will use in the various stages of cruising, turning, berthing and loading. Ferries also need to be relatively light in weight, stable (both when intact and damaged), capable of operating reliably in all weathers (except the occasional and most extreme gales), and able to accommodate sufficient passengers, vehicles and cargo to be commercially viable in an increasingly competitive market. Every new ferry represents a considerable financial risk and must be designed and built to optimise payload – efficiency which makes sound economic and environmental sense.

Only when these many primary concerns have been defined is it possible to consider the details of what the ship will actually look like when built and how she will be laid out internally in terms of cargo holds, trailer decks, passenger and crew accommodation, propulsive and auxiliary machinery, fuel and ballast tanks, stores areas and safety equipment.

In undertaking this long process, individual shipyards and

Illustrating the pleasure of short-sea travel, passengers line the **Stena Danica**'s deck rail as she leaves Gothenburg for Frederikshavn in the early 1990s. The **Stena Germanica** and the **Stena Carrier** await evening sailings to Germany. (Bruce Peter)

Top left: A British ferry interior of the 1970s: the Scotia Bar on Sealink's Stranraer-Larne Irish Sea ferry *Ailsa Princess*, designed by Ward & Austin with a 'lunar landscape' ceiling. *(Bruce Peter collection)*

Top right: A First Class cabin on the London & North Eastern Railway's Harwich-Hook of Holland overnight ferry *Arnhem* of 1947 shows a standard of design similar to ocean liners of the same era. *(Matthew Murtland collection)*

Above left: Estuarial and coastal railway-owned steamers of the late-Victorian and Edwardian were designed to impress - as the Caledonian Steam Packet Company's 1889-built *Galatea* demonstrates. *(Bruce Peter collection)*

Above right: Manoeuvring a car on the turntable of a Dover Strait passenger vessel in the early-1950s at that time cars to the Continent were mainly loaded by crane, then manhandled by stevedores - a time-consuming and costly process. *(Bruce Peter collection)*

Right: From the latter nineteenth century onwards, passenger journeys to the Continent began with a ride on the boat train. Here, 'The Hook Continental' prepares to leave London Liverpool Street in the latter 1950s. *(Bruce Peter collection)*

Baltic cruise ferries carry vast numbers all year round. Their ice-breaking capabilities are sometimes put to the test in severe winter weather, as Viking line's **Mariella** demonstrates here in the Stockholm archipelago in March 2010. *(Bruce Peter)*

naval architects inevitably develop their own favoured design solutions – sometimes inspired by rivals' innovations – but the principles governing the creation of a new passenger ferry are the same.

The short-sea ferry first emerged in the mid-nineteenth century – the height of the railway age – when society and culture were changing rapidly. The expanding railway network was arguably the most potent force in the modernisation of the western world, delivering goods to warehouses and shops in unprecedented quantities – the dawn of mass consumerism.

The era's emergent social hierarchies could afford to take holidays, and the trains and steamers provided their means of escape. But as railways originated in mining areas, the early railway companies had something of an image problem in persuading the upwardly mobile that train travel was safe and respectable. The answer? Perpetuating the design language of the stagecoach – in the shape of First Class carriages.

As the railways reached the coast, packet steamer services to offshore islands and to the near Continent were introduced. The term 'packet' denoted that these ships also carried packets of Royal Mail. In layout, service and dining options (especially in First Class), the steamers were miniaturised versions of deep-sea ocean liners, an approach soon copied in the interiors of Continental Wagon-Lits and British Pullman trains connecting the major European cities.

On the Clyde estuary, several railway fleets and a number of private entrepreneurs competed for business. The majority of their vessels were paddle-steamers with lofty funnels and named after royal and aristocratic ladies such as the Duchess of Rothesay and the Marchioness of Lorne.

The roll on-roll off (ro-ro) ferry also had its origins in Scotland. The pioneering *Leviathan* of 1850 was designed to carry freight wagons efficiently across the Firth of Forth between Granton, near Edinburgh, and Burntisland in Fife. Her highly innovative design enabled her to move freight in great quantities and with minimal labour, signalling the way ahead for seaborne transport and, in time, establishing the ro-ro ferry as an efficient, highly cost-effective vessel for the carriage of passengers, vehicles and goods by sea.

Aesthetically, when compared with a traditional ocean liner or modern tropical cruise ship, the typical ferry may at a glance appear banal – even ugly. Too short, too broad, too bluff, surrounded by broad rubbing strakes and the functional paraphernalia of modern marine safety legislation: modern ferries do not – as a rule – equate with traditionally-understood conceptions of romance and beauty. Yet they encompass a bewildering array of inventive design solutions.

Ferries are infinitely varied, each generation possessing its own design characteristics. Impressive in scale, they tower over port facilities and display intriguing details, some satisfyingly chunky and others remarkably delicate. Add to this an amazing variety of colourful liveries and bold graphic designs and it is easy to see why so many people with enquiring minds find modern ferries a fascinating phenomenon.

Moreover, in naval architecture as with many other design and engineering genre, true innovations are most often manifested in smaller and less prestigious ships for the simple reason that designers would be nervous of incorporating radically new ideas into prestigious high-profile vessels such as large warships or flagship transatlantic liners. As this book shows, many innovations in planning, construction, propulsion and passenger comfort were pioneered in ferry design.

So far as ferry design development is concerned, this book follows two main themes. One begins with barge-type vessels with entirely open vehicle decks which, between the 1900s and the 1930s, became increasingly enclosed with topsides, forecastles and superstructures resembling those of conventional passenger ships, especially when viewed side-on. Even so, their hull forms were determined by the need to maintain regularly-shaped and unobstructed vehicle decks, meaning that usually they had very pronounced knuckle-joints and belting only a couple of metres above the waterline. Typically, ferries of this kind were developed for use on high-density short crossings, often in fairly sheltered waters where the need for a large capacity and rapid loading and discharge of vehicles took precedence over the requirement for good sea-keeping characteristics.

The other and subsequent aspect of development relates to the 1930s-60s period and saw a gradual move from traditional coastal packet steamers – or small overnight passenger liners – to vessels capable of loading cars. Rather than a process of enclosure, this could be viewed as more a procedure of 'burrowing out' vehicle deck space within the constraints of typically fine-lined passenger liner hull forms.

During the first half of the twentieth century, the few cars that were carried on 'overnight' vessels were loaded by crane into forward cargo holds, or were parked on deck. Later, holds were equipped with side-hatches, through which cars could be driven directly onboard. Later still, in the early 1960s, a number of larger vessels appeared with side-loading car decks running the entire length of the hull along the centreline, usually inboard of cabins.

As ferries of this kind tended to operate on longer routes, speed was often of the essence and so, to accommodate more powerful machinery, the engine room casings cut through several decks amidships, making the provision of relatively unobstructed vehicle decks more of a challenge. One solution was to locate these high up in the hull, leaving sufficient space below for large slow-speed, direct-drive diesel engines. Another was to fit four smaller, medium-speed diesels, coupled in pairs via gearboxes to each propeller shaft. A third, rarer answer was to use V-diesels, with the pistons and cylinders angled so as not to protrude into the vehicle deck space.

The development of more compact yet powerful medium-speed engines during the 1960s enabled ferries to travel faster without sacrificing vehicle capacity, and it became typical that all ferries, whether intended for short or long crossings, should carry trucks and buses as well as cars.

A further key consideration in designing a ferry is the

The port of Gothenburg is home to Stena Line's headquarters and the company has brought the city great prosperity. Here, the funnels and superstructures of five Stena vessels dominate the skyline. *(Bruce Peter)*

Color Line's ***Superspeed 1*** and ***2*** are state-of-the-art ro-pax ferries linking Denmark and Norway. The ***Superspeed 2*** is seen departing from Hirtshals on another crossing to Larvik in October 2010. *(Bruce Peter)*

optimisation of deadweight capacity – that is, the payload a ship can carry. For naval architects, the challenge is to devise hulls with sufficient excess buoyancy to enable an optimal weight of cars, lorries, passengers and ship's stores to be transported within the parameters set out by the classification societies, as well as those of national governments and international conventions such as SOLAS (the international convention for the Safety of Life at Sea). Essentially, to enable a bigger deadweight capacity, more hull volume needs to be provided below the waterline by increasing a ship's length or breadth – but a broad, bluff vessel will be neither as comfortable in heavy seas nor as fuel-efficient as one with fine lines. Consequently, a balance must be struck, depending on the typical sea conditions in which a ferry will operate or the expected service speed.

For example, a vessel intended to cross the stormy northern North Sea at high speed will need a fine-lined hull, meaning either that some deadweight capacity has to be sacrificed or that the hull will need to be longer to compensate for the more slender fore and aftbody configurations. Yet, constructing a fine-lined hull may be more expensive than one of more regular shape and, with less internal volume, the payload will also be lower.

On the other hand, a ferry designed to serve on the Stockholm-Turku route through the Swedish and Finnish archipelagos will be relatively shorter and broader, with a more bluff forebody. To mitigate the slowing effects of this to some extent, a bulbous bow (a torpedo-shaped 'snout' fitted to the front of the hull at and below the waterline) helps to alter the amplitude of the waves ahead of the hull's entry point, lowering resistance and thus enabling the ship to sail through more ideal conditions.

Since the 1960s, the development of bulbous bows has been an important aspect of the general advancement in ferry hydrodynamics – as has the subsequent development of so-called 'duck-tail' sponsons. These slightly increase a hull's length at the stern, not only reducing drag but also providing

When displaced by new tonnage, older ferries tend to migrate either to the Mediterranean or to the Red Sea before being sold for scrap. Here, the ***Bakarat*** (ex ***Travemünde***) approaches Port Sudan with a steam-hauled train in the foreground. *(Colin Meill)*

more buoyancy and consequently an enhanced deadweight capacity.

Ferries, uniquely, can load and unload considerable weights of cargo within minutes, meaning that hidden systems of pumps work constantly to trim their hulls to maintain an even keel and uniform buoyancy. At the same time, powerful ventilation plants keep the vehicle decks free of exhaust fumes, and hydraulic systems open and close the bow and stern doors, the internal flood control doors, and the ramps which link the various vehicle deck levels and retractable platform decks.

Technology aside, ferries are also intriguing sociological phenomena. With prosperity increasing generally after the Second World War, private car ownership grew too and ferries became ever larger and better appointed – particularly overnight vessels serving routes between UK, West German and Scandinavian ports. Their modern comforts, efficient design and manoeuvrability meant that many had the potential to be redeployed as cruise ships during winter months. Indeed, these ships were the pioneers of today's mass cruise industry and the many technological advances and design features they introduced helped to make cruising an affordable mainstream activity. It is questionable whether, without the impetus of ferry design developments, the popularity of cruising would have increased as it has, becoming nowadays the world's fastest-expanding leisure activity.

In fact, today's cruise ferries are the latest manifestation of a tradition of providing short pleasure cruises dating back to the latter 19th century. In America, Mississippi stern-wheelers were among the first places where jazz music was heard, as depicted in the 1927 musical *Show Boat*. The layouts of American river and coastal steamers anticipated those of Scandinavian cruise ferries by the best part of a century.

In Europe too, lake, river and coastal steamers of the Edwardian era offered entertainment as an added attraction and were judged not only by that but also by the cuisine in their restaurants and, especially, the relative cheapness of their bar tariffs. On the Clyde, the *Ivanhoe* (Firth of Clyde Steam Packet Company, 1880) was the only teetotal ship.

It was not until 1960 that the 'booze cruise' really took off, in northern Europe. Lower duties levied on alcohol and tobacco persuaded large numbers to indulge in tax-free shopping at sea. The Finns went to Sweden, the Swedes and the Norwegians went to Denmark, the Danes went to West Germany and, later, the Brits went to France.

On Scandinavian routes in the 1960s, dining passengers were spoilt for choice – à la carte, 'smorgasbord' buffet or self-service cafeteria – options which, along with duty-free shopping, made a ferry short break even more appealing. Successive larger ferries, of which many were built, introduced other innovations, notably self-service supermarkets. For ferry entrepreneurs and passengers alike, the 1960s was a truly golden age.

Come the 1970s, the northern European ferry industry was hit by a series of stern challenges: wage inflation, increasing shipbuilding costs and the 1973 Oil Crisis in the wake of the Yom Kippur war. As companies merged and uneconomic services were cut, a new generation of 'jumbo' ferries (as in the then very popular Boeing 747 jumbo jet) was developed, designed to maximise passenger and freight capacity and to accommodate as many revenue-earning attractions as possible – bars, restaurants, shops, discos, cinemas and slot machines.

With the 1980s came deregulation, growth of the service sector and a new consumerism – trends on which that decade's new ferries were designed to capitalise. Particularly on the mid-Baltic routes between Sweden and Finland, a remarkable number of increasingly large and opulently-appointed vessels were built to carry millions of mainly Swedes and Finns on short cruises, combining shopping, drinking, dining, dancing and entertainment.

In 1999 the northern European ferry industry was hit by a most unwelcome development – the abolition by the European Union of the sale of duty-free goods on journeys between EU member states. The overall result was a greater emphasis on freight traffic and the rise to prominence of ro-pax ferries – large and often fast freight carriers with only a limited amount of passenger accommodation (albeit usually of high quality).

The ro-pax concept dated back to the latter 1950s and the Atlantic Steam Navigation Company. Typically, a ro-pax has two or three vehicle decks big enough to take freight lorries and trailers. Then there are 'ro-cruise' ferries – ro-pax ferries on which the passenger accommodation and facilities resemble those of boutique hotels. Some of the most impressive ro-cruise ferries are to be found on routes between Italy and Greece.

Other significant chapters in ferry design and development include the emergence of Japan, South Korea and China as economic and industrial powers; the EU's Motorways of the Sea initiative to transport vast numbers of lorries and so save energy and reduce pollution and road congestion; and the determination by naval architects and ferry operators to further address environmental issues by developing vessels powered by LNG (liquified natural gas) or solar energy.

Thus the story of the ferry is dynamic, new trends constantly emerging. Today, the world's largest passenger ro-ro vessels are the giant 69,000-ton Color Line cruise ferries *Color Fantasy* and *Color Magic*, each boasting impressive manoeuvrability, rapid loading and unloading of vehicles, and facilities to rival the most modern mass-market cruise ships. In terms of naval architecture and design development, these glamorous hi-tech ships are a world away from the earliest ro-ros of the mid-nineteenth century.

Yet, as this book shows, they are further evidence of an unbroken ferry design tradition dating back more than 150 years.

With the beach at Laboe in the foreground, the **Color Magic** gathers speed as she heads for Oslo in September 2010. *(Bruce Peter)*

CHAPTER TWO

The Ro-Ro Pioneers

On 7th February 1850, the SS *Leviathan* left Burntisland Harbour in Fife and headed south across the Forth estuary to Granton, near Edinburgh – the world's first open-sea roll on-roll off ferry service. The *Leviathan* carried mainly freight wagons, passengers encouraged to traverse instead on the railway's fleet of saloon paddle-steamers.

The concept of the ro-ro ferry was used during the American Civil War, primitive forms of landing craft being successfully deployed to carry troops and supplies and unloaded directly ashore via hinged bow ramps. In Britain, a side-loading ferry had crossed the River Tyne between North and South Shields since the latter 1820s. This carried passengers and horse-drawn vehicles, loaded via ramps – raised and lowered by pulleys – fitted to the ship's sides so that the ferry could load and unload at different states of the tide. Similar ferries were already established across Portsmouth Harbour and the Hamoaze, between Devonport and Torpoint. Elsewhere in Britain, horsedrawn canal barges carried coal wagons. So by the time the *Leviathan* was built, the basic design elements of the modern ferry were already in place, and she made her debut when the railway age was at its height and lines were fanning out all over the British Isles.

The Edinburgh, Perth & Dundee Railway had set itself the difficult task of establishing train services along Scotland's serrated east coast, meaning that the River Forth and the River Tay would need to be bridged in order to reach Dundee. The roll on-roll off solution to this problem had been suggested in 1845 by Mr Bateman, the railway's Chief Engineer. He proposed a flat-decked vessel to carry ten carriages, shunted aboard by a steam locomotive via a 1-in-12 ramp, to operate at Queensferry, where the River Forth was only three-quarters of a mile wide and much more sheltered than the four-and-a-half mile passage

between Granton and Burntisland. However, as the railway had an established passenger steamer route between these ports, this longer crossing was chosen as the better option.

The design for the port infrastructure was the work of two of the most inventive railway engineers of the era – Thomas Grainger (1794-1829) and Thomas Bouch (1822-1880) – and the *Leviathan* was drawn up and built by the eminent ship designer and builder Robert Napier (1791-1876).

Grainger, one of the first to realise the potential of railways – particularly in mining areas – was entrusted to build the Monkland & Kirkintilloch Railway in 1824. The line ended at a basin beside the Forth & Clyde Canal, where coal was trans-shipped on to barges. In the early 1830s, the railway and canal companies (who shared some directors) decided that this process would be more efficient if they constructed a barge on to which coal wagons could be loaded directly.

Built by Paisley-based Reid and Hannah, specialists in so-called 'passage boats' for use on canals, this innovative but nameless horsedrawn vessel was completed in October 1835. Records suggest that it was a success and that the Monkland & Kirkintilloch Railway (M&K) and the Forth & Clyde Canal Company benefited equally from the considerable efficiencies embodied in the design. Thomas Grainger also built several other railway lines to carry coal in west central Scotland.

In England the success of the Liverpool & Manchester Railway (opened in 1830) had shown that inter-city routes could carry passengers too and so Grainger became involved in the planning for such a line between Edinburgh and Glasgow. He was held in considerable esteem for his railway engineering work, which extended into the north of England, but at the height of his career he died from injuries suffered in a railway

An etching showing the shore arrangements for loading the **Leviathan** and her sisters; the platform was winched up the ramp to adjust its height depending on the tide. *(The Illustrated London News, Bruce Peter collection)*

collision near Stockton-on-Tees.

Tragedy of a different – but no less terminal – kind struck Cumbria-born engineer Thomas Bouch. During his career he worked on the Lancaster & Carlisle Railway, the Stockton & Darlington Railway and (in 1849) as Manager and Engineer of the Edinburgh, Perth & Dundee Railway. In the latter post he focused on the problem of carrying trains across the Forth and Tay, and within two years had set himself up as a consulting railway engineer, designing numerous lines, often through difficult terrain. Budget-conscious Bouch frequently produced quite daring solutions, such as spanning deep valleys with iron trestles and lattice girders rather than with masonry viaducts. His most audacious scheme was to construct a railway bridge over the River Tay, completed in 1878 and earning him a knighthood. But the design was not robust enough and, coupled with shoddy workmanship in casting iron components on site, the bridge collapsed in December 1879 – only six months after Queen Victoria had crossed in the Royal Train en route to Balmoral. The downfall destroyed Bouch's reputation and his pioneering work in railway and ferry design was largely forgotten.

Robert Napier, born in Dumbarton, was the son of a blacksmith and became one too, setting up in Glasgow's East End and opening an iron foundry. Here, in 1823, a steam-powered engine was built for the Clyde passenger vessel *Leven*. Further marine engine orders followed and Napier bought shares in the City of Glasgow Steam Packet Company (which introduced coastal services from Glasgow to Liverpool) and supplied engines for its vessels.

In 1841 Napier acquired his own shipyard at Govan, where the *Leviathan* was subsequently designed and built. By the time he retired a few years later, his contribution to the development of steam navigation worldwide, and to Glasgow's reputation as the leading centre of marine engineering excellence, was considerable.

When it came to designing the infrastructure for the ferry service that the *Leviathan* would in time operate across the River Forth, railway engineer Thomas Grainger's initial proposal was that hydraulic cranes could load wagons on to the deck of the vessel. But Thomas Bouch deemed this idea inefficient, as it would severely limit the throughput of wagons in a working day. For the railway and ferry to work effectively in bringing coal from Fife to Edinburgh, a much higher throughput was essential.

Graingers then proposed that wagons could be shunted directly on to the ship's deck via large girders out from the shore, resting on floating pontoons. But for reasons such as cost, the 20-foot tidal range and the ferry berth's exposure to North Sea storms and rough sea conditions, this idea too was scotched – as was the suggestion that ramps could be attached to each end of the ferry's hull. Thus Bouch decided that the most effective solution would be to construct 'moveable platforms' which could be winched up and down fixed ramps (an idea already being developed by a fellow civil engineer, Scott Russell, to cross the River Thames). The ramps were duly constructed at Granton and Burntisland by the Edinburgh, Perth & Dundee Railway.

The *Leviathan*, a double-ended iron-hulled paddle-steamer, was 172 feet long and had a deck width of 34 feet between the paddle-boxes. What was so remarkable about Napier's design was his vision in bringing together in that pioneering vessel all the basic design characteristics of the modern ferry.

The flat-bottomed hull had a draft of only 6 feet 6 inches when fully laden. The train deck, entirely unobstructed, enabled two trains to load simultaneously on parallel tracks. On either beam, independent forward and reverse operation of each paddle wheel meant that the ferry could manoeuvre very quickly and turn around practically within her own length. The commanding view from the bridge, 13 feet aloft on a gantry spanning the train deck, was perfect for overseeing loading and unloading.

Upon delivery to the Edinburgh, Perth & Dundee Railway at Granton, the *Leviathan* was quickly pressed into service in adverse winter weather but 'went along as smoothly and steadily as if the sea had been placid and calm.' Indeed, she proved to be a tremendous success, making four or five return trips a day with up to 40 wagons at a time. Not only was crossing time a mere 25 minutes each way; her heavy mineral freight rates were considerably cheaper than those for break-bulk shipping by steam collier.

In the autumn of 1850 a second ferry, the *Robert Napier* (140 feet long) was introduced across the River Tay, using the same features pioneered on the Forth crossing. A third example of the type, the *Carrier*, arrived in 1851, constructed by Scott's of Greenock rather than by Napier's shipyard. Three further ferries – the *Balbirnie* (1861), the *Kinloch* (1865) and the *Midlothian* (1881) – were added as demand grew before, eventually, all were superseded by bridges on both routes.

Although derailments during loading and unloading were rare, it was not unknown for wagons (which did not have brakes) to overshoot the deck and tumble into the harbour. Thus ferry decks came to be fitted with buffer stops at one end, which negated the original 'drive-through' principle and meant loading and unloading at one end only, their manoeuvrability enabling them to turn quickly in each harbour.

The Forth Railway Bridge was completed in 1890, bringing to an end 40 years of constant and reliable service by the ferry fleet. The *Leviathan* and her sisters were sold for scrap but the *Carrier* forged a second but short life with the London, Brighton & South Coast Railway.

TRAIN FERRIES IN SCANDINAVIA AND GERMANY

The pioneering train ferries across the River Forth provided the inspiration for subsequent early ferry designs.

One was the *Danish Lillebælt*, built by J. Wigham Richardson in Newcastle for service between Fredericia and Strib and delivered in 1872 to the Jydsk-Fyenske Statsbaner. Further similar ferries followed in the 1883-1900 period in the form of the *Korsør*, the *Nyborg*, the *Sjælland*, the *Jylland* and the *Store-Bælt* – all used on the short Nyborg-Korsør route over the Great Belt. These too were essentially paddle-propelled barges with tracks built into a flat train deck and some passenger accommodation below. Although they appeared to be double-ended, their paddles actually worked much more effectively in one direction than in the other.

The Danish railways also developed ferry berth design which differed from that created by Bouch and Grainger on the Forth. At train deck level, the hulls of the Great Belt ferries were elongated hexagons in plan, the tapering ends of which snugly fitted V-shaped inlets in the quay wall, into which the ferries sailed until the belting hit the berth, meaning that the hull was perfectly aligned to load and to discharge railway vehicles. Further examples of the type were built to link Denmark and Sweden via Helsingør and Helsingborg. Until as recently as 1997 – when the *Prins Richard* and the *Prinsesse Benedikte*

Top: Even before the *Leviathan* entered service, a horse-drawn ro-ro vessel was in use on the Forth & Clyde Canal in Scotland to carry coal wagons and cattle. This etching is inaccurate, as written evidence suggests that the craft was broad and capable of loading wagons on three tracks. *(Bruce Peter collection)*

Above left: The pioneering ro-ro ferry, *Leviathan*, was a very functional-looking ship, designed principally to carry freight wagons. *(Bruce Peter collection)*

Above right: The ro-ro concept in its most primitive form: a skiff with a wagon loaded on planks of wood is rowed across a river somewhere in America in the early years of the nineteenth century. *(Bruce Peter collection)*

Right: One of the subsequent Forth train ferries, the *Carrier*, is seen receiving attention to her rail deck. *(Bruce Peter collection)*

The DSB train ferries **Fredericia** and **Lillebælt** at Nykobing Mors: the latter was delivered in 1872 and was the first such vessel in Scandinavian waters. *(Thomas N. Olesen collection)*

were introduced on the Rødby-Puttgarden route – Danish train ferries were built to this configuration.

NEW MODES OF PROPULSION

In 1903, train ferries were introduced between Gedser in Denmark and Warnemünde in Germany, a route operated by Danish-owned and German-owned vessels.

For comparative analysis, each operator built one paddle-propelled ferry and one screw-propelled ferry. Thus, while the Danish *Prinsesse Alexandrine* and the German *Friedrich Franz IV* were essentially enlarged versions of existing train ferry precedents, their screw-driven fleetmates – the *Mecklenburg* (built in Germany by Schichau) and the *Prins Christian* (built in Denmark at Helsingør) – were far more innovative. Indeed, they were the first of a 'second generation' of train ferries, the design of which then developed further.

Along with a more sophisticated propulsion system, these screw-driven ferries also had more substantial superstructures, filling the entire hull width above their train decks. Unlike the route's paddle-propelled ferries, which had only a single train track down the centreline, the screw vessels had twin tracks and therefore greater capacity. Passenger facilities comprised dining and smoking saloons, a non-smoking ladies' lounge for First and Second Class passengers, and cabins with berths for around 38. With funnels located amidships, and silhouettes that were more built up at the bow than at the stern, they introduced the typical general arrangement and aesthetic elements of the modern short-sea ferry.

Both paddle-driven and screw-driven were propelled by twin triple-expansion steam engines. By the 1900s, two new and superior methods of ship propulsion were emerging – steam turbines and diesel motors.

The Newcastle engineer Charles Parsons (1854-1931) developed his turbine electric generator into a geared propulsion system for ships – sets of angled rotating blades turning a propeller shaft. The process was relatively efficient, near silent,

gave a higher power output than a steam-expansion plant and, best of all, the turbines were vibration-free. In 1894 a small experimental vessel called the *Turbinia* showed off his invention and attracted considerable interest. In 1897, as the fastest ship in the world, the *Turbinia* proved a sensation when demonstrated at the Diamond Jubilee Naval Review off Spithead.

The first commercial turbine steamer was the *King Edward*. Built by William Denny & Bros of Dumbarton, she was delivered in 1901 and not only became the prototype in propulsion for practically every major British ship thereafter but also remained the favoured mode of propulsion for the majority of British passenger ships, ferries included, until the mid-1960s.

Motor propulsion also made its debut in commercial shipping in short-sea passenger vessels. Although the origins of the internal combustion engine are still debated, most agree that the true inventor was German engineer Dr Rudolf Diesel (1858-1913). Diesel licensed his invention to manufacturers in Europe and the USA, but early work to develop a marine version was conducted by the Sulzer company in Winterthur, Switzerland, and Burmeister & Wain shipyard and engine works in Copenhagen, Denmark. One of the first motor ships with Sulzer engines was a Lake Geneva cargo vessel, the 1905 *Venoge*.

Shortly after, in Scotland, the *Comet* became the first vessel sailing in UK inshore and coastal waters with an internal combustion engine. She was operated by David MacBrayne Ltd, which ran steamer services on the Clyde and to the Western Isles. The *Comet*, built in 1905 by Robertson of Canning Town in London, was a modest 43 tons, powered by two paraffin-fuelled motors, manufactured by Gardner of Manchester and generating 90 kW. Whilst she needed far less attention than the lengthy preparation time demanded by steamers, the *Comet*'s downside was that the engines and exhaust were irritatingly noisy, though the latter problem was rectified by improved silencing. Thanks to her compact machinery, she also offered relatively commodious passenger accommodation and served her owners well. In 1928, her paraffin engines were replaced with new Gardner 8-cylinder diesels. She remained in the MacBrayne fleet until 1947 and, remarkably, still exists today as the *Gradely* – a houseboat at Shoreham.

In Denmark, the development of Rudolf Diesel's internal combusion engine by Burmeister & Wain led to the installation of the first marine diesel for an ocean-going ship – the 4,964-ton passenger-cargo liner *Selandia*, delivered to the East Asiatic Company in 1912.

The First World War and its aftermath slowed down marine diesel engine development until the 1920s. Both leading exponents – B&W and Sulzer – sought to achieve the same goals: greater reliability, fuel economy and power output, and reduced maintenance and engine size (the latter to require less space onboard ship).

It was in 1905 that Sulzer first demonstrated its innovative (non-marine) two-stroke diesel, which had twice the power output of a four-stroke engine and mechanically was more straightforward. From this came the successful marine applications for two-stroke diesels. B&W, the market leader in four-stroke marine diesels, lagged slightly behind Sulzer in two-stroke development and argued that two-stroke achieved less combustion than four-stroke and, furthermore, that two-stroke engines would wear out more quickly. Two-stroke also seemed noisier due to higher sound frequency.

B&W's first diesels with trunk pistons for marine use came in 1921 and were advantageous for vessels with engine rooms of constricted height, such as ferries. It was quickly realised that feeding engines with low-pressure compressed air could increase their power output by up to ten per cent. Shortly after, B&W developed a range of four-stroke, double-acting engines, each cylinder having ignition at either end. Although mechanically complex compared with Sulzer's two-stroke single-acting designs, they were – for their time – fairly efficient in terms of power output.

More economical than steam turbines and needing no large boilers, diesels were a more profitable option, creating space for more passengers or cargo. Against this, they were noisier than turbines and early designs were slower, making them a better choice for freighters than for passenger ships. Using motor propulsion also had implications for ships' appearance. As with MacBrayne's little ferry the *Comet*, the *Selandia* and her later sisters for the East Asiatic Company (EAC) had no funnels, the exhaust discharging up pipes attached to one of the masts.

EAC was principally a 'deep-sea' liner company, trading from Denmark to the Far East and to North America, and owned a number of subsidiaries. One – the Det Sønderjydske Kompagni – operated coastal steamer services between ports in Southern Jylland, Fyn and nearby islands. In the early 1920s it set up a subsidiary of its own, called Mommark Færgeri, to operate a train and vehicular ferry service from Mommark to Faaborg, and ordered a small 331-ton motor ferry from the Nakskov Skibsværft for delivery in 1922.

Named the *Mommark*, it could carry up to 300 passengers and either three railway vehicles or 20 cars. The engines were two 4-cylinder Holeby diesels, delivering a speed of 11 knots. As the engines were non-reversible, the *Mommark* was notable for her pioneering use of a primitive form of variable-pitch propeller, whereby a gear system altered the angle of the blades, not only reversing the thrust but also giving finer control over speed and manoeuvrability. Such advantages were highly desirable for a vessel which loaded and unloaded via the stern only and had to rotate within the confines of each harbour.

It was 25 years down the line before variable-pitch propeller technology was sufficiently reliable and efficient to be used on significant numbers of merchant ships. The first was the 1948 Swedish Johnson Line refrigerated cargo vessel *Los Angeles*, built by Kockums of Malmö and fitted with KaMeWa (Karlstads Mekaniska Werkstad) propellers. In 1951 the Norwegian single-screw coastal passenger ferry, the *Sandnes*, was likewise equipped, but the next application on a ro-ro ferry was not until delivery of the 1958 French-owned Dover Strait vessel the *Compiègne*. Thereafter, specifying KaMeWa propellers on ferries became commonplace.

The *Mommark* looked quaintly home-made, her superstructure consisting of a wooden deckhouse held aloft by steel poles above the otherwise open vehicle deck. She had no

Four subsequent DSB ferries on the Storstrøm crossing at Masnedø. Nearest the camera are the **Alexandra** (1892) and **Thyra** (1893), while the **Ørhoved** (1916) and **Fyn** (1919) are in the background. The latter two utilised screw propulsion rather than paddles. *(Thomas N. Olesen collection)*

In the inter-war era, train ferry design progressed rapidly in Denmark. Motor vessels, with funnels along the centre line and streamlined forward superstructures, led progressive naval architectural trends, as illustrated here by DSB's *Storebælt* of 1939. *(Ann Glen)*

funnel and her engine exhausts were slender pipes attached to the aft mast. Yet she was so successful that when sold for scrap in 1965 she had served the Mommark-Faaborg route for over forty years.

Motor ships without funnels had become the exception even in the 1920s, the funnel signifying modernity and seaworthiness. By the middle of that decade, many fashionable motor passenger vessels of all sizes were distinguished by their shorter, wider funnels (compared with steamers), capable of housing generators, ventilators and other unsightly machinery and creating a more modern, uncluttered and even slightly streamlined profile.

Subsequent Danish railway-owned train ferries, such as the *Korsør* (1927), the *Nyborg* (1931) and the *Sjælland* (1933), each of which had twin 8-cylinder B&W trunk engines, followed suit. The basic design of these Helsingør-built three-track ships was done by the Royal Danish Navy's drawing office at the Orlogsværftet and all were employed on DSB's important Nyborg-Korsør route across the Great Belt. A distinguishing characteristic of this type of ferry was the large overhang of the train deck, additionally protected from damage during docking by a broad band of steel and hardwood belting.

As such vessels typically sailed in sheltered waters and were unlikely to encounter even moderately high waves, the optimal hull design gave a slender entry at the waterline with a relatively broad train deck above. Cars – and even trucks and buses – were more easily manoeuvred and could be much more tightly packed compared with railway vehicles, meaning that car ferries were substantially more efficient in terms of pay-load than rail-orientated vessels.

THE EMERGENCE OF THE CAR FERRY

As Henry Ford so ably demonstrated with his ubiquitous Model T, the American System of Manufacture made it possible to produce, relatively cheaply, large quantities of cars to a standard design. Hence it is no surprise that the car ferry phenomenon first emerged in North America.

The first ferry built specifically to carry cars was the Canadian *Motor Princess*, built by the Yarrows Shipbuilding Company of Esquimalt for the Canadian Pacific Railway Company and delivered in early 1924 for service on the Sidney-Bellingham route between Vancouver Island and the United States. The ferry's design was a collaboration between Captain J.W. Troup and Norman Yarrow (son of the shipyard owner).

The *Motor Princess* was steel-framed but her hull was timber-clad and the deckhouses entirely wooden. She could accommodate 250 passengers and, by utilising the main deck plus additional space on the shelter deck, 45 cars, loaded and unloaded via sliding doors in the bow and stern quarters.

As the vessel was nearing completion, Sir Alfred Yarrow returned from a lengthy business trip and was reputedly struck with horror at the 'monstrosity' that his son and Captain Troup had created in his absence. Troup considered the ferry an experiment – but, nicknamed 'The Galloping Dishpan' on account of her short length and bluff lines, she soon proved her worth. Her two McIntosh-Seymour six-cylinder diesels were noisy and prone to cause vibration, and her short funnel did little to prevent fumes and soot from falling on deck. Fortunately, her passenger accommodation – comprising dining saloon, social hall, promenade lounges and two private staterooms – was comfortably appointed.

In 1926, after only three years in international service, she was switched to operate between Vancouver and Nanaimo on Vancouver Island. In 1929 she transferred again, to a more southerly route between Stevenston (south of Vancouver) and Sidney. But fuel rationing during the Second World War produced a general decline in car usage. In addition, new safety regulations governing wooden passenger vessels resulted in the *Motor Princess*'s withdrawal from passenger service in 1950, temporarily becoming a freight carrier. In 1955 she was substantially rebuilt, renamed the *Pender Queen* and served as an open-decked vessel for short ferry crossings between British Columbia's Gulf Islands. In later years she became a freight barge and in 2003 sank in the Gulf Islands.

CARS ACROSS THE DOVER STRAIT

The railway-owned steamer fleets connecting Britain with Ireland and the Continent were intended for foot passengers, brought by train directly to the quayside, plus mail and general cargo. The idea of carrying motor cars was taboo. Furthermore, loading a car by crane on to a packet vessel deck was an awkward operation.

In 1927, frustrated by the difficulties and expense of taking his car abroad on Southern Railway vessels, and having worked out that he could reduce fares by 50% compared with theirs and still earn a profit, youthful entrepreneur Stuart Townsend introduced his own rival car ferry service across the Dover Strait.

Initially he chartered the steam coaster *Artificer* to carry cars between Dover and Calais. His aim was to operate this for a couple of months only and so force the Southern Railway to reduce its prices – but his enterprise was a success. When his first charter expired he repeated the exercise with the *Royal Firth*. In 1930 Townsend purchased a former Royal Navy minesweeper, the *Ford*, converted it into a car ferry for 28 cars and 168 passengers, and renamed it the *Forde*. The use of an ex-Navy ship as a ferry was perhaps unusual, but apart from costing him an affordable £5,000, (plus £14,000 for the rebuild) it fitted the bill in various ways, from meeting Board of Trade regulations to boasting an impressive turn of speed and a spacious flat area of open deck towards the stern, ideal for cars. With the *Forde* established between Dover and Calais, Townsend commissioned naval architect Norman M. Dewar (who designed the converted *Forde*) to produce speculative drawings for a new Dover Strait steam turbine ferry, capable of side-loading cars by means of an aft-located hoistable ramp, fitted with a turntable – so eliminating the need for any special shore-based facilities. This project never came to fruition but illustrated Townsend's desire to introduce drive-on vessels.

Meanwhile, the Southern Railway's attempts to hit back by carrying cars included chartering two elderly steam colliers (the *Abington* and the *Dublin*) and building their own car-carrying vessel, the *Autocarrier*, introduced in 1931 and able to transport 35 crane-loaded cars and 120 passengers.

Three years later the *Twickenham Ferry* – the first of a trio of Southern Railway steam turbine-powered train ferries – was delivered by Swan Hunter & Wigham Richardson on the River Tyne for service between Dover and Dunkerque. She had four tracks, loaded via the stern and accommodating either 12 Wagon-Lits sleeping cars or up to 40 goods wagons, plus an upper garage on her aft deck for 25 cars – arguably, the first multi-purpose ferry. Her funnels were athwartships, the casings located between the train tracks.

The *Twickenham Ferry* and her sisters – the *Hampton Ferry* (delivered in 1934) and the *Shepperton Ferry* (1935) – did not actually enter service in 1936 due to unforeseen difficulties at Dover in constructing a special dock for their use. Unlike the packet steamers, which formed the bulk of the Southern Railway's Channel fleet, the train ferries were slow (capable of around 16 knots) but employed 24 hours a day.

In 1936, to transport cars between Dover and Oostende, the Belgian state-owned Regie voor Maritiem Transport (RMT, or Belgian Marine Administration) converted its 1913-vintage turbine steamer the *Ville de Liège* into a side-loading ferry and renamed it the *London-Istanbul*. The aft section of the superstructure was gutted, two boilers removed and a new vertical funnel and masts fitted, so creating a better resemblance to RMT's latest motor packet vessels such as the 1934 25-knot Sulzer-powered *Prince Baudouin*. But despite all this, there was still no doubt that passengers with cars were considered less important than those arriving at the dockside by train, the latter in those days very much in the majority. The *London-Istanbul*'s name reflected the new trunk road between Brussels and the Turkish capital – so going by ferry meant it was possible for motorists to drive between the two.

The world's first purpose-built car ferry was the Canadian Pacific-owned ***Motor Princess*** (1923). *(Bruce Peter collection)*

DENMARK'S CAR FERRY PIONEERS

Ferry traffic in Denmark was likewise dominated by railway-owned vessels dedicated to carrying trains, much to the frustration of the increasing number of motorists. DSB, the Danish State Railway, had no desire to transport cars in competition with their own rail services on the shortest Great Belt ferry crossing between Nyborg and Korsør, so concentrated instead on a longer northerly route from Århus to Kalundborg, for which a new motor vessel, the 1,359-ton *Kalundborg*, was ordered from Burmeister & Wain in Copenhagen for delivery in 1931.

In 1929, to get the better of DSB on the Great Belt, a private company called Motorejernes Færgefart A/S (The Motor Owners' Ferry Service Ltd) was established and it too ordered a car ferry, to be named the *Heimdal*, from Aalborg Værft. But before taking delivery, an agreement was reached with DSB, who purchased the vessel.

These two ships demonstrated very different approaches to ferry design. DSB's *Kalundborg* appeared to be a conventional short-sea packet liner with a relatively fine-lined hull, straight stem and a counter stern, much like the previous generation of steamers she displaced. But both mechanically and in her car-carrying ability, she embodied notable innovations.

A single-screw ship, she was equipped with a new type of two-stroke, single-acting 2,850 bhp Burmeister & Wain engine, giving a 15-knot service speed. (After further refinement, engines of this type became standard on most subsequent DSB ferries until the mid-1960s.) Although primarily a passenger carrier with space for 1,200 and operating a rail-connected service to give travellers from Northern Jylland a short cut to Copenhagen, she had garage space for 40 cars. Only one deck in height with a centre casing, it was accessed through hatches in the bow and stern quarters of the hull, and located well above the waterline to avoid being obstructed by the engine room. The Third Class saloons were below, making good use of the substantial freeboard.

In complete contrast, the layout of the privately-financed *Heimdal*, delivered to DSB in 1930, followed the precedent of train ferry design practice. Her car deck was relatively tall, wide and unobstructed and, as there were bow and stern doors, cars could drive on and off with minimal inconvenience. In addition, a small onboard car repair workshop offered motorists a valuable service en route. The *Heimdal* was powered by two 6-cylinder Frichs diesels, with the exhausts and passenger access staircases routed through short casings on either beam. While the *Kalundborg* and her subsequent near-sister, the *Jylland* (built

DSB's ferry loading procedures were highly efficient - particularly on the Nyborg-Korsør route across the Great Belt. *(Ann Glen)*

The first of the Southern Railway's train ferries, the **Twickenham Ferry**, also carried cars. These vessels were operated much more intensively than the railway's packet vessels. *(Bruce Peter collection)*

by the Nakskov Skibsværft) remained almost unique in the annals of Danish domestic ferry design, the *Heimdal* effectively became the prototype for nearly all subsequent car ferries. The *Kalundborg* did, however, provide a useful alternative approach to ferry design for longer, more exposed routes.

By the mid-1930s, a number of other car ferries were employed in Danish domestic service. Entrepreneur Jens Peder Jensen, who owned a bus company, decided to open a ferry link across the Great Belt to compete with DSB's *Heimdal* and the various train ferries on which road vehicles were carried when space permitted. When that proved too difficult, he concentrated his efforts on establishing a more northerly Kattegat crossing between Grenaa in western Jylland and Hundested in northern Sjælland – a route on which there was no direct competition from DSB's own ferries. In 1933, supported by a small group of fellow bus operators and other local worthies, Jensen founded Grenaa-Hundested Færgefart A/S and ordered a small car ferry (the *Djursland*) from the Nakskov Skibsværft for delivery the following year.

The *Djursland* could carry 400 passengers and 40 cars, loaded via bow and stern doors. Powered by two 5-cylinder Vølund diesels, the little ferry could manage just 12.5 knots. The route's owners, taken aback by the success of their enterprise, ordered a second and larger ferry, the *Isefjord*, built by Aalborg Værft. It accommodated 500 passengers and 52 cars, and both ferries were remarkably well appointed, with smoking saloons and rather elegant restaurants, and thoughtful timetabling enabled motorists to take day trips to either north-east Jylland or Sjælland.

Once Grenaa-Hundested Færgefart was a successful competitor, DSB suddenly noticed that some motorists were buying single tickets for the railway's Great Belt ferry and returning via Grenaa-Hundested, making a circular tour. Rather than welcoming this innovative touring of Denmark by car and ferry, DSB refused to sell single tickets to motorists and slapped a heavy supplementary fare on returns, which was only refunded when car drivers checked in for their homeward ferry crossings.

Nevertheless, DSB realised that car ferries represented a growing market, even though their loyalty was to rail-connected shipping services. Their response was to build a new multi-purpose Great Belt ferry (to be named the *Freia*) to carry road and rail vehicles, and to deputise when necessary on the Århus-Kalundborg route. Construction of this new vessel's hull and superstructure was sub-contracted to Aalborg Værft, builder of

the *Heimdal* and *Isefjord*.

The *Freia*'s design was a joint effort by DSB's own technical staff and the drawing offices at Helsingør and Aalborg. In the Helsingør office, a young naval architect called Knud E. Hansen was notably proficient in drawing up short-sea passenger ships and he was asked to take charge of the design. Over the next quarter of a century Hansen was destined to become one of the most important names in the field of ferry design.

Hansen was born nearby in Espergærde in 1900, the son of Eduard Hansen, a skipper of coastal sailing ships. He studied naval architecture at the Polyteknisk Læreanstalt in Copenhagen (nowadays Danmark's Tekniske Universitet or DTU). Upon graduation in 1925, he gained experience in shipbuilding by working in a number of yards in Denmark and abroad, initially at Københavns Flydedok & Skibsværft. Thereafter, he travelled to Britain and the Netherlands to experience their ship design practices. From 1927 until 1929, he worked in the drawing office of Burmeister & Wain and went on to join the Helsingørs Jernskibs og Maskinbyggeri, where he remained until 1937.

In designing the *Freia*, Hansen and his colleagues at Helsingør were influenced by the *Heimdal* and *Isefjord*, as well as by recent DSB train ferries. For example, the forward superstructure was curved in much the same manner as on DSB's recent *Sjælland*. The black hull livery stepped down abaft the bow – a tactic subsequently employed many times by Hansen to make fairly compact ferry hulls appear longer than they actually were.

As with the *Heimdal*, the *Freia*'s 55-car vehicle deck was arranged on the drive-through principle, with a lifting bow visor installed as well as folding doors in the bow quarters for use when operating between Århus and Kalundborg. At the upper level, wide casings containing sitting saloons flanked a double-height space along the centreline. There, a single railway track was installed as DSB had requested that the *Freia* should be built to carry a three-coach diesel 'Lyntog' express train, loaded via the stern. In the event this was seldom used but, as a symbolic gesture, demonstrated DSB's continuing desire for ferries capable of transporting even one relatively short train. To protect against fire, the vehicle deck was fitted with a sprinkler system, split into fourteen loops, each of which would activate separately in the event of cars igniting below. Installations of this kind – a major safety development – became standard features of most subsequent ro-ro ferries. Able to also carry up to 1,000 passengers, the *Freia* proved to be an extremely useful vessel.

After her launch in Aalborg, the *Freia* was towed to Helsingør

The Southern Railway-owned **Autocarrier** was actually a modified cargo vessel design. *(Ferry Publications Library)*

A side-on view of the **Forde**, showing the open deck area towards her stern. *(Ambrose Greenway collection).*

for fitting out prior to her introduction between Nyborg and Korsør in 1936. She went on to achieve a very long and lucrative career in the DSB fleet, serving on a variety of Danish domestic routes. Little altered, she continued in DSB service until 1975. She then passed to Italian owners to operate across the Bay of Naples as the *Ischia Express*, and was withdrawn for scrap in 2007 – by which time her hull was over 70 years old.

Meanwhile, attention turned to establishing international ferry routes from Denmark to Sweden and Norway. Until the mid-1920s, Det Forenede Dampskibs-Selskab (DFDS, or the United Steamship Company) had maintained a daily steamer service from Frederikshavn in Northern Jylland to the important Swedish city and port of Gothenburg. Thereafter, Hallandsbolaget (a subsidiary of the famous Gothenburg-based Broström AB) had taken over. Hallandsbolaget director Harry Trapp realised that to make the service more successful, and attract Sewdish day trippers to visit Denmark, it would be profitable to offer a return trip every day, rather than just a single crossing. By the mid-1930s, even sceptical Chairman Dan Broström realised that there was increasing interest in taking short sea trips for pleasure as well as for getting from A to B. So Harry Trapp set about establishing a new ferry company to link Frederikshavn with Sweden's Second City – an initiative in which the Danish government not only showed keen interest but also subscribed to a third of the share capital.

A new ferry (the *Kronprinsessan Ingrid*) was ordered from the Frederikshavn Værft og Flyvedok A/S for delivery in time for the 1936 summer season. The 794-ton vessel could carry up to 572 passengers and 40 cars, loaded through folding side-hatches in the bow and stern topsides. As with DSB's *Kalundborg* and *Jylland*, the car deck was only one deck high and split into port and starboard sections by a centreline casing. Two Swedish-built 6-cylinder Alpha diesels gave a 16-knot service speed and enabled two return trips a day to be made at the height of the summer season. Passenger accommodation consisted of a smoking saloon and a restaurant, both designed by well-known Gothenburg architect Gustav Alde, whose previous interiors included those for the Bergen Line cruise ship *Stella Polaris*.

Externally, the *Kronprinsessan Ingrid* was quite a tubby little ship but, unlike previous ferries built for service within sheltered Danish territorial waters, her hull lines more closely resembled those of conventional packet vessels, with no knuckle joint or belting at vehicle deck height. Sporting an all-white livery and a buff funnel, from certain angles she resembled a modern motor

yacht. The new ferry service was officially registered as the Göteborg-Frederikshavn Linjen, but it was popularly known as 'Sessanlinjen', an abbreviation of the ship's name.

Although the *Kronprinsessan Ingrid*'s operations were suspended during the Second World War, she subsequently enjoyed considerable success – to the extent that in 1950-51 she was lengthened by eight metres by Burmeister & Wain in Copenhagen to increase her capacity. Three years later, she carried her millionth passenger and, by the mid-1950s, the Frederikshavn-Gothenburg route was the second busiest Swedish ferry line (after the short Helsingør-Helsingborg route across The Sound). Replaced by larger tonnage in 1955, the *Kronprinsessan Ingrid* was sold to other Swedish owners for use on routes to Gotland and to the Åland Islands in the Baltic Sea. Later still, in 1969, she passed to Yugoslavian owners and operated along Croatia's Dalmatian Coast until the end of the 2006 summer season. She was little changed since her early-1950s' lengthening except for rebuilding of the stern to create a new aft-facing vehicle access door. After her withdrawal, she was laid up in the charming Croatian town of Mali Losinj, where she was converted into a floating restaurant and night-club complete with pole and lap dancing.

While the *Kronprinsessan Ingrid* was being designed, various bus-operating interests were rapidly developing plans for a second new car ferry initiative – to introduce a service across the Skagerrak from Denmark to Norway. The route chosen was from Frederikshavn to Larvik, a small port near the mouth of the

Belgium's first car ferry, the **London-Istanbul**, was converted from the packet steamer **Ville de Liege**. Here she is seen reversing into Oostende harbour. *(Ambrose Greenway collection)*

DSB's **Kalundborg** (1931) loaded cars through side ports, the forward of which is partially open and with passengers looking out. Note the large car deck ventilators protruding ahead of the superstructure. *(Thomas N. Olesen collection)*

The Danish car ferry **Heimdal** was a very forward-looking and efficient drive-through motor vessel. *(Bruce Peter collection)*

Oslofjord. A/S Larvik-Frederikshavn Færgefart was established in April 1936 and on 8th June the Grenaa-Hundested ferry *Isefjord* undertook a trial trip between the two ports to demonstrate to local dignitaries and investors what such a ferry service would be like. When the little ferry arrived in Larvik it seemed that the entire town had turned out at the dockside to welcome her. However, to cope with the open water of the Skagerrak, any new car ferry needed to be far more substantial than the *Isefjord*. In fact, it required a vessel similar in scale and dimensions to DSB's Great Belt train ferries. Given his experience and involvement in designing the newest of these vessels, Knud E. Hansen was invited to design the new Larvik-Frederikshavn ferry, to be named the *Peter Wessel*. He accepted the challenge on a freelance basis but to complete the task set up his own independent naval architectural consultancy.

Although Hansen's design clearly owed a great debt to the previous Aalborg newbuild the *Freia*, the 1,415-ton *Peter Wessel* was more than twice her size – indeed, the biggest car ferry to date. She accommodated 60 cars and 500 passengers, 141 of whom were berthed in cabins mainly squeezed in below the car deck, forward and aft of the engine room, and the boat

deck had a small additional number of superior cabins.

Powered by two Atlas-Polar diesels, the *Peter Wessel* was capable of 16 knots. As on the *Kronprinsessan Ingrid*, a casing containing machinery, pipework and stairways ran down the centreline, splitting the vehicle deck into two areas on either beam. A significant difference from the Swedish ferry was the fact that the entire vehicle deck had sufficient free height for buses and trucks to drive straight through, reflecting the fact that her majority owners were bus operators. Immediately above, on the main deck, was the passenger accommodation – a smoking saloon and cocktail bar forward, and a dining saloon with a buffet counter aft of amidships, where passengers would be slightly less likely to feel the ship's motion.

Her bow had a more pronounced rake than had been typical of ferries for domestic routes (such as the *Isefjord* and the *Freia*), so the bow visor also needed to have flared rather than flat sides and a straight stem. Unlike the *Kronprinsessan Ingrid*, whose hull more resembled a conventional small motor passenger vessel, the configuration of the *Peter Wessel* (and of subsequent ferries designed by Knud E. Hansen) featured a knuckle joint at vehicle deck height. Although less pronounced

The **Jylland**, the **Kalundborg**'s near-sister and operating mate, crosses the Kattegat in the 1950s. Again, the forward car-loading hatch is open. *(Bruce Peter collection)*

The Grenaa-Hundested ferry **Djursland** was, like the **Heimdal**, a drive-through ship, capable of carrying commercial vehicles. *(Ambrose Greenway collection)*

The DSB vehicle ferry **Freia** had a long and successful career. This vessel was the naval architect Knud E. Hansen's first attempt to design a car-carrying vessel. *(Trevor Jones)*

than on ferries serving in sheltered waters, it demonstrated the need to compromise between fine lines at water level and a relatively broad and regular vehicle deck above to optimise capacity. Such designs were very effective in relatively calm conditions but, above a certain wave height, the knuckle joint tended to cause a degree of 'slamming' motion.

With only a low hinged door, similar to that on DSB's Great Belt ferries, the *Peter Wessel*'s vehicle deck appeared to be open at the stern, but a further set of watertight folding doors beneath the rear of her superstructure ensured complete protection from following seas. She thus established the preferred Scandinavian means of avoiding free surface effect by keeping water out through full enclosure of the garage space. To remove small amounts of water, drains with non-return valves (known as scuppers) piped the water overboard above the load waterline. Free surface effect causes a rapid loss of stability due to water sloshing around the expansive surface of a ferry's vehicle deck. On other types of passenger and cargo ships, hulls are divided to shelterdeck height by transverse watertight bulkheads which on ferries reach no higher than the vehicle deck.

In contrast, the tendency on British cross-Channel ferries was to specify partially-open stern designs. Freeing ports (holes cut into the shell plating immediately above the belting) drained away excess water. Each method had its advantages and disadvantages. In the event of flooding through collision or hatches breaking open, ferries without freeing ports were liable to quickly become unstable, whereas in rough weather freeing

ports could also let water flood in and this too was potentially dangerous.

The *Peter Wessel*'s drive-through ability and opening bow visor enabled very rapid loading and discharge of cars – but to an extent were also the ship's Achilles heel. In safety terms, both her designer and operator were entering largely uncharted territory and she was considered best suited to the Kattegat's relatively calm summer conditions, operating between late May and mid-September – the key period for vehicle traffic. (Car ownership in Denmark was then around 100,000.) For the rest of the year she was laid up – a situation which subsequently suggested she was not earning enough in revenue to offset her construction cost.

In 1939, with Europe's political situation worsening, she was put up for sale. Entrepreneur Captain Stuart Townsend inspected her but the British maritime safety authorities were unconvinced of the security of her opening bow and lack of forward collision bulkhead. Furthermore, the outbreak of war precluded any sale. Thus she remained on the summer-only Larvik-Frederikshavn route until she was damaged during the 1940 German invasion and subsequent occupation of Norway.

The German Marines realised the value of the ship's design and she was seized, modified at Stettin as military transport and put to work between Oslo and Århus and, occasionally, to Baltic ports. She was later converted to a minesweeper and then to a minelayer before being laid up at Sønderborg in Denmark in April 1945. After the German capitulation she was rescued by a Norwegian crew, repaired in Aalborg by her original builder and

A dockside scene in Gothenburg with the **Kronprinsessan Ingrid** loading cars for Frederikshavn in Denmark via one of her side hatches. *(Rickard Sahlsten collection)*

The Swedish **Kronprinsessan Ingrid** manoeuvres off her berth in Gothenburg in the latter 1930s. *(Rickard Sahlsten collection)*

A stern-quarter view of the **Peter Wessel**: as well as bow and stern doors, she was also fitted with side hatches. *(Bruce Peter collection)*

returned to the Larvik-Frederikshavn route. In 1956 she was lengthened at Aalborg to increase capacity and remained in summer service until completion of a new ship of the same name in 1968, when she was laid up again. Six years later she was sold to Italian owners and served in the western Mediterranean as the *Jollyeme*. In 1981, 44 years after her introduction, the *Peter Wessel* was broken up.

In 1939 a second Denmark-Norway ferry route was inaugurated between Hirtshals and Kristiansand by the Kristiansands Dampskipsselskap, which hitherto had operated passenger, cargo and mail steamers to ports in northern Denmark. As with the *Freia* and the *Peter Wessel*, their new ship – the 1,281-ton *Skagerak I* – was built by Aalborg Værft. A stern- and side-loader, she could carry 30 cars and up to 1,200 passengers but, unlike previous Aalborg-built ferries, whose vehicle decks were high enough for trucks and buses to drive

straight through, only her aft section could take either commercial vehicles or two railway wagons on a single short track. (In this respect she was a rare example at that time of a train ferry not owned by a railway company.) Forward, only cars could be accommodated as the space above was taken by passenger cabins.

Alas, after just one brief summer season, in which she made 313 crossings and carried 14,591 cars, the *Skagerak I*'s ferry life was all but over. The outbreak of war enforced the suspension of Kristiansands Dampskipsselskap's operation and in May 1940 the *Skagerak I* was seized by the Germans and sunk four years later by Allied bombing off Egersund.

While the *Skagerak I*'s multi-purpose specification was precisely tailored to serve the Kristiansand Dampskipsselskap's very particular requirements, the *Peter Wessel*'s design became a standard reference for numerous subsequent Scandinavian drive-through ferries. Furthermore, as car ownership increased, her eventual success established Knud E. Hansen as the leading Scandinavian ferry designer.

Hansen's next project was to draw up a similar vessel – the 1,217-ton *Marsk Stig* – for Grenaa-Hundested Færgefart's expanding Danish domestic service. Delivered from Aalborg Værft in 1940, she was laid up for two years because of the German invasion and, thereafter, was seized and placed in service between Warnemünde and Gedser, carrying supplies and equipment for the Kriegsmarine. In June 1944, while unloading tanks in Helsinki, she tipped over and sank, allegedly because the German officer in charge did not allow time for her trim to be adjusted to compensate for the changing weight distribution on her vehicle deck. This was the first of several similar accidents to afflict the ship throughout her career, suggesting that she was unforgiving of human error.

After the war, the *Marsk Stig* was restored for her original

The **Skagerak I** briefly operated between Kristiansand in Norway and Hirtshals in Denmark, carrying cars and railway wagons. *(Ambrose Greenway collection)*

The Grenaa-Hundested ferry **Marsk Stig** in post-World War 2 condition. *(Jan Vinter Christiansen collection)*

intended service, continuing until 1964 when she was sold to Europafærgen Service A/S for a route between Grenaa and Varberg in Sweden and renamed the *Varberg*. This phase lasted for only two years because the ship keeled over again, this time while in dry-dock, and was sold to Swedish shipbreakers.

That might have been the end of the story, but the damaged ferry was resold to an up-and-coming Baltic ferry entrepreneur, Rederi AB Sally of Mariehamn, and rebuilt as the *Viking 2* – one of the first of the now famous red-hulled ferries of the Viking Line brand. In April 1970, whilst in winter lay-up at Mariehamn, she sank for a third time after another member of the Viking Line fleet rammed and holed her hull. She was again repaired and continued in seasonal service until the autumn of 1977. In the following February she was seriously damaged by fire at Mariehamn and, deemed not worthy of repair, was sold for scrap. By this time, dozens of considerably more sophisticated ferries designed by Hansen were operating successfully not only in Scandinavian waters but also around the British Isles and in North America.

In Britain, shortly before the outbreak of war, the London, Midland & Scottish Railway's Caledonian Steam Packet Company subsidiary commissioned the then largest short-sea car ferry – the 2,197-ton *Princess Victoria* – built by William Denny & Bros of Dumbarton for the LMS Stranraer-Larne route across the northern Irish Sea. A notoriously difficult crossing, exposed to south-westerly gales and made more challenging by strong coastal currents and shallow water, this demanded a vessel of very robust design. Indeed, ferries constructed for short-sea services in the British Isles generally faced much more testing conditions than were typically encountered in Danish waters by ships such as the *Marsk Stig*.

Powered by two 14-cylinder Sulzer diesels, the *Princess Victoria* was the first large motor ship to be owned by a British railway company and was described in LMS publicity material as a 'floating garage'. As with the majority of ferries of the era, she sailed astern up to linkspans, which were adjusted with the tide to align perfectly with her belting at the stern. Her vehicle deck, like those on most of her Scandinavian counterparts, was only partially enclosed at the after end – this being achieved by means of a guillotine-type door shutting from above. So in order to drain away excess water from spray in rough weather, freeing ports were cut in the shell plating of the vehicle deck. The deck's forward section was fitted with pens for livestock, which boarded through side-hatches, located towards the bow.

Requisitioning the *Princess Victoria* for war service, the British Army found her ideal for transporting military vehicles. In May 1940 (at just 13 months old) she was sunk off the Humber by an enemy mine. But her design survived, forming the blueprint for British railway-owned Channel car ferries in the post-war era.

CAR FERRIES IN NORTH AMERICA

In America, in the wake of the Great Depression, President Roosevelt's New Deal helped to kick-start the US economy and create a sustained consumer boom. It also brought about a new discpline – industrial design. Unlike engineers, whose interest

The **Princess Victoria**, the London, Midland & Scottish Railway's Stranraer-Larne ferry, operated only briefly before the advent of the Second World War. *(Ambrose Greenway collection)*

DSB's 1952-built **Broen** was designed by Knud E. Hansen and incorporated elements from both the pre-war **Freia** and the unbuilt Fehmarn projects. *(Ambrose Greenway collection)*

was primarily in mechanical matters, industrial designers set about the task of creating objects and experiences that looked and felt more appealing to prospective customers. This was in a climate of international competition to develop the fastest trains, ocean liners and cars.

Wind-tunnel testing determined that the shape with least wind resistance was a tear-drop – rounded at the front and tapering at the rear to reduce drag. But the materials then available often meant that fitting 'streamform' casings to fast cars and locomotives made them heavier, thus negating any advantages.

The only entirely streamformed ship was the 1,417-ton *Kalakala*, a ferry which operated between Seattle and Vancouver Island. She was actually a radical reconstruction of a fire-damaged San Francisco Bay ferry called the *Perlata* which was the victim of a 1933 arson attack on San Francisco's wooden ferry terminal. The wreck was bought by Captain Alexander Peabody (Chairman of the Puget Sound Navigation Co of Seattle, otherwise known as the Black Ball Line) and he employed Boeing engineer Louis Proctor to construct a large model showing how the ferry might look with a streamlined superstructure. This was then translated into a full set of construction drawings, and with her streamformed silvertopsides, large porthole windows and viewing galleries, the rebuilt ferry was 'The Shape of Things to Come'. The name *Kalakala* meant 'flying bird' in the local Chinook Native American language, and an advertising campaign promoted 'the world's most futuristic-looking ship'.

Of light monocoque construction, her streamformed upperworks gave her a greater deadweight capacity and a larger payload than a conventional build could achieve. Although this design did not increase her 17.5-knot service speed, it meant far fewer awkward corners for salt water to gather and cause corrosion, and so had the potential to make maintenance easier.

The *Kalakala*'s maiden sailing was attended by a crowd estimated at over 100,000. In regular service between Seattle

and Bremerton, she was a great success. Her saloon deck had comfortable lounges, a fashionable circular cocktail bar and a dance saloon featuring The Flying Bird Orchestra to entertain passengers. Nothing of this kind had been offered on a car ferry and the *Kalakala* became a national sensation. In 1967 she was sold as a crab-processing vessel in Alaska and in 1998 was rescued for preservation.

Only a year after the *Kalakala* first entered service, Sun Shipbuilding delivered the *Princess Anne* to the Virginia Ferry Corporation for operation between Norfolk and Cape Charles. Although designed by W.R. Elsey of the Pennsylvania Railroad, the industrial designer Raymond Loewy was consulted regarding the streamlining of the superstructure. Of more conventional appearance than the *Kalakala*, the *Princess Anne* had a short domed funnel with the navigation bridge, forward superstructure and the bow styled to match.

In daily ferry service, the *Princess Anne* proved to be anything but practical. Her funnel was too short and sooty smoke from her steam reciprocating engines was dragged down on to the after decks. Consequently, she was gradually de-streamlined and ended her days in the 1970s working on the Delaware River as the *New Jersey*. In 1993, after withdrawal from service and a period laid up, she was sunk off Palm Beach on the Floridian coast to create an artificial reef for divers.

From the latter 1930s onwards, what really distinguished American ships such as the *Kalakala* and the *Princess Anne* was not so much their contrived streamlining as their emphasis on fire safety through the specification of fire-resistant fittings and finishes, as opposed to the British method of fighting fires using sprinklers. This created two rival camps in ship design that endured until the 1990s: fire proofing versus fire fighting. Today, a combination of both techniques is mandated in ship construction.

The American preference for fireproof ships was the result of bitter experience. On the night of 8th September 1934, an arsonist set fire to the 1930-built coastal liner *Morro Castle* of the New York & Cuba Mail Steamship Co. The fire spread from

The Virginia Ferry Corporation's **Princess Anne**, with external styling by Raymond Loewy, made a bold and futuristic impression. *(Bruce Peter collection)*

The remarkable streamformed **Kalakala** caused a mild sensation when introduced by Puget Sound Navigation between Seattle and Vancouver Island in 1935. *(Bruce Peter collection)*

stem to stern and killed 133 people, most of them passengers. Thereafter, America introduced the 'Method 1' fire safety standards on all US-flagged tonnage, whereas the British model (also employed elsewhere in the world) became known as 'Method 2'. (The French, uniquely, combined aspects of US and British standards in what they called 'Method 3'.)

The streamlined appearance of the *Kalakala* and the *Princess Anne* was much admired in Scandinavia – influence reflected in unrealised designs for car and train ferries to serve a projected route between Rødby and the island of Fehmarn, off the north German coast. Known as 'Fugleflugtslinien' (Bird-flight Line), the project was first promoted in 1940, with completion set for 1945. By 1942, three tentative general arrangement drawings, known as 'Project no. 1.1', 'Project no. 1.2' and 'Project no. 1.3' had been produced. Each scheme was for a vessel 113 metres long and 19 metres broad, capable of transporting five-coach 'Lyntog' express diesel trains. Above the train deck would be three elliptically-shaped saloons with hallways, promenades and service facilities, such as the galley, in the

'negative' spaces between. The forward ellipse would contain a First Class saloon, with the restaurant amidships and a Second Class saloon aft. But because of the war, these schemes did not materialise, although their influence was felt in numerous ferries introduced in the post-war era in Denmark and beyond – commencing with DSB's 1,581-ton *Broen* (1952) and followed by the much larger DSB 4,084-ton *King Frederik IX* (1954), a three-track train and vehicle ferry for the Gedser-Grossenbrode route between Denmark and West Germany.

Equally, the Spanish Empresa Nacional Elcano's stern-loading 3,392-ton 'Type H' car ferries the *Victoria* (1952) and the *Virgen de Africa* (1953) had similar external styling and machinery to their Danish counterparts.

The increasing use of streamlining reflected wider trends in the design of merchant ships of all types and also related to the shipbuilding industry's development of more sophisticated techniques for working steel and aluminium alloy.

The Spanish Empesa Naçional Elcano ferry **Virgen De Africa** was another early post-war ferry to display streamlined external styling. Here she is seen at Algeciras. *(Bruce Peter collection)*

CHAPTER THREE

From Packet Liner to Overnight Ferry

On longer overnight services, vehicle-carrying ferries gradually evolved from existing packet liner designs and progress in the inter-war years was in fits and starts.

Developments occurred in three main areas: propulsion technology, increases in car capacity and advances in the comfort, amenity and style of passenger accommodation. In theory all three were related, but in practice certain vessels were significant for progress in some respects but not others.

The balance of power in engine rooms shifted in turn from steam reciprocating engines to steam turbines and, slightly later, to diesel motors. The need to carry more cars created a variety of responses from ferry operators, some ignoring this potentially lucrative market altogether and others either converting existing vessels or commissioning dedicated car-carrying tonnage of one sort or another.

In 1909 the Dutch Stoomvaart Maatschappij Zeeland (SMZ or the Zeeland Steamship Company), which operated between Folkestone and Vlissingen (Flushing), introduced a trio of 2,885-ton steamers with reciprocating engines – the *Oranje Nassau*, the *Mecklenburg* and the *Prinses Juliana*, all built in Govan by the Fairfield Shipbuilding & Engineering Company. Of the three, only the *Oranje Nassau* survived the First World War and in the early 1920s she was joined by Dutch-built near-replicas of the *Mecklenburg* and the *Prinses Juliana*, constructed by the Koninklijke Maatschappij 'De Schelde' shipyard at Vlissingen and fitted with turbines rather than reciprocating engines.

By the mid-1920s, the SMZ service was carrying cars driven directly on to the steamers' promenade decks via a ramp at Vlissingen, where the fairly constant water level facilitated wet dock berthing – a method unique until the mid-1930s. Cars at the other end of the operation, Folkestone, were crane-loaded because of the far greater tidal range.

In National Socialist Germany, technological innovation in marine engineering was celebrated as a sign of national virility. Between 1932 and 1935 the number of private cars (mainly in society's upper echelons) more than doubled to 1,272,000 and a nationwide 'Reichsautobahn' motorway network was developed.

The first large purpose-built German overnight car-carrying vessel was the 5,504 grt *Tannenberg*, delivered in 1935 by the Stettiner Oderwerken to the Hamburg-Amerika Line (HAPAG). A famous transatlantic liner company, HAPAG also contributed to a jointly-operated network of services between German Baltic ports – Helsinki in Finland and Königsberg in the German enclave of East Prussia, routes first established in 1926. The other partners were Norddeutscher Lloyd and Braeunlich of Stettin.

Up to 100 cars could be loaded through side hatches into the *Tannenberg*'s commodious garage spaces, which were spread over two decks connected by hydraulic lift. The lower garage filled only the forward section of her hull while the upper extended aft on either side of a broad centre casing. In

THE Dutch Stoomvaart Maatschapij Zeeland packet vessel **Oranje Nassau** (1909) operated between Vlissingen and Folkestone. By the inter-war era, the service was being heavily promoted to motorists in the UK. *(Bruce Peter collection)*

comparison, the Seedienst Ostpreussen vessels, the *Hansestadt Danzig* and the *Preussen*, could only carry limited numbers of cars crane-loaded on deck – and only if each weighed less than a ton, so as not to affect the ships' stability.

As the *Tannenberg*'s garage was not fitted with sprinklers, before cars were loaded onboard petrol tanks had to be emptied on the quay to minimise the fire risk. A seven-strong deck crew pushed each car up the ramp and into the garage, while an eighth man steered.

Passenger accommodation consisted of 21 three-berth cabins, 60 two-berth cabins and 72 fold-down beds in dormitories, somewhat akin to couchettes in railway carriages. More slept on metal-framed hammocks resembling German Youth Hostel 'vanderkoge' and the berths on troop ships. Canvas-covered reclining chairs in the sheltered promenade decks gave additional space – hence the 2,000-passenger capacity. The *Tannenberg*'s public rooms, designed by architect Max Wittmaack, were decorated in a variety of Nazi-approved traditional Germanic styles – from a Prussian baroque smoking saloon to a ladies' lounge in the Biedermeier manner. The main staircase, adjacent to the passenger entrance hall, was hung with portraits of Hindenburg, Ludendorf and Hitler.

When the ship was not carrying cars, the Hitler Youth used the *Tannenberg*'s garage. The idea was to give them a gratis taste of life at sea in an environment somewhat akin to the dormitories onboard the warships of the Kriegsmarine, in the hope that it would encourage them to sign up for military service. Although the restrictions of the *Tannenberg*'s small car hatches and garage spaces made her unusable for transporting military hardware, she would have been very effective as a high-capacity troop carrier or civilian evacuation ship.

The specification of turbine propulsion rather than diesel motors was intriguing, not only because the *Tannenberg*'s fleetmates (the *Hansestadt Danzig* and the *Preussen*) were

A car is manhandled up a ramp on the *Tannenberg* in the mid-1930s. *(Bruce Peter collection)*

Loading a car onboard the prestigious French transatlantic liner *Normandie* in the latter 1930s. *(Les Streater collection)*

motor ships but also because HAPAG were early diesel enthusiasts, even going so far as to purchase the newly-built East Asiatic Company passenger-cargo liner *Fionia* on first sight at Kiel in 1912.

Moreover, during the National Socialist period, numerous notable German passenger liners were constructed with diesel propulsion – not least the large Kraft durch Freude cruise ships of 1938 and 1939 respectively: the *Wilhelm Gustloff*, which appeared to be a much-enlarged version of the *Tannenberg*, and the *Robert Ley*. All had fairly straight hull lines and four-square superstructures, with little of the curvaceousness of the period's latest Scandinavian and American passenger ships. The Nazis' conservative ideology apparently deplored the streamlining of ship exteriors.

The *Tannenberg*'s career was short. In 1940 she was mined off the Swedish coast – ironically while in use as a minelayer.

Thereafter, elements of her design influenced initial proposals by Deutsche Reichsbahn (German Railways) for train ferries to operate the planned Fugleflugtslinien service from Puttgarten to Rødby in Denmark. These eventually came to fruition in the form of the 3,863-ton *Deutschland*, delivered in 1953.

In 1935 – the year that the *Tannenberg* entered service – the world's most famous car-carrying passenger liner (if not the most famous liner of all time) commenced transatlantic operation between Le Havre and New York via Southampton. The Compagnie Géneralé Transatlantique's giant 79,280-ton *Normandie* was a vessel of statistical superlatives, and much has been written about her magnificently opulent interior decoration, as well as her innovative hydrodynamic and technical design. Less has been said about the fact that she could load cars via side-hatches into her forward hull where the garage turntable enabled them to be manoeuvred with relative ease.

The *Tannenberg* as she appeared in the latter 1930s once the large windows in her hull topsides had been plated in, possibly because they were prone to damage in poor weather. *(Bruce Peter collection)*

Delivered in 1937, DFDS' *Kronprins Olav* operated between Copenhagen and Oslo. Cars could be driven onboard via hatches in her bow quarters. *(Bruce Peter collection)*

Of course, the *Normandie* attracted an elite clientele; how well-to-do Americans must have loved the idea of taking their car to Europe for a motoring holiday. Besides, as with Hamburg-Amerika who owned the *Tannenberg*, CGT clearly had an eye on a future in which car ownership would increase exponentially. Alas, the *Normandie*'s untimely destruction by fire in New York Harbour in 1942, coupled with post-war austerity in Europe, nullified the possibility of car traffic forming a significant element of transatlantic liner services.

In Denmark, the headquarters of Det Forenede Dampskibs-Selskab (DFDS, or The United Steamship Company), whose services then reached all over the western hemisphere, looked across Copenhagen's busy harbour towards the Burmeister & Wain shipyard and marine diesel engine works. During the 1920s, DFDS became enthusiastic proponents of B&W diesel propulsion for passenger and cargo vessels, introducing numerous examples not only on routes within Scandinavia but also to Britain, the Faeroe Islands and Greenland.

In the mid-1930s, DFDS turned its attention to building a new flagship for the prestigious Copenhagen-Oslo route. It was to be a floating showcase of progressive Danish architecture, technical developments and interior design. For inspiration they turned to progressive Copenhagen-based architect Kay Fisker, whose very impressive track record included the acclaimed and strikingly modern 1,726-ton passenger motor ship *Hammerhus* (1936) for the Dampskibs-Selskabet paa Bornholm af 1866 (popularly known as the '66 Company). Fisker was also entrusted with the new vessel's interior design, working in close collaboration with Knud E. Hansen.

Delivered in 1937, the new flagship – the 3,038-ton *Kronprins Olav* – was similarly striking and contemporary. Mounted on her curved stem was a DFDS crest, and the combination of high forecastle, broad tapering funnel and cruiser stern created a sense of urgent forward movement and

reflected her relatively high service speed of 18.5 knots (the fastest in the DFDS fleet). This was delivered by twin 7-cylinder B&W diesels. Her forward superstructure was semi-circular, emphasised by Fisker in the First Class smoking saloon's furniture and lighting. An open-plan approach was used throughout, the saloons separated by plate glass doors. Light and uncluttered, the interiors appeared deceptively spacious. Passengers and architectural critics alike acclaimed her elegance and modernity – a wonderful advertisement for Danish design, and a great influence on subsequent DFDS ships until the latter 1960s.

The *Kronprins Olav* was also progressive in respect of carrying cars. As with the *Tannenberg*, hatches were cut into her bow quarters but the inclusion of a sprinkler system enabled vehicles to be driven directly into her forward hold. They were then raised, one at a time, to the deck above by hydraulic lift – an approach repeated in several post-war DFDS vessels.

In late summer 1939, the Dutch Stoomvaart Maatschappij Zeeland (SMZ), which jointly operated the Harwich-Hook of Holland service with Britain's London & North Eastern Railway (LNER), took delivery of two fast new motor ships – the 4,353 grt *Koningin Emma* and the *Prinses Beatrix*. Powered by 10-cylinder Sulzer engines, they were built by the Koninklijke Maatschappij 'De Schelde' shipyard at Vlissingen and operated day-time sailings. Although there were berths for only 297 passengers, the public rooms were commodious. Up to 35 cars could be driven directly into the cargo holds.

Their civilian service was brief. Laid up after summer, they were then converted to transport British troops, returning to commercial operation in 1948. Packet liners of this type continued to be built until the early 1960s, but in the post-war era overnight services were increasingly dominated by vessels with a much greater vehicle capacity.

Top: The *Koningin Emma* during her brief period of civilian service in the summer of 1939. *(Matthew Murtland collection)*

Above left: The First Class cocktail bar on the *Koningin Emma*. *(Matthew Murtland collection)*

Above right: A corner of a First Class cabin on the *Koningin Emma*, convertible for daytime use. *(Matthew Murtland collection)*

Right: The First Class dining saloon on the *Koningin Emma* - the height of 1930s shipboard elegance. *(Matthew Murtland collection)*

CHAPTER FOUR

Short-Sea Ferry Design in the Post-War Era

In contrast to war-ravaged Europe, North America had enjoyed sustained economic growth since the mid-1930s. By 1945, the United States was the world's pre-eminent superpower and the source of all that was fashionable and desirable.

Of the many American ferry operators 'bridging' lakes, gulfs and river estuaries, the Puget Sound Navigation Company was arguably the most innovative. In addition to its daytime service from Seattle to Bremerton by the streamformed *Kalakala*, the company decided to build a substantial new overnight ferry with luxurious passenger facilities comparable with the most modern ocean liners in the US merchant fleet. To achieve this, it enlisted the services of distinguished American naval architect William Francis Gibbs.

Born in Philadelphia in 1886, he earned a science degree from Harvard and graduated from Columbia in 1913. In 1922 he formed the naval architecture and marine engineering consultancy Gibbs Bros, which in 1929 became Gibbs & Cox. During the 1930s he designed or converted a succession of passenger and cargo liners for America's leading shipping companies, including United States Lines, Matson Line and Grace Line. Unusually for a naval architect, Gibbs was a commanding public figure and had a very singular opinion of how ships should be designed.

He was also obsessive about safety – particularly the threat of fire – and his designs were both physically robust and often technologically visionary. Up to his involvement with the PSNC, he was best known for overseeing the development of the United States Lines' transatlantic flagship liner *America* (1939), which put in distinguished war service as the troop-transport USS *West Point*.

The new Puget Sound ferry, named the *Chinook*, was built by the Todd Shipyard in Seattle and delivered in 1947. Modest in scale in comparison with Gibbs' large deep-sea liners, for a ferry of her era she was substantial and proved to be prophetic in terms of ferry design development over ensuing decades.

The *Chinook* was also structurally and technically innovative. Gibbs was a pioneer in using aluminium alloy for passenger ship superstructures, appreciating its weight-saving qualities. On a ferry, it helped to lower the centre of gravity and thus increase the potential vehicle payload. Furthermore, the innovative use of diesel-electric propulsion gave the *Chinook* an 18-knot service speed and a car deck largely unobstructed by machinery casings. Four relatively compact yet powerful 16-cylinder General Motors high-speed diesel engines were arranged across the ship's beam. They drove generators to power electric motors, connected in pairs via gearboxes to the two propeller shafts. By the latter 1940s, GM's Electromotive Division (known as GM-EMD) was the acknowledged world leader in designing reliable machinery of this type. The small cylinders and short piston-throw made them ideal for ferries, as they could be fitted into the constricted spaces below the vehicle deck.

On the *Chinook*, machinery uptakes were routed through a casing, running along the centreline. On either beam were three lanes. The two inboard had sufficient vertical height to accommodate trucks and buses, while the outboard lanes, next to the shell plating, were only one deck high with blocks of cabins above – a layout which from the early 1960s onwards became typical on overnight ferries.

More cabins were located amidships on the Main Deck, the shapes of lounges forward and aft reflecting the semi-circular streamlined superstructure. Further cabins were above, on Boat Deck, where the large windows of the aft-facing circular restaurant gave panoramic views of the changing coastal scenery. Adjacent was a coffee shop. Not only was the *Chinook* ingeniously planned but also very contemporary in appearance – clean modern lines, a low streamlined funnel and a striking all-white livery, accented with bright red stripes.

Her interiors were designed by Smyth, Urquhart & Marckwald – an all-female company headed by Dorothy Marckwald, who had previously worked to Gibbs' stringent safety specifications on a number of prestigious American liner projects. This feminine touch perfectly complemented the technological innovations.

As with all US-flagged vessels, the *Chinook* had to comply with American 'Method 1' safety restrictions, forbidding the use of any combustible materials. The result was deckheads of bare aluminium, with all service ducting in full view. But her passenger accommodation was of a very high standard, the interior designers using bright fabrics, showy laminates and tubular metal-framed furniture. Gibbs described the *Chinook* as 'the *Queen Elizabeth* of the inland seas', and her ability to carry 100 American-sized cars, loaded through stern and side-ports in her bow quarters, was remarkable for that time. It was another decade before more vessels of this size and type were introduced in appreciable numbers. In the interim, the majority of European shipping lines engaged in short-sea services re-equipped with

The Puget Sound ferry **Chinook** shows off her modern lines. This vessel set the trend for subsequent day and night ferries in the 1950s and 60s. *(Bruce Peter collection)*

conventional small passenger and cargo liners rather than ferries.

While the *Chinook* was widely acclaimed, she was probably too well-appointed for operations in the Puget Sound area. Better roads meant that short crossings, such as from Port Angeles to Victoria, were more lucrative than longer overnight services all the way from Seattle. Moreover, the Puget Sound Navigation Company's operation faced stiff competition from the mighty Canadian Pacific Railway, whose steamers on the Vancouver-Victoria-Seattle 'Triangle' route were far less progressive than the *Chinook* in comfort and design.

Canadian Pacific had a long-standing relationship with the Fairfield Shipbuilding & Engineering Company in Glasgow's Govan district in Scotland. For CP's initial post-war newbuilds, Fairfield constructed a pair of 5,911-ton steam turbine-powered coastal liners, the *Princess Marguerite* and the *Princess Patricia*, delivered in 1949. Rather traditional in appearance, each carried up to 1,800 passengers and 50 cars, loaded through side-ports.

Apart from the *Chinook*, the Puget Sound Navigation Company's wider ferry fleet consisted mainly of older vessels maintaining the core network of short routes that were considered vital to the regional transport infrastructure of Washington State and British Columbia. The company could ill afford the required fleet renewal programme, particularly with wage inflation and industrial unrest afflicting operations in the early 1950s. The State of Washington therefore took over the majority of PSNC's beleaguered fleet in 1951, forming Washington State Ferries.

BRITISH FERRIES IN THE POST-WAR ERA

After all the trials and tribulations of the war, Britain was economically and physically exhausted, and although getting shipping services up and running again was considered an achievement, the reality was that in ship design and construction the country was falling behind its major competitors.

Britain's first new post-war ro-ro ferry service was inaugurated in September 1946 using a trio of hastily-converted ex-Royal Navy LST (Landing Ship, Tank) craft to carry mainly freight – plus small numbers of passengers – from Tilbury to Rotterdam. These nameless flat-bottomed vessels, designed to deliver tanks and other military equipment directly on to beaches, were known by their pennant numbers – 3519, 3534 and 3512 – and operated by the Transport Ferry Service, the brainchild of former White Star Line Passenger Traffic Manager Colonel Frank Bustard.

Born in Liverpool in 1886, he was awarded a military OBE for distinguished service in the First World War, overseeing the opening of the ports of Beirut, Tripoli, Alexandria and Mersin to enable the British Army to advance through Palestine and Syria. Post-war, he was employed by White Star and involved in the design of its Belfast-built motor ships, the *Britannic* and the *Georgic* and introduced a Tourist Class as a lucrative new source of revenue. Bustard also pioneered White Star's cruise business in the wake of the Great Depression, but was not enamoured by the British government's insistence that White Star should merge with Cunard in order to fund the completion of the latter's new transatlantic flagship, the *Queen Mary*.

In 1934 Bustard formed his own business, the Atlantic Steam Navigation Company, aiming to build or acquire a fleet of liners with which to operate a one-class tourist service from Europe to America. But he failed to raise the necessary funds.

During the Second World War, Bustard was promoted to Lieutenant-Colonel, in charge of logistics, firstly at Southampton and then at Holyhead, Birkenhead, Liverpool, Manchester and other ports in England's north-west. The possibilities of using flat-bottomed LSTs to ferry commercial vehicles intrigued him.

His first three ex-Navy LST acquisitions were renamed the *Empire Baltic*, the *Empire Cedric* and the *Empire Celtic*, reflecting Bustard's own White Star Line pedigree. Following initial success in carrying freight between Tilbury and Rotterdam, a second route was inaugurated in 1948 across the Irish Sea from Preston to Larne. Two more LST craft were purchased – the *Empire Doric* and the *Empire Gaelic*.

RAILWAY FLEET RENEWAL

In terms of passenger and car ferries, the most urgent priority for Britain's railway fleets was to cover for war losses as best possible until newbuilds could be commissioned. Thus, in 1946, the 22-year-old Southern Railway Dover Strait turbine steamer *Dinard* was rebuilt on the River Tyne as a crane-loaded car ferry for the Dover-Boulogne service. In June 1947 the LMS (London, Midland & Scottish Railway) took delivery of the *Princess Victoria* – a new Stranraer-Larne car ferry built by William Denny & Bros of Dumbarton. Compared with the new state-of-the-art American Puget Sound vessel *Chinook*, the new LMS ship was merely a replica of her predecessor, also named the *Princess Victoria*, and shortly after she entered service the four neglected and struggling railway companies were nationalised to form British Railways – the organisation for which the next large British car ferry was built.

Delivered in 1952 by William Denny & Bros, the 3,333-ton *Lord Warden* closely followed the layout of the 1939 *Princess Victoria*. Intended mainly for daytime operation between Dover and Boulogne, she too was a stern-loader, her vehicle deck having a central casing around which cars drove in a U-shape, with a fixed upper car deck filling the forward two-thirds of the hull. Where the *Lord Warden* differed significantly was in her steam turbine propulsion and this, rather than diesel, became standard for the larger units of the British Railways ferry fleet until the mid-1960s. By then, practically every other shipping company operating short-sea routes – and many deep-sea lines as well – had rejected turbines due to their higher operational costs. The *Lord Warden* was a one-class steamer with space for up to 1,000 passengers and 120 cars.

British Railways' initial post-war vessels were drawn up by their builders, working to capacity and speed specifications supplied by the British Transport Commission's London-headquartered Shipping & International Services Department. Interiors were also left largely to the shipyards and had not really progressed in terms of comfort and facilities since the early 1930s.

Both the *Princess Victoria* and the *Lord Warden* had only partially-enclosed stern arrangements, with freeing ports to drain excess water from their vehicle decks. On 31st January 1953, disaster struck the *Princess Victoria* during a stormy crossing, her vehicle deck flooding at such a rate that the freeing ports could not cope, resulting in free surface effect and a rapid capsize. The loss of 128 lives included that of her Captain, James Ferguson. This was the first of a number of similar tragedies to befall ro-ro ferries; indeed, at the accident enquiry in Belfast, it was revealed that previously, spillage from a milk tanker had shown the *Princess Victoria*'s freeing ports to be inadequate – yet no modifications had been made. Similarly, only a week after the tragedy, the stern gates of the *Lord*

Left: The Atlantic Steam Navigation Company's converted landing craft **Empire Cedric** was one of a fleet of such vessels to introduce dedicated services for commercial vehicles from Britain to the Continent and Northern Ireland. *(Ferry Publications Library)*

Below: A 1970s view of British Rail's Dover Strait ferry **Lord Warden** leaving Dover. *(Bruce Peter collection)*

Bottom left: British Railways' **Princess Victoria** replaced her war-loss namesake between Stranraer and Larne in 1947 but sank in tragic circumstances in 1953. *(Ambrose Greenway collection)*

Bottom right: A 1960-vintage brochure advertising British Railways' Dover Strait ferry services. *(Bruce Peter collection)*

Warden were smashed open by waves while she was leaving Boulogne, but only temporary repairs were made and she quickly returned to service without any modification.

The British Transport Commission, determined that none of its vessels should ever be lost again in similar circumstances, adopted an admirably cautious approach to building substantial safety margins into all future vessels. As an immediate solution, existing ferries, such as the *Lord Warden*, were fitted with larger freeing ports to increase the speed of run-off from the car deck (although, in certain sea conditions, these also tended to let more water in).

Another consequence of the *Princess Victoria* tragedy was that the BTC took over control from their regional subsidiaries and the shipyards of the specification of new ships, centralising design through the formation of a new Naval Architecture Department in December 1956. This followed the 1955 announcement of a far-reaching Modernisation Plan for British Railways, establishing a Design Panel to advise on aesthetic matters affecting all aspects of the railway's operations. Centralised design also brought about the possibility of British Railways ships having a more co-ordinated appearance, particularly in interior design.

The 3,920-ton *Maid of Kent*, delivered in 1959 for Dover Strait service, was the first ship completed under the Modernisation Plan. As with the *Lord Warden*, she was a stern-loading turbine steamer, retaining the traditional external appearance of her fleetmates but with contemporary interiors, designed by the Panel-recommended Ward & Austin. Their work was praised by the architectural press for its appropriately workmanlike but graceful style, with clean lines, simple forms and solid colours in soft tones. The *Maid of Kent* also had seating for her entire complement of 1,000 passengers.

In December 1958, Prime Minister Harold Macmillan opened Britain's first motorway, the M6 Preston Bypass, and his controversial Secretary of State for Transport, Ernest Marples, strongly supported development of a nationwide network. In November 1959, the M1 motorway was opened between Birmingham and St Albans and, as car ownership soared, a succession of similar developments was announced.

Hence more car ferries were required and the *Maid of Kent* became the prototype for British Railways newbuilds, including the *Caledonian Princess* (1961), the *Dover* and the *Holyhead Ferry I* (both 1965). Notwithstanding their robust construction and high safety standards, these ships had short active lives, all

Newly completed, the ***Saint-Germain*** leaves Helsingor harbour in Denmark at the commencement of her delivery voyage. *(Bruce Peter collection)*

withdrawn prematurely in the early 1980s. With fuel prices rising sharply, their steam turbines were no longer economically viable – particularly as each ferry had limited freight capacity.

British Railways' Belgian and French partners on the Dover Strait, RMT and SNCF, developed different approaches to the expansion of their post-war ferry fleets. The Belgians returned to Cockerill of Hoboken for a further fast and powerful Sulzer-engined motor vessel, based on the design of the 1934 *Prince Baudouin* and her sisters. The new ship, however, had space for 100 cars, loaded via the stern and parked on either side of a wide central casing, but as the entire vehicle space was only one deck high commercial vehicles could not be accommodated. Her superstructure, with space for a mere 700 passengers, was far less substantial than that of the company's packet vessels. Delivered in 1949, the new ship was named (imaginatively!) the *Car Ferry* but three years later renamed the *Prinses Josephine-Charlotte*.

For the majority of their post-war newbuilds, RMT specified six packet motor ships, also developed from the *Prince Baudouin*'s design and delivered between 1947 and 1966. RMT additionally took delivery of four stern-loading car ferries – the *Artevelde* (1958), the *Koningin Fabiola* (1962), the *Roi Baudouin* (1965) and the *Princesse Astrid* (1968) – all of which carried commercial vehicles in the aft sections of their vehicle decks. They were of similar appearance to their passenger-only fleetmates, except that spaces given over to lower saloon decks on the latter type were used as upper car decks on the ferries,

The First Class dining saloon on the ***Caledonian Princess***, designed by Ward & Austin and featuring decorative panels by David Gentleman. *(Bruce Peter collection)*

Part of the First Class lounge and bar on the ***Caledonian Princess***, exemplifying the bright décor found throughout the vessel. *(Bruce Peter collection)*

Top: The *Maid of Kent* (1959) was the first large ferry to be delivered to British Railways under its Modernisation Plan. Externally and inboard, the vessel was considered a design success. *(Bruce Peter collection)*

Above left: Part of the *Maid of Kent*'s vehicle deck showing the ramp to the fixed upper level. *(Bruce Peter collection)*

Above right: The *Maid of Kent* offered indoor seating for her entire passenger complement, many being accommodated in lounges arranged along each side of the saloon deck. *(Bruce Peter collection)*

Right: The Stranraer-Larne ferry *Caledonian Princess* was delivered in 1961, replacing the lost *Princess Victoria*. *(Bruce Peter collection)*

with commercial vehicles occupying double-height sections towards the stern.

SNCF's first priority was to acquire a new train ferry for the Dover-Dunkerque route and, as Denmark was at the leading edge with regard to train ferry design, in 1950 SNCF ordered a large four-track passenger and train ferry, the *Saint-Germain*, from the Helsingør Skibsværft, which had built many of DSB's key ships. Delivered the following year, the *Saint-Germain* was inevitably a motor vessel with Burmeister & Wain engines – but, unlike DSB's train ferries, she was a stern-loader only, reflecting the existing port infrastructure for train ferries at Dover and Dunkerque. (As with the Southern Railway's 1934 *Twickenham Ferry* and her sisters, a 30-car garage was provided in the aft superstructure.) The *Saint-Germain* proved to be robust and economical, inspiring plans for Helsingør to build SNCF two more ferries of the same type.

French shipyard management and trade unions protested strongly that SNCF should be supporting French yards, not Danish, and all subsequent newbuilds were constructed on home territory – albeit owing a great deal in design terms to the *Saint-Germain*.

In 1958 SNCF introduced its pioneering car ferry, the *Compiègne*, on the Calais-Dover route. A Pielstick-engined motor ship built by the Chargeurs Reunis Loire-Normandie Shipyard at Grand Quevilly, she was obviously a cousin of the *Saint-Germain*. The *Compiègne* also featured several notable

The Atlantic Steam Navigation Company's **Ionic Ferry** was an early example of a vessel purpose-built to carry lorries and trailers, as well as passengers and cars. *(Ferry Publications Library)*

innovations for a cross-Channel ferry. For example, she was of fully-welded construction and was the first ro-ro vessel to have KaMeWa variable-pitch propellers, controlled by the officers on the bridge. She also had an aft docking bridge to ease navigation astern. Her manoeuvrability was welcomed, as Calais has an awkward entrance with strong cross currents. The *Compiègne* set the tone for subsequent SNCF ferries such as the *Villandry* and the *Valençay*, delivered in 1965 by the Dubigeon-Normandie shipyard in Nantes for the Newhaven-Dieppe service, and the *Chantilly* of 1966, which operated on the Dover Strait.

ATLANTIC STEAM NAVIGATION JOINS THE BRITISH TRANSPORT COMMISSION

By the latter 1950s, the British Transport Commission had grown into a public transport monopoly, perpetuating state control over Britain's rail, road and short-sea shipping operations. Only the government could afford to borrow money in sufficient quantities to invest in expensive new assets and infrastructure.

In 1954 Colonel Frank Bustard's ferry business, the Atlantic Steam Navigation Company, was nationalised. Although notably successful it was under-capitalised, banks refusing loans sufficient to pay for new tonnage. In nationalised form, within the Transport Ferry Service operation, ASN would form only a small part of the British Transport Commission's mighty, railway-dominated shipping empire, and it came under the control of the BTC's British Road Services subsidiary, bringing lorries and ferries together under a single administration.

Nationalisation enabled the construction of a much-needed fleet of new vessels, the existing converted ex-Naval landing craft, with their steam reciprocating engines, being rather

A notably modern-looking ship for her time, the **Compiègne**'s design was clearly developed from the earlier, Danish-built train ferry **Saint-Germain**. This image shows her following a 1969 rebuilding to heighten her aft vehicle deck to give more space for trucks, hence the broken window line. *(FotoFlite)*

Top: The *Europic Ferry* was the final example of ASN's series of ro-ro vessels. She was longer and therefore more capacious than her older fleetmates - and, unlike them, there was no crane to handle lift-on cargo. *(Ferry Publications Library)*

Above: An Australian cousin of the Atlantic Steam Navigation ferries was Australian National Line's *Bass Trader*, a vessel propelled by compact high-speed Napier Deltic engines. *(Bruce Peter collection)*

Right: The Union Steamship Company of New Zealand's *Wanaka*, built in Hong Kong, was a further example of a ro-ro ferry inspired by the layout of ASN's vessels. *(Bruce Peter collection)*

primitive and not particularly seaworthy. Thus, two combined passenger-freight ferries of a completely new type were drawn up by British Railways' in-house Naval Architecture Department and built by William Denny & Bros of Dumbarton. The first, the 2,550-ton *Bardic Ferry*, was delivered in August 1957 for the Preston-Larne route.

The *Bardic Ferry* was a stern-loader with 295 lane metres of freight capacity and a generous 4.4 metre free height. Power came from two 10-cylinder Sulzer diesels, located forward of amidships and exhausted via a short casing, to the rear of which was a clear internal span in the aft two-thirds of the hull's length. This arrangement proved satisfactory but meant that the propeller shafts were relatively long. The superstructure, piled up forward in receding layers, accommodated 55 passengers in considerable comfort, in some ways resembling a small motel at sea. Aft of the superstructure was an open deck for additional lorries. There was also a cargo hatch and an electric crane to load general cargo in the traditional manner.

In 1958 the *Ionic Ferry* joined the *Bardic Ferry* in service across the Irish Sea. Next, two further near-sisters, the *Cerdic Ferry* and the *Doric Ferry*, were built at the Ailsa Shipbuilding yard at Troon, also on the Clyde, and delivered in 1961-62.

Although the Transport Ferry Service was notably successful, the British Transport Commission's losses from British Railways grew year on year and the need for reform was urgent. In 1961 the BTC was abolished and replaced by a new British Railways Board, chaired by Dr Richard Beeching, whose mandate was to drastically cut the size of Britain's rail network – a controversial task which exacerbated the shift from rail to road as the preferred means of moving people and goods around Britain and overseas. This in turn led to an accelerating decline of train ferry and rail-connected packet steamer operation and a parallel growth in the use of ro-ro ferries. For the international road haulage industry the future looked bright.

Meanwhile, further vessels were built for the Atlantic Steam Navigation fleet – the *Gaelic Ferry* (1964) and the somewhat longer 4,190-ton *Europic Ferry* (1968), both the product of the Swan, Hunter & Wigham Richardson shipyard on the River Tyne. Allegedly, ASN (Atlantic Steam Navigation) believed that lorry traffic would be only a short interlude in the development of full inter-modal container shipping, and so the *Europic Ferry* was designed with frame spacing optimised for subsequent conversion into a container ship. Lorries were not considered ideal due to the wasted space between their wheels and the fact that each required to be lashed down for safety. Although the BTC did build some small container ships, the ro-ro advantage in fast loading and unloading was considerable.

The *Bardic Ferry*'s overall layout was quickly emulated by a recently-formed state-owned ferry operator on the other side of the world – the Australian National Line, which operated between Melbourne and Devonport in Tasmania. The 1,653-ton *Bass Trader*, built by the New South Wales Dockyard Co at Newcastle, was delivered in 1961 and, most unusually, was powered by two very compact 2,100 bhp high-speed Napier Deltic diesels of a design more commonly found on naval gunboats and minesweepers. Mechanically complex, these engines were located in the ferry's aftbody and connected via gearboxes to her consequently very short propeller shafts. This saved weight and space, freeing up more deadweight capacity for freight, but such high-speed diesels were likely to wear out quickly. For ferries – especially those like the *Bass Trader* operating in harsh weather conditions – robust slow-speed or medium-speed engines were best.

Normandy Ferries' 1967-built Southampton-Le Havre vessels the *Dragon* and the *Leopard* also had a similar layout to ASN ships, albeit with superstructures extending further towards the stern and machinery aft of amidships. In 1970 the Union Steamship Company in New Zealand (like Normandy Ferries, a P&O subsidiary) commissioned the freight ferries *Wanaka* and *Hawea*, built by the Taikoo Dockyard & Engineering Company of Hong Kong and also inspired by the ASN fleet's design. By then, freight-orientated ro-ro ships of various shapes and sizes were being built in large numbers, replacing general cargo ships on short-sea routes all over the world.

The Normandy Ferries Southampton-Le Havre vessel **Dragon** had a similar hull configuration and open shelter deck as on the ASN vessels, but with her machinery space further aft. (*Bruce Peter collection*)

DSB's innovative 1956-built car ferry **Halsskov** was built to operate between Halsskov and Knudshoved across the Great Belt. A drive-through vessel, she could load cars simultaneously on two levels. *(Bruce Peter collection)*

DANISH STATE RAILWAY DEVELOPMENTS

While British Railways and its partners were taking a rather conservative approach to Channel ferry design in the 1950s, Danish State Railways (DSB) was simultaneously developing some of the most capacious and fast-loading car ferries in the world. DSB's post-war ferry newbuild programme was part of a general modernisation of the entire railway system, which also saw the first of many 'MY' class diesel locomotives delivered in 1954. By the end of the decade, this class had superseded much of the railway's steam locomotive fleet.

DSB modestly believed that it led the world in ferry design standards, and its ships exhibited many unique features – the inspiration of DSB's Technical Department working jointly with Helsingør Skibsværft's drawing office. Whereas independently-owned ferries berthed at protruding linkspans, DSB vessels sailed into V-shaped inlets, cut into the quay wall, their hulls formed to fit. In plan, all DSB ferries were shaped like elongated hexagons, the hulls and superstructures narrowing from approximately one third forward and one third aft of amidships.

Typically, DSB's Great Belt and Fehmarn Belt ferries were powered by robust and reliable 9- or 10-cylinder direct-drive B&W diesels – well-proven design favoured over newer and more mechanically complex engines. DSB also focused sharply on the need for a quick turnround in port, so loading and unloading were well organised and efficient.

DSB's train ferries of the 1900-60s period were divided by class, but its car ferries were one-class vessels with all passenger accommodation topsides. Usually, dining saloons were located forward on the saloon deck with seating arcades on either beam amidships and lounges aft. Throughout, the specification of fine hardwood veneers, modern furniture and lighting created a distinctly elegant onboard environment.

From the mid-195os, as car traffic across the Great Belt increased, DSB decided to open dedicated new ports at Halsskov and Knudshoved, adjacent to the main train ferry ports of Nyborg and Korsør respectively and each to be equipped with double-level linkspans. A new car ferry, the 3,194-ton *Halsskov*, was ordered from Helsingør for delivery in 1956, although until the new ports were inaugurated in 1957 she sailed between Nyborg and Korsør

The *Halsskov* was the first double-deck ferry on the Great Belt. She could carry 200 cars – more than twice as many as the single-decked train and car ferry *King Frederik IX*, and almost as many passengers (1,000 compared with 1,200). Moreover, she was able to load and unload cars simultaneously on two levels via the new linkspans, and her main vehicle deck could take a combination of cars and commercial vehicles as dictated by demand – an operational benefit perpetuated by other new Great Belt ferries which followed .

If there was a slight downside to this highly effective arrangement, it was that the linkspans necessitated a squared-off bow with side-hinged doors, which somewhat spoiled the ferries' appearance. Mechanically, the *Halsskov* was equally progressive – the first large ferry to be fitted with B&W's newly-developed turbocharged diesels, their enhanced combustion achieving increased power output and better fuel economy.

In 1961-62, two further multi-purpose car and train ferries – the *Knudshoved* and the *Sprogø*, the latter named after an island in the Great Belt – followed the *Halsskov* into service. Built at Helsingør and clearly developed from the *Halsskov*'s

The sisters **Sprogø** and **Knudshoved** operated as car ferries by day but were additionally fitted with railway tracks to carry freight wagons at night. *(Bruce Peter collection)*

When delivered in 1963, the **Arveprins Knud** was the world's most capacious car ferry. Here, the new vessel is seen crossing the Great Belt. *(Ann Glen)*

planning and layout, both additionally had railway tracks to carry night freight wagons between Nyborg and Korsør.

In 1959, before the advent of the *Halsskov*, the 3,667-ton *Prinsesse Benedikte* was introduced on the parallel Nyborg-Korsør train ferry route. To enhance manoeuvrability in port, she pioneered a new type of lateral-thrust bow propeller. Made by Swedish manufacturer KaMeWa, it was a development of – and a better solution than – the German-made Voith-Schneider propellers used increasingly on ferries. In essence, this KaMeWa innovation was a propeller installed in a tunnel across the breadth of the hull at the bow. It was so successful that it quickly dominated the global market and became standard specification on the vast majority of ferries.

Two other noteworthy DSB ferries, operating on the northerly Århus-Kalundborg route, were the 3,412-ton *Prinsesse Anne-Marie* (1960) and the 3,506-ton *Prinsesse Elisabeth* (1964). Hitherto, this rail-connected service had been served by the *Kalundborg* (1931) and the *Jylland* (1933). Constructed by Aalborg Værft, the new *Prinsesse* sisters were unusually fast, capable of well over 20 knots. DSB's other larger units could only manage around 16-18 knots, the theory being that crossing the Great Belt or the Fehmarn Belt in anything less than an hour would not give passengers time to enjoy lunch or dinner. But as the Århus-Kalundborg route was longer, the higher speed was justified.

By 1959, car ownership in Denmark had increased from 200,000 in 1946 to 370,000. There had also been a steep rise in the number of lorries, and the Danish Ministry of Transport produced a long-term plan to improve and enlarge the country's road network. Danes also enjoyed more disposable income for holidays and short breaks and trips. To capitalise, DSB ordered from Helsingør a significantly larger new car ferry for the Halsskov-Knudshoved route. When introduced, the 4,836-ton *Arveprins Knud* was the world's largest double-decker car ferry, able to carry 1,500 passengers and 341 cars per crossing, and her main vehicle deck had hoistable platforms which, when

lowered, accommodated a third level for cars. These were loaded and unloaded via separate shore-based spiral ramps, connecting with side-hatches in the hull's upper shell plating. Thus three separate traffic flows could be handled simultaneously and the ferry achieve a turnround of less than 30 minutes – a remarkable achievement, demonstrating the value of efficient, co-ordinated port infrastructure. To control vehicle movements onboard, and for the first time ever on a ferry anywhere in the world, traffic lights were fitted in the deckheads.

TOWNSEND'S FREE ENTERPRISE FERRIES

The state-owned ferry fleets on the Dover Strait had a single competitor in the form of Townsend Bros, which in 1950 replaced its existing converted minesweeper, the *Forde,* with a larger and fast ex-naval craft, the 1944 River Class frigate *Halladale*, built on the River Clyde by A & J Inglis.

The *Halladale* was converted by the Cork Drydock Company into a 355-passenger ferry with an open deck at the stern, on to which 60 cars could be driven. The *Halladale's* four Parsons turbines gave a service speed of over 20 knots, but her lightweight construction meant a deadweight capacity of only around 50 tons. She operated between Dover and Calais, the British Railways ferries serving Boulogne.

In 1956 Townsend Bros was taken over by Coventry-based entrepreneur George Nott, who had no previous knowledge of shipping, let alone the car ferry business. With traffic volumes increasing exponentially on the Dover Strait, and the railways introducing their own substantial ferries, the company decided that the best way forward was to build anew and sought the assistance of Norman Dewar & Son Ltd – designers of the *Forde* and *Halladale* conversions.

That firm's new owner was W. James Ayers, a youthful naval architect who joined Dewar's staff in 1958 from the Ministry of Transport and bought the business two years later when Norman Dewar died.

Older members of Ayers' immediate family had been

Top: The *Free Enterprise I* is shown berthed in front of SNCF's *Chantilly* at Calais in the latter 1960s. *(Ferry Publications Library)*

Middle left: A lounge onboard the *Free Enterprise I*, showing the open-plan layout typical of Townsend ferries. *(Ferry Publications Library)*

Middle right: Loading cars into the *Free Enterprise I*'s upper vehicle deck by means of a rather steep ramp. *(Ferry Publications Library)*

Right: A further view of the *Free Enterprise I*'s somewhat spartan interior. *(Ferry Publications Library)*

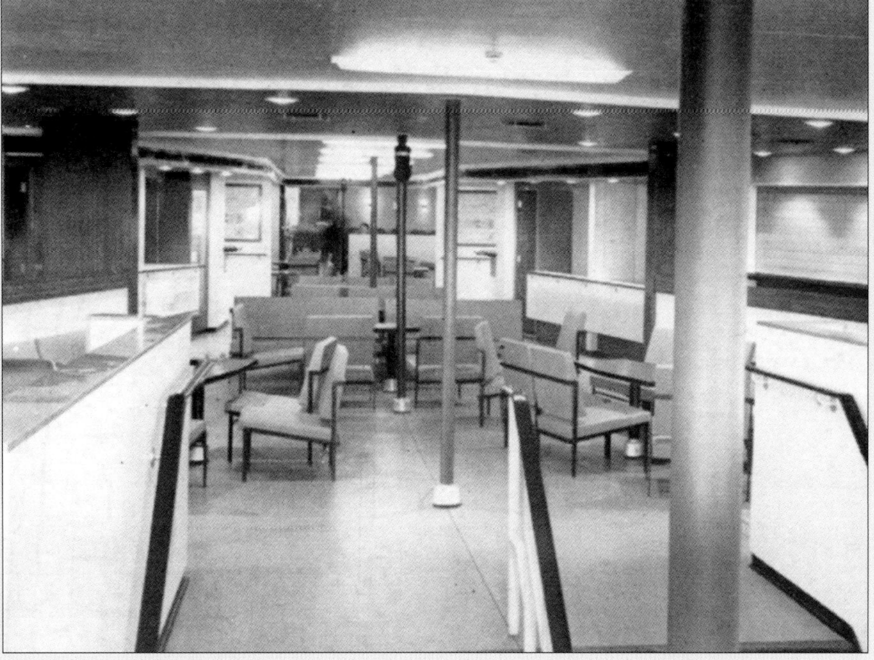

A contrast between rail-operated and private sector ferry design on the Dover Strait: SNCF's *Compiegne* and Townsend's *Free Enterprise II* at Calais in the mid-1960s. *(Ferry Publications Library)*

employed at the Royal Navy's Chatham Dockyard, and he maintained this maritime tradition by becoming an apprentice in Thornycroft's Southampton shipyard during the Second World War. When the yard switched from naval to merchant ship construction, he was involved in detailed design of significant passenger vessels, including Red Funnel's *Solent* ferry and excursion ship the *Balmoral*, the French CGT passenger-cargo liner the *Commandante Quere* and the Egyptian Khedivial Mail liner the *El Malek Fouad*. In 1954 he joined the Ministry of Transport as a ship surveyor in Southampton, working onboard many of the famous liners which regularly called there.

Acutely aware that it was imperative to have any new vessel in service in time to capitalise on the coming summer season, Ayers ordered Townsend's new ferry as soon as his design was approved. The builder was the Werf Gusto shipyard at Schiedam in the Netherlands, delivery scheduled for April 1962. Named the *Free Enterprise*, she was a 2,680-ton stern-loader with capacity for 850 passengers and 120 cars (just slightly less than her rival, British Railways' *Maid of Kent*) and had two powerful 12-cylinder MAN diesels, with KaMeWa variable-pitch propellers for enhanced manoeuvrability. Competitive speed and manoeuvrability were particularly important for Townsend ferries, as they had to negotiate the strong lateral currents at the entrance to Calais Harbour, whereas the British Railways-owned vessels serving Boulogne had an easier harbour entrance through which to navigate.

A constant theme of Ayers' ferry design was to find ingenious ways to lower vessels' centres of gravity and increase stability while carrying the maximum possible payload. To help achieve this, the *Free Enterprise*'s engines were positioned close to the shell plating on either beam with single lanes for cars above each. The middle vehicle lanes were in a well deck between the engines and had sufficient height to take trucks

and buses. Casings separated the inner commercial vehicle lanes from the outer car lanes. Above was an additional upper car deck, accessed via internal ramps – a first on a Dover Strait car ferry and a feature perpetuated on all subsequent Townsend ships.

Externally, the *Free Enterprise* was equally remarkable and, perhaps because of Ayers' formative experience with Thornycrofts, had a silhouette slightly reminiscent of a naval destroyer. She was brightly painted with a light green hull and twin red funnels, forward of amidships. The funnels and the forward superstructure were slightly streamlined and her open-plan interiors, offering single-class accommodation, were calculated to give passengers a greater sense of freedom than in the more compartmentalised railway vessels.

Following the delivery of the *Free Enterprise*, Ayers went to Denmark to research the country's latest ferries and to meet the managers and technical staffs of the Aalborg and Helsingør

The *Free Enterprise III* had a taller vehicle deck better suited to accommodating commercial vehicles. *(James Ayers collection)*

The newly-completed **Free Enterprise II** displays her smart green, white and red livery to advantage shortly after delivery from her Dutch builders. *(Bruce Peter collection)*

shipyards. The operational efficiency and solid construction of DSB's Great Belt fleet particularly impressed him – but he noted that their bow door arrangements would not comply with British safety regulations as they had neither collision bulkheads above vehicle deck height nor watertight inner doors behind their bow visors. Nonetheless, Ayers was keen that Townsend should introduce drive-through operation on the Dover Strait as quickly as possible and devised an acceptable solution. This comprised a straight-sided bow visor – similar to those on DSB's train ferries – and a collision bulkhead some distance behind, fitted with locking watertight inner doors. Consequently, Townsend's second purpose-built ferry, the 4,122-ton *Free Enterprise II*, also constructed by Werf Gusto, was the first British-flag drive-through vessel. In terms of layout and external aesthetics, DSB's fleet heavily influenced her overall design and so she looked very different from the existing *Free Enterprise*. As there had been less commercial vehicle traffic than Townsend had expected, her vehicle deck was of insufficient height to accommodate trucks and buses. This proved to be her undoing: no sooner had she entered service in 1965 than there was a leap in demand to carry lorries and tourist coaches.

As a direct result, the otherwise similar *Free Enterprise III* of 1966 had a taller garage space with three vertically-stacked car decks along her centreline and double-height lanes for commercial vehicles located between her casings and shell plating. This was a complete reversal of the usual arrangement on short-sea ferries but gave a total capacity of up to 250 cars – although her compact dimensions made the task of turning lorries and buses into the side lanes something of a challenge for her crew.

With three modern ships, Townsend could now offer services from Dover to Calais and to Zeebrugge. During the latter 1960s, Townsend and the state-owned ferry fleets were fairly equally matched – but in the 1970s the private company surged ahead. British Railways' predominantly steam-powered vessels were more affected by sharply-increased fuel costs and, in addition,

ongoing investment depended directly on government priorities, whereas Townsend could make more strategic decisions based on forecast traffic growth. By the mid-1970s, the company had built no less than eight *Free Enterprise* ferries for its Dover Strait routes.

THE CANADIAN AND ALASKAN FERRY NETWORK

In 1955 Canadian Pacific returned to the Clyde for the construction of a large four-track train, car and commercial vehicle ferry, ordered from Alexander Stephen & Sons of Linthouse. The new ferry, the *Princess of Vancouver*, was a 5,554-ton motor ship for day-time operation on a relatively short road- and rail-connected crossing to Vancouver Island between Vancouver and Nanaimo. She was propelled by four 7-cylinder diesels of an unusual type, manufactured by the National Gas & Oil Engine Company of Ashton-under-Lyne in Cheshire, England. Designed to burn heavy-grade marine bunker oil, the engines were coupled in pairs to each propeller shaft – a novel solution to the conundrum of how best to provide an acceptable power output for ferries, and avoiding the obstruction of the vehicle deck by casings, or a high freeboard, which complicated loading and unloading procedures due to the consequent need for steep or long shore-based linkspans. In addition, four engines allowed the ferry to remain in service and nigh on schedule even with an engine failure. Hence this engine specification was widely emulated on numerous ferries of the early 1960s, before more powerful and compact engines were developed later in the decade.

In appearance, the *Princess of Vancouver* was rather more progressive than the steamers making up much of the existing CP coastal fleet, but there was none of the streamlining of the most recent American and Danish vessels. Inboard, she was a high-density ship with row upon row of fixed seating and a fast-food diner with stools arranged around long servery counters. As with the *Chinook*, the deckheads – and all the pipework and electric wiring – were exposed throughout the passenger

Canadian Pacific's **Princess of Vancouver** (1955) was fitted with four diesels, coupled in pairs to each propeller shaft - a solution which found popularity during the subsequent decade. *(Bruce Peter collection)*

accommodation. She could accommodate 1,000 passengers and 130 cars, loaded and unloaded via the stern. Her vehicle deck arrangement was similar to British Railways' Channel ferries of the same era, with cars filling a U-shaped space around a central casing or, alternatively, two trains on either side.

Meanwhile, the former Chairman of the Puget Sound Navigation Company, Captain Peabody, had set up a new firm called Black Ball Ferries, for which he retained the *Chinook* and a couple of his other vessels and re-registered them in Canada, where crewing costs were slightly lower than in the USA. Black Ball's focus was centred on short ferry crossings within British Columbia where car traffic volumes were growing rapidly and Canadian Pacific, with only one really substantial ferry, appeared to be struggling to keep up with demand. In 1955, the *Chinook* was rebuilt with the removal of the overnight cabins in the upper level of her hull and the bow cut away for installation of a drive-through door. She was then transferred to Black Ball's Horseshoe Bay-Nanaimo route, competing with Canadian

Pacific's service from Vancouver.

In 1957 Black Ball Ferries decided to build a new vessel, especially tailored for this short crossing. The 5,315-ton *Coho* was designed by up-and-coming Seattle-based naval architect Philip F. Spaulding. Born in Washington State in 1913 into a family of master mariners, he grew up in Seattle and studied industrial engineering at the University of Washington and took a Master's degree in Naval Architecture and Marine Engineering at the University of Michigan. Employment at the Bethlehem Steel Shipyard in Maryland was followed by a spell with Todd's Shipyards in Tacoma, New York, Alameda and Chicago. He founded his own naval architecture firm, Philip F. Spaulding & Associates, in Seattle in 1952, specialising in the design of car ferries, coastal cargo vessels and tugs.

The *Coho*'s capacity was 750 passengers and 110 cars, the latter loaded through a stern door and side-ports in the bow quarters. Powered by two 8-cylinder Cooper-Bessemer diesels, she had a 16-knots service speed. Although her overall design owed much to the *Chinook*, she also demonstrated the basic

Black Ball Line's 1957-built car ferry **Coho** sailing between Victoria and Port Angeles. *(Bruce Peter collection)*

BC Ferries' **Queen of Victoria**, delivered in 1962 as the **City of Victoria**, was a drive-through vessel for operation in fairly shetered waters, hence the bluff bow configuration. *(Bruce Peter collection)*

The Alaska Marine Highway stern- and side-loading coastal ferry **Matanuska** was a fine example of Philip Spaulding's approach to ferry design. *(Andrew Kilk)*

features of what would become recognisable as Spaulding's distinctive approach to coastal ro-ro ferry design. Her hull had fine lines at water level but at vehicle deck height it was broad and bluff, especially towards the bow. On either beam, her vehicle deck had large overhangs with sponson tanks between the waterline and the belting to add buoyancy and to give protection from side-on collisions. Apart from fuel economy, one welcome additional advantage of maintaining slender bow and stern profiles at the waterline on a ferry intended for service in inshore waters was that the amount of wash was kept to a minimum, reducing the ship's impact on the coastal environment.

The *Coho*'s superstructure was slightly streamlined, with a large forward-facing observation saloon, side arcades with seating amidships and a diner facing the stern. Introduced in 1959, the ferry was an outstanding success and, remarkably, she is still maintained in pristine condition and remains in daily operation on her original route, although her engines were replaced in 2004.

The *Coho* was the first of a whole series of ferries designed by Spaulding for routes north of Seattle on the American and Canadian Pacific seaboard. In 1961, the government of British Columbia acquired all Black Ball Ferries operations – with the exception of the Port Angeles-Victoria route – as well as Canadian Pacific's coastal steamer and ferry routes.

In 1960, under the premiership of W.A.C. Bennett, BC Ferries was formed. The intention was to commission a substantial fleet of new car ferries and, in parallel, to develop numerous ferry ports, making a comprehensive route network tied in with the wider highway system. The first new BC Ferries route was from Tsawassen to Swartz Bay, linking Vancouver with Vancouver Island – still the company's most intensive operation. Simultaneously, the State of Alaska set up Alaska Marine Highway to link America's 49th State with the USA proper. Philip F. Spaulding was the ferry designer favoured by both companies.

BC Ferries' the *Tsawassen* and the *Sidney* entered service in 1960, followed two years later by the *City of Victoria* and the *City of Vancouver*. Built by the Victoria Machinery Depot Co Ltd, these 3,128-ton sisters could each carry 989 passengers and

138 cars. In terms of overall design, they owed much to the smaller *Coho*. Each was powered by twin 16-cylinder medium-speed Mirrlees diesels, coupled to KaMeWa variable-pitch propellers and delivering an 18-knot service speed.

They had very spacious drive-through vehicle decks, divided by centre casings, which were accessed via two-part bow and stern doors on rollers, each half of which retracted into the hull on either beam. As with the *Coho*, they were high-density no-frills transport ships, with basic facilities, built to carry large numbers. A whole series of similar craft followed, many of which are still in operation today. Some have been lengthened and others lengthened and heightened, creating a rather strange appearance.

For Alaska Marine Highway's direct 'coastal express' service from Seattle to Alaskan ports, Spaulding developed a ferry type tailored for this relatively lengthy overnight route with cabin accommodation as well as lounge and dining facilities. Three vessels – the *Malaspina*, the *Matanuska* and the *Taku* (all names of Alaskan glaciers) – were built by the Puget Sound Bridge & Drydock Co in Seattle for delivery in the 1963-65 period. At 2,928 tons, they were propelled by two 12-cylinder Enterprise medium-speed V-diesels, and each could carry 500 passengers (100 berthed) and 109 cars.

The Gothenburg-Frederikshavn ferry **Kronprinsessan Ingrid** following lengthening in 1950. In this form, the vessel survived in active service until 2006. *(Rickard Sahlsten collection)*

THE SESSANLINJEN TYPE

The Göteborg-Frederikshavn Linjen, popularly known as Sessanlinjen, commenced operations across the Kattegat in 1936 with the pioneering *Kronprinsessan Ingrid*.

In 1955 the company took delivery of a second, larger ferry, the 2,176-ton *Prinsessan Margaretha*, built by the Helsingør Skibsværft. She was not only a side-loader but also fitted with a stern door. Additionally, she was the first of many Scandinavian ferries with an off-centre machinery casing so that five lanes of cars could be catered for – three to port and two to starboard – although, allegedly, this asymmetrical arrangement made her more difficult to trim on an even keel. Her vehicle deck was double-height to accommodate eight commercial vehicles on the casing's port side and, consequently, large turntables were installed fore and aft to turn them within the hull's constricted dimensions. Below, power came from twin 5-cylinder Nohab-Polar main engines, coupled to twin screws.

Typically of ferries designed and built at Helsingør, the *Prinsessan Margaretha* was streamlined in appearance and passenger accommodation was to a high standard. Yet, due to exponential traffic growth, she was replaced by more efficient and capacious drive-through tonnage after only seven years.

For its next ferry, the 2,240-ton *Prinsessan Christina* of 1960, Sessanlinjen placed an order with Aalborg Værft, whose drawing office developed a remarkable design solution to greatly increase the vehicle capacity within hull dimensions similar to those of the *Prinsessan Margaretha*. Much credit for this goes to Ulf Trapp, son of Harry Trapp, a founding director of Sessan. Trapp Junior served on Swedish submarines during the Second World War. On joining Sessanlinjen he rose quickly to the rank of captain and took command of the *Prinsessan Margaretha*. He later followed in his father's footsteps and became a Board member, taking a keen personal interest in the development of

In this dramatic aerial view, the **Prinsessan Margaretha** motors through the archipelago out from Gothenburg. *(Rickard Sahlsten collection)*

all subsequent newbuilds. He also contributed to the distinctive appearance of Sessan ferries of the 1960s, such as superstructures angled forward rather than back to reduce window glare and to improve the view ahead.

The *Prinsessan Christina*'s engines were placed as far aft as possible, exhausting through short side-casings in her stern quarters – the first time that such an arrangement was specified on a ferry. Forward of these, virtually the full width and depth of the hull's mid-body accommodated cars and commercial vehicles. In fact, the main vehicle deck actually consisted of three large double-level vehicle lifts. When loading cars, these were placed in the 'raised' position, with the 'main' deck level hoisted up to mezzanine height so that cars could drive directly on to the 'lower' levels which, when filled, were hoisted down to rest on the hull's double bottom. Once this was done on all

The **Prinsessan Margaretha** (II) and the **Prinsessan Christina**: the former has a forward-slanted superstructure to reduce glare in the interiors. *(Rickard Sahlsten collection)*

three lifts, the main deck could also be filled with cars and commercial vehicles. If required, retractable platform decks could additionally accommodate yet more cars, giving the *Prinsessan Christina* a total capacity of 152 – fifty per cent more than the *Prinsessan Margaretha*. (This layout was widely copied for numerous freight ferries built between the latter 1960s and the 1980s – albeit with open trailer decks between their forward-located superstructures and funnels.)

Furthermore, the *Prinsessan Christina* was a drive-through vessel. At that time, Swedish regulations governing ferry design did not stipulate either a watertight inner bow door or a collision bulkhead extending above vehicle deck height. Thus, when the *Prinsessan Christina*'s visor was raised, it left a gaping hole with only a small flip-down loading ramp to connect with the linkspan. With an open stern, similar to that of the *Prinsessan Margaretha*, it would have been relatively easy for the vehicle deck to flood. (The *Prinsessan Christina* was the second ferry with a KaMeWa lateral-thrust propeller and the first carrier of road vehicles to be so equipped.)

The forward-facing smoking saloon on the ***Prinsessan Margaretha*** typifies the high design standard onboard Sessanlinjen ferries. *(Rickard Sahlsten collection)*

Sessanlinjen, pleased with the high capacity and profit potential of the *Prinsessan Christina*'s design, ordered two near-sisters from Aalborg Værft – the second *Prinsessan Margaretha* (delivered in 1963) and the *Prinsessan Desirée* (1965). Apart from their relatively high vehicle capacities, all three were notable for well-appointed passenger accommodation, including around 50 cabin berths located forward on Boat Deck.

THE KNUD E. HANSEN TYPE

The railways dominated short-sea shipping until the 1960s and were initially ambivalent about the need to develop car ferry services. Established commercial shipping lines were also frequently slow to grasp the new reality of mass car ownership. Indeed, throughout northern Europe, private entrepreneurs – some with no background in shipping – often became the most successful car ferry pioneers and required state-of-the-art ships, designed for maximum efficiency. It was through serving this niche market that Danish naval architect Knud E. Hansen became the leading independent ferry designer, mainly serving Danish, Swedish and Norwegian private sector owners. As a consulting naval architect, Hansen offered a complete package, from initial layout design to project supervision up to the point of delivery, leaving owners to concentrate on running their businesses.

So successful was Hansen's firm that he was able to employ a number of talented colleagues who went on to make their own important contributions to ferry design during the 1960s. The most significant of these were Svend Aage Bertelsen, Tage Wandborg, Dag Rogne and Poul Erik Rasmussen – all graduates of the Helsingør Technicum and accomplished in complementary areas of expertise.

Bertelsen, who became the Managing Director of Knud E. Hansen A/S, was an effective administrator as well as expert in calculating optimal overall dimensions and costings of newbuilds. Wandborg was an exceptionally talented designer of ships' profiles and interiors. Rogne's speciality was in layout planning and Rasmussen's in hydrodynamics and forming the lower parts of ferry hulls below their vehicle decks.

The first design project allotted to Wandborg by Hansen, in 1958, was to draw up two small passenger ferries – the *Sundbuss Henrik* and *Sundbuss Pernille* – for Norwegian tanker owner Ragnar Moltzau. Known as 'Sundbusserne' (or 'Sound buses'), these each carried 100 passengers and were for service between Helsingør and Helsingborg. Moltzau was to become one of KEH's best clients.

That same year, Grenaa-Hundested Færgefart A/S, a client of KEH since the latter 1930s, took delivery of the 1,619-ton *Djursland* from Aalborg Værft. For her size, this compact new car ferry, built to supplement the *Isefjord* and the *Marsk Stig*, had a remarkably high capacity of 1,100 passengers and 95 cars. She was followed later the same year by the *Skagen*, a combined car and train ferry for the Kristiansands Dampskipsselskap's Kristiansand-Hirtshals route.

KEH's next significant car ferries – the 1,064-ton *Primula* (1960) and the 2,375-ton *Kattegat* (1961) – set the tone for the design team's output during the first half of the 1960s. The *Primula* was built for Linjebuss, a subsidiary of Stockholm's Rederi AB Svea, which operated between Helsingør and Helsingborg in competition with the state-owned car and train ferries of DSB and Moltzau's passenger-only 'Sundbusserne'. She was constructed by the Finnboda shipyard at Nacka.

The *Primula* was a short and broad craft, only 48 metres

Top: The Grenaa-Hundested ferry **Djursland**, designed by Knud E. Hansen A/S and delivered in 1958. *(Jan Vinter Christiansen collection)*

Above: The Kristiansands Dampskipsselskap's car and train ferry **Skagen**, also delivered in 1958, for service across the Skagerrak. *(Bruce Peter collection)*

Right: The short, broad Linjebuss ferry **Primula** (1960) transformed ferry travel on the Helsingor-Helsingborg route. *(Rickard Sahlsten collection)*

The **Kalle** of Juelsminde-Kalundborg Linien had her exhaust uptakes routed through narrow side casings and a dummy funnel to balance her profile. *(Jan Vinter Christiansen collection)*

long yet 15.36 metres wide. This gave her a toy-like quality when seen from a distance. Nevertheless, she could manoeuvre quickly and easily in what were relatively confined harbours. In order to simplify and speed up loading, the car deck was a single span from side to side, a web-frame construction adding greater strength and rigidity to the superstructure. Although the hull was open at the bow and stern, the superstructure, housing a spacious cafeteria and smoking saloon, covered most of its length. From the passengers' point of view, the *Primula* was infinitely more attractive than DSB's ferries, which were almost entirely open to the elements. The *Primula* was the first of numerous short and broad ferries designed by KEH for routes across the Øresund – not only between Helsingør and Helsingborg but also from Tuborghavn to Landskrona and from Dragør to Limhamn.

The *Kattegat*, a fourth ferry for Grenaa-Hundested Færgefart A/S, became the prototype for an even larger series of similar vessels to be deployed on various routes across the southern Kattegat between Jylland and Sjælland. Built by Marinens Hovedverft at Horten in Norway, she was very much an improved half-sister of the *Djursland*, but with a larger capacity of 1,500 passengers and 120 cars. An aft docking bridge was fitted and there was also a solarium, consisting of perspex panels, in front of the funnel to give passengers a fine view forward while they sunbathed. Another novelty was a fully-enclosed wheelhouse, extending over the bridge wings.

Tage Wandborg gave the *Kattegat* a slightly forward-weighted teardrop-shaped silhouette, accentuated by the horizontal elongation of the solarium, funnel and aft sun-decks – a form he describes as his "hungry look". He observed that

Grenaa-Hundested Faergefart's **Kattegat** (1961) further developed the elements which were to typify Knud E. Hansen A/S-designed ferries during the remainder of the decade. *(Jan Vinter Christiansen collection)*

The same can be said of the elegant Grenaa-Hundested ferry **Grenaa** (1964). *(Bruce Peter collection)*

The Rederi AB Gotland ferry **Gotland** (1964) was one of several ferries designed by Knud E. Hansen A/S for various Swedish owners. *(Shippax archive)*

"modern ferries such as these should look eager to proceed and should, in fact, appear to be proceeding, even when tied up at their moorings." This became the signature of all subsequent KEH A/S ferry designs until the latter 1960s.

Tragically, Hansen did not survive to enjoy the growing reputation of his naval architecture consultancy. In 1960 he drowned when sailing his yacht the *Sollys* through rough weather in the Kattegat. In his will he left his firm to ten of his longest-serving employees. Svend Aage Bertelsen took over the helm as Managing Director.

Not long after, the Juelsminde-Kalundborg Linien announced the opening of a new cross-Kattegat route between Jylland and Sjælland, an initiative first suggested in 1959. It appeared that the Norwegian Ragnar Moltzau (of Sundbuss fame) was ready to invest 25 million Danish kroner (just under £3 million) in two new ferries plus a linkspan at Juelsminde, but the Norwegian authorities objected to such a large investment in Danish domestic transport infrastructure. No more was heard about the project until the Dansk-Fransk Dampskibs-Selskab of Copenhagen expressed interest and directors Eigil and Leif Hahn-Petersen sought the expertise of KEH to design two new ships for the route. They were ordered from the Adler Werft at Bremen in West Germany, delivery of the first expected in time for the 1962 summer season and the second after autumn.

Named the *Julle* and the *Kalle*, the new 2,301-ton ferries had much in common with Grenaa-Hundested Færgefart's *Kattegat*, but featured casings on either beam rather than along the centreline, giving an unobstructed vehicle deck. Fold-away platform decks at the upper level could carry either commercial vehicles or two levels of cars, depending on demand and the time of year. This arrangement also protected the car decks from side collisions and reduced the free surface area for water

to slosh around in the event of accidental flooding. Below, four 9-cylinder MAN medium-speed diesels gave a 16.5-knot service speed. Twin rudders increased manoeuvrability as, when turned, they forced the wash of each propeller to the side more effectively than a centre rudder (fitted to the majority of ferries at that time). There was also a bow rudder and a lateral-thrust propeller, enabling the *Julle* and the *Kalle* to turn quickly within their own length.

Routeing the exhaust uptakes through side-casings impacted on each ship's external appearance as there was no need for a conventional funnel amidships. But, as funnels are of great symbolic importance to shipowners and passengers alike, the *Julle* and the *Kalle* were fitted with streamlined funnel-like structures (housing ventilation equipment and generators) slightly forward of amidships between foremasts and exhaust stacks.

Each ferry could carry 1,200 passengers and 120 cars. The Main Deck had a cafeteria forward with a hallway amidships and a restaurant aft. The galley, supplying food to both, was on the Boat Deck above, as on DSB's Great Belt ferries. The remainder of the Boat Deck had a small number of passenger cabins and a smoking saloon, with officer accommodation occupying the full width of the superstructure further forward. Although the crossing time was only 2 hours and 35 minutes, more passenger cabins were located below the car deck to enable drivers to rest before disembarking.

The *Julle* and the *Kalle* became important reference ships for subsequent KEH ferry designs such as Ragnar Moltzau's 2,494-ton *Gedser* (1963) and *Travemünde* (1964), built by Orenstein & Koppel und Lübecker Machinenbau of Lübeck, and Grenaa-Hundested Færgefart's 3,061-ton *Grenaa* (1964) and *Hundested* (1965), built by Schiffbau-Gesellschaft Unterweser AG in

Bremerhaven. These had the further refinement of so-called 'sky bars' in their dummy funnels – cocktail lounges with large panoramic windows giving views of the passing coast and seascape.

Between 1964 and 1968, Aalborg Værft constructed a further series of five ferries to modified KEH designs. The first, the 2,360-ton *Lasse*, joined the Juelsminde-Kalundborg service, while the remainder – named the *Mette Mols*, *Maren Mols*, *Mikkel Mols* and *Morten Mols* – were built for DFDS' Mols Linien subsidiary, which operated between Ebeltoft and Sjællands Odde. Although their general arrangements were similar to other KEH-designed ferries in their size range, an ingenious space-saving innovation on these Mols Linien vessels was to omit a galley in favour of preparing food in shore-based kitchens in the ferry terminals – a very effective solution to catering for very large numbers of passengers quickly and to a high standard. Sailing on ferries such as these specifically to dine became an established pastime, particularly on the short and scenic routes across The Sound between Denmark and Sweden.

By the mid-1960s, a dozen KEH-designed ferries were operating across the southern Kattegat between Jylland and Sjælland. Variations of these ferries were also produced for overnight services, with cabins squeezed in on either side of vehicle deck upper levels and in superstructure forward sections. Examples were Larvik-Frederikshavn Fergen's 2,913-ton *Cort Adeler* (1961), Bornholmsfærgen's 2,964-ton *Jens Kofoed* (1963) and Rederi AB Gotland's 2,825-ton *Visby* (1964). Other ferry entrepreneurs quickly began to take notice and they too commissioned KEH to create their own examples.

One such company, newly established, was Thoresen Car Ferries, founded by Otto Thoresen, who planned to operate frequent cross-Channel routes between Southampton, Le Havre and Cherbourg. Reputedly, Thoresen experienced a severely-delayed crossing on a down-at-heel British Railways steamer and decided he could do much better in terms of efficiency, catering and onboard style. He approached KEH for a design for three new ferries. The 3,670-ton *Viking I* and *Viking II* were delivered by the Kaldnes Mekaniske Verksted A/S at Tønsberg in Norway in 1964, and the 3,824-ton *Viking III* (June 1965) was built by the Orenstein & Koppel und Lübecker Machinenbau of Lübeck. All three were larger than previous KEH-designed vessels. Overnight accommodation for 300 was provided in cabins above and below the car decks, other passengers sleeping in aircraft-style reclining chairs aft on the main deck. Each could carry 180 cars, loaded through both bow and stern doors. They were, in fact, the first drive-through ferries to serve international routes from a British port, albeit flying the Norwegian flag and therefore exempt from British regulations.

When the *Viking I* made her maiden arrival in Southampton, she caused a mild sensation. Apart from her strikingly modern design, she was painted in a remarkable livery – a bright orange hull with 'Thoresen Car Ferries' painted along either side, and the topmost decks of her superstructure and her exhaust stacks were turquoise green. As she shared Southampton, Le Havre and Cherbourg harbours with such legendary ships as the *Queen Mary*, the *Queen Elizabeth* and the *France* – as well as the Union-Castle, P&O and Orient liners – the extreme stylistic contrast could hardly have been more pronounced.

The ***Viking I*** is seen approaching Southampton in the early 1970s. By this time, she is displaying the unified 'Townsend Thoresen' brand name on her hull. *(Ambrose Greenway)*

The move from traditional black or grey hull liveries for packet steamers to brighter alternatives was widespread in the early 1960s. At the time that Thoresen's vessels were turning heads in Channel ports, Swedish ferry entrepreneur Carl Bertil Myrsten had taken delivery from Sölvesborg Varv of a 1,291-ton ferry, the *Apollo*, for Baltic Sea operation between Simpnäs in Sweden and Mariehamn in the Åland Islands. Her hull was painted bright red – a striking colour applied to all ferries marketed under the now very familiar Viking Line brand.

Thoresen's *Vikings*, as they became known, were one-class and open-plan in layout. Plate glass doors between the saloons, modern Scandinavian designer furniture with brightly-coloured upholstery and dark wood panelling added a touch of luxury and modernity. Passengers had three dining options – enjoying waiter service in the à la carte 'Le Commandant' restaurant, eating as much as they liked for a fixed price from the Scandinavian smorgasbord buffet, or tucking into 'good familiar British fare' in the self-service cafeteria.

Similar vessels were created for other operators, such as the 1966 4,018-ton *Svea Drott* (built by Öresundsvarvet in Landskrona) for Rederi AB Svea's Trave Line subsidiary, and the 1966 3,500-ton *Queen of Prince Rupert* (built by the Victoria Machinery Company) for BC Ferries in Canada to operate on the scenic 'Inside Passage' route from Prince Rupert to Port Hardy.

Another KEH-designed ferry delivered in 1966 was the 2,890-ton *Ibn Batouta* for a new ferry company – Lignes Maritimes du Detroit, known as 'Limadet' – established by Otto Thoresen. Built at Le Trait in France, she served on a route connecting Malaga and Algeciras with Tangier in Morocco.

In Halmstad in southern Sweden, Lion Ferry – a subsidiary of the Bonnier newpaper and publishing empire – had invited KEH to draw up plans for a whole series of new ferries. As the Swedish government provided tax breaks for investors in shipping, Bonnier no doubt thought that the ferry business could prove very lucrative – especially with the growing popularity of tax-free onboard shopping and 'booze cruises'. Indeed, these helped to bring about the construction of significant numbers of increasingly commodious ferries – economies of scale resulting in lower fares and bigger onboard self-service supermarkets.

Lion Ferry, established in 1958, ordered its first ferry – the 2,196-ton *Prins Bertil* – from the Helsingør Skibsværft in Denmark which (due to a full order book) sub-contracted it to another Danish shipyard, Århus Flydedok, and she was delivered in 1960. The *Prins Bertil* accommodated 900 passengers and 80 cars, her two Nohab diesels giving a moderate 17.5-knot service speed. She was the first Swedish-owned ferry with KaMeWa variable-pitch propellers. Lion Ferry's plan was to operate her on a shorter hop between Halmstad and Grenaa, but in the event they established instead a new Halmstad-Århus route. Although not an obvious ferry link, and difficult to timetable attractively as it was somewhat longer than other Sweden-Denmark crossings, the lure of onboard tax-free shopping, and of Århus as a destination, made the operation successful – at least for a time. Then there was additional income from freight business, such as a lucrative contract to carry frozen fish waste from Danish processing plants to Sweden for use as mink farm animal feed.

Other Lion Ferry income was generated by selling and chartering ships, so few of its vessels were in the fleet for long. This aggressively commercial approach to business meant that the company soon desired larger vessels and enlisted the help of KEH to design a more substantial ferry type, with increased car and freight capacity and significantly faster service speed. The resulting new design was to become a standard ship type for Lion Ferry and for other clients of builder Werft Nobiskrug at Rendsburg in West Germany.

The first of this series, also named the *Prins Bertil* (3,625 tons), was completed in 1964. Her vehicle deck had a clear span for almost the entire hull length, save for a short narrow casing aft of amidships, giving five unobstructed lanes on which lorries could be parked. To increase the length of parallel lane metres, the bow had a pronounced knuckle joint and the stern was squared-off. Indeed, the vehicle capacity of 162 cars or 24 trucks represented a significant increase over previous KEH designs. As there was very little supporting framework in the hull, it was necessary to build robust diagonal cross-bracing into the deckhead to prevent the structure from flexing unduly.

The superstructure only covered two-thirds of the hull, with an open deck to the rear, upon which cars were loaded via a side ramp. According to one former Lion Ferry captain, this area had another (unofficial) use – as an outdoor prison for aggressive drunks who had overdone the tax-free booze and were handcuffed to the aft deck railing to cool off!

Externally, the *Prins Bertil*'s superstructure was built up in layers and the effect was accentuated by a large 'sky bar' above the bridge, the exhaust being routed through a broad rear mast with a tapering black-painted top and a smoke-deflecting fin, somewhat resembling a witch's hat. The principal saloons were on the main and boat decks, with a large restaurant forward, overlooking the bow. Throughout, the ship's light wood veneers, glassfibre furniture and bright colours created a fresh and contemporary ambience. The sleek external design was reflected by the relatively high speed of 20.5 knots, delivered by four MAN diesels coupled in pairs to each propeller shaft.

The *Prins Bertil* was followed by two half-sisters, the *Gustav Vasa* (1965) and the *Kronprins Carl Gustav* (1966), and two similar vessels for the British & Irish Line's Irish Sea ferry routes – the *Munster* (1968) and the *Innisfallen* (1969). The turbulent Irish Sea severely tested these ferries, however, and their 'slamming' motion became notorious. More alarmingly, there were occasions when their bow visor locking pins sheared, but fortunately British and Irish regulations stipulated that they had watertight inner doors providing a second layer of protection.

In Gothenburg, scrap metal dealer and entrepreneur Sten Allan Olsson had recently taken over the operation of tax-free shopping day cruises to Skagen at the northern tip of Jylland in Denmark. In 1963 he introduced on this route two vintage former Baltic steamers, the *Skagen I* (1914) and the *Skagen II* (dating from 1924). This was the beginning of Stena Line, today one of the world's leading ferry companies.

While there was no difficulty in attracting Swedes to sail to Denmark to cash in on duty-free shopping, Olsson must have realised that to be really successful he needed to encourage Danes to sail in the opposite direction – not easy, as Danes were perceived to be nationalistic and a little uneasy with Swedish culture. His clever solution was to give his ships Danish names and to paint them in their national colours of red and white.

Stena Line ordered new tonnage and commissioned KEH to design its ships. The first of these was the *Poseidon*, a small passenger vessel built at Ulsteinvik in Norway and delivered in

1963. This was followed by three car ferries – the sister vessels *Stena Danica* and *Stena Nordica* (built at Le Trait in France in 1965 and each around 2,700 tons) and the smaller 1,156-ton *Stena Baltica*, constructed at Langesund in Norway and delivered in 1966. The *Stena Danica* inaugurated Stena's car ferry service from Gothenburg to Frederikshavn, in direct competition with the incumbent Sessanlinjen, whose vessels offered passengers high-quality accommodation. In order to provide a similar standard, Stena employed up-and-coming architect Robert Tillberg. At that time he was also engaged by the Swedish American Line to design the First Class ballroom on the prestigious transatlantic liner the *Kungsholm*, and he became an important designer of ferry interiors for a variety of Swedish operators.

The *Stena Baltica* was intended to operate between Nakskov in southern Denmark and Kiel in Germany, but after a severe delay at the shipyard she was redeployed between Gothenburg and Skagen. The *Stena Nordica* was sent to the Channel to inaugurate a new Tilbury-Calais route marketed as 'The Londoner' to invite British passengers to sample the delights of tax-free shopping trips to France – a concept probably ahead of its time for most Brits.

In these early years, Stena Line was less a conventional ferry operator and more a ferry dealer, acting immediately if a good offer came along from a buyer or charterer – even if that meant leaving passengers waiting on the quay for a ferry which would never arrive. The Danish Port Manager once rang Stena's head office in Gothenburg to find out why the *Stena Baltica* had failed to arrive, only to hear: "We've hired her to Swedish Television today – haven't you been told?'

Typically, Stena vessels were built cheaply but to a high standard and sold on at a profit. Working closely with KEH naval architects, Stena acquired ferries which were state-of-the-art in efficiency and aesthetics, and very attractive to prospective buyers. Another example of these dealings occurred in the 1960s, when Stena's Danish Marketing Manager telephoned HQ to complain about the sudden sale of a new vessel which had been vigorously publicised. Reputedly, Sten Allan Olsson advised him to "go and take a rest and dream about all the money we've earned from that sale."

In January 1966, Stena negotiated a very lucrative charter for the *Stena Nordica* to the Caledonian Steam Packet Company – British Rail's Scottish Shipping Division – to serve opposite its 1961-built steam turbine-driven ferry the *Caledonian Princess*, which was struggling to cope with increasing demand on the Stranraer-Larne route. The CSP were prepared to pay a charter rate of £1,000 per day – an offer too good for Stena to refuse and so she was withdrawn from her Tilbury-Calais route and dispatched to Scotland. Her introduction there made it possible to draw a fascinating and direct comparison between typical modern British and Scandinavian short-sea ferry design practice.

The *Stena Nordica* was 90 feet shorter than the *Caledonian Princess* but had a greater free height in her drive-through vehicle deck. The British ship was a stern-loader with turntables. Whereas the *Stena Nordica* could carry 935 passengers and 120 cars, the respective capacities of the *Caledonian Princess* were 1,400 and 104.

The *Stena Nordica* was powered by two economical 12-cylinder Deutz V-diesels, rather than fuel-hungry turbines, and her open-plan passenger accommodation, with saloons spanning the full width of the superstructure, was rather more luxurious than that of the robustly-outfitted, though elegant, *Caledonian Princess*. One unexpected advantage of chartering a Swedish ship was that, during a National Union of Seamen's strike later in 1966, the *Stena Nordica* remained in service while the *Caledonian Princess* lay strike-bound at Stranraer. The CSP was so pleased with its chartered Swedish ferry that it retained her on the Stranraer-Larne route for over five years before purchasing her outright, and British Rail's Shipping Division also chartered KEH-designed ferries from Stena Line.

THE WARTSILA TYPE

While KEH cornered the ferry design market on routes between Denmark, Norway, Sweden and West Germany, in the mid-Baltic area it was the Finnish Wärtsilä shipyards in Helsinki and Turku which made the most significant contribution to car ferry design and, later, to cruise ship development.

The Helsinki yard's origins date from 1867, with the foundation of the Heitalahti Shipyard. A dry dock, completed in

As with Thoresen's 'Vikings', Rederi AB Slite's Baltic ferry **Apollo** (1964) was brightly painted and featured bold graphic design on her hull. *(Micke Asklander collection)*

Top: The **Prins Bertil** shows off her smart, modern lines in this trials photograph. *(Werft Nobiskrug Rendsburg)*

Middle left: A mid-1960s deck scene on the second **Prins Bertil** with passengers relaxing abaft the sky bar. *(Bruce Peter collection)*

Middle right: The cafeteria on the **Prins Bertil**. *(Werft Nobiskrug Rendsburg)*

Right: Crisp modern design inside the **Prins Bertil**'s sky bar. *(Werft Nobiskrug Rendsburg)*

The B&I ferry *Innisfallen* (1969) represents the ultimate version of the Knud E. Hansen A/S-designed ferries built at Rendsburg in the latter 1960s. *(Werft Nobiskrug Rendsburg)*

1868 and filled and emptied using steam pumps, was ideal for ship repairs and the construction of new steamships. In 1939 Wärtsilä was established, its numerous industrial enterprises mainly involved in shipbuilding, supply and outfitting. At a time when long-established British yards, traditionally builders of much of the world's passenger fleet, were struggling for survival, the Finns became serious competitors, working in a climate which produces winter temperatures often lower than -20° Celsius.

Wärtsilä's first ferries were the 3,593-ton *Skandia* and *Nordia*, delivered to Silja Line in 1961-62 to link Norrtälje (a town north-east of Stockholm) with Mariehamn in the Åland Islands and Turku. Silja was created in 1957 as a jointly-owned subsidiary of three long-established shipping companies engaged in the passenger and cargo trades across the mid-Baltic between Sweden and Finland: the Finska Ångfartygs Aktiebolaget (Finland Steamship Company, or FÅA for short), formed in 1883 in Helsinki; the Ångfartygs AB Bore, founded in 1897 in Turku; and Stockholm's Rederi AB Svea, established in 1872. Since

1918, all three had co-operated in providing steamers to work the Stockholm-Helsinki and Stockholm-Turku routes – a joint operation marketed as 'De Samseglande Rederierna'.

During the mid-20th century, political instability prevented significant development of these services and it was only in 1952, when Soviet President Kruschev formally recognised Finland as an independent nation, that significant investments in new tonnage could be contemplated. Meanwhile, three new passenger and cargo steamers, one for each owner, had been built to coincide with that year's Helsinki Olympic Games. These vessels – the *Aallotar*, the *Bore III* and the *Birger Jarl* – operated the traditional overnight service from Skeppsbron Quay in Stockholms city centre to the new Olympia Terminal in the heart of Helsinki. Small single-screw steamers with rather old-fashioned triple-expansion steam engines, the trio had limited passenger facilities and space for just fifteen cars, loaded by crane. At that time, Finland was a relatively poor country compared with her Nordic neighbours and many Finns migrated to work in Sweden, returning home in large numbers for

BC Ferries' Knud E. Hansen A/S-designed 'Inside passage' ferry *Queen of Prince Rupert* used a design based on the Thoresen 'Vikings'. *(Bruce Peter collection)*

The **Stena Nordica** (1965) - one of two sisters built to Knud E. Hansen A/S designs at Le Tait in France. Here, she is seen operating 'The Londoner' service on the Dover Strait. *(Bruce Peter collection)*

holidays and special occasions. For Baltic operators, this clientele was at first important but, as Finland rapidly prospered during the 1960s, there was also an increase in tourist traffic.

Silja Line's *Skandia* and *Nordia* were drive-through ferries with capacity for up to 1,200 passengers and 175 cars. Twin 9-cylinder Wärtsilä-Sulzer diesels, located towards the stern, gave an 18-knot service speed, the exhaust uptakes routed though a narrow centre casing. Their hull construction was exceptionally robust. Wärtsilä were expert builders of ice-breakers and, as the ferries were intended for year-round service, they had ice-breaker bows thickly plated and cut back below the waterline to make a 'knife edge' to smash through sheet ice. These vessels were also notable for their very bright, fresh and modern passenger accommodation, an outstanding feature of which was an oval-shaped observation lounge in a 'dummy funnel' amidships, giving panoramic views of the changing archipelago scenery.

Externally and inboard, these ferries were radically different from the steamers they indirectly replaced, some of which dated back to the Edwardian era. Unlike their predecessors they were one-class vessels, the entire passenger accommodation air-conditioned and finished in light, contemporary colours and comfortable, relaxing furniture. For the first time, crossing the Baltic by sea became a pleasure rather than a necessity. Eating, drinking, shopping, the sauna and the children's playroom were all welcome attractions. Yet, reflecting the budget-conscious clientele, the majority of overnight accommodation was in the form of reclining seats, with only 136 berths. However, these ferries' combination of relatively high capacity, efficient diesel propulsion and increased onboard sales created a demand for short cruises. Over ensuing decades, the Baltic ferry industry expanded rapidly and Wärtsilä was well placed to design and construct a succession of larger and more sophisticated vessels.

Children enjoy the view forward from the **Skandia**'s panorama lounge, as their parents relax in reclining seats. *(Shippax Archive)*

Silja Line's **Skandia** (1961) motors through the Baltic archipelago early in her career. *(Shippax Archive)*

CHAPTER FIVE

Larger Ferries for Longer Routes

Throughout the 1950s the steady growth in car ownership created new opportunities for vehicle-carrying ferry services. The ferries built to capitalise on this demand, for both short and longer overnight routes, emulated the layout and aesthetics of the passenger and cargo ships they superseded, with one vital addition – a vehicle deck.

Towards the end of this decade, Norwegian shipowners Fred Olsen & Co initiated plans to introduce a pioneering long-distance car ferry service in northern Europe – between Kiel in West Germany and Oslo in Norway. The commercial potential was obvious: the West German economy was booming, the autobahn network had been extended, and Norway was already a popular destination for German travellers – even though it meant sailing from Amsterdam or going via Sweden to get there. Olsen's proposed new direct Kiel-Oslo service was a far more attractive alternative, particularly as much of the route was in sheltered waters.

In the event this innovative idea was brought to fruition by another Norwegian shipping entrepreneur, Anders Jahre, with a new ferry the *Kronprins Harald*. Jahre had made his money in whaling and the very lucrative oil tanker business, and Jahre Line was a traditional First and Second Class operation. The new 7,034-ton *Kronprins Harald* was delivered in 1961. Built at Kiel by HDW (the Howaldtswerke Deutsche Werft) to a basic design by Knud E. Hansen A/S, she had a service speed of 20 knots and space for 120 cars, loaded through ports in the side of the hull. Passenger capacity was 577 and almost all could be accommodated in cabin berths. Other onboard features included smoking saloons, restaurants and a large galley.

Shortly after the *Kronprins Harald* entered service, a slightly larger fleetmate – the *Prinsesse Ragnhild* – was ordered from HDW for delivery in 1966. Both ships were at least as well

appointed as the majority of 'deep-sea' liners of this era. In winter the *Prinsesse Ragnhild* cruised to the Canary Islands, Madeira, the Mediterranean and the Norwegian Fjords – relatively long voyages carrying mainly German passengers, and an ideal solution for Jahre Line in coping with the perennial industry problem of lower winter demand.

Meanwhile, in the Mediterranean, another new ferry service had been established, introduced for the 1960 summer tourist season. It was a joint enterprise between the Greek line HML (Hellenic Mediterranean Lines) and the Italian state-owned Adriatica di Navigazione, each contributing a new large purpose-built car ferry.

The service was across the Adriatic, linking southern Italy (Brindisi) and Greece (Corfu, Igoumenitsa and Patras). Its birth was due to two key factors: the keeness of the National Tourist Organisation of Greece to promote motoring holidays, and the fact that many Italians were car owners for the first time given the country's expansive new post-war automotive industry.

The first of the two large ferries in service was the *Egnatia*, built at the Chantiers Reunis Loire-Normandie shipyard at Grand Quevilly in France. The design was similar to that of the then recently-completed SNCF Dover Strait vessel the *Compiègne*. While under construction, the *Egnatia* was purchased at auction by HML.

HML's own origins dated from 1901 with the foundation of the Constantinople Steamship Company to link Italian, Greek and Black Sea ports. In 1929 it became The Steamship Company of Greece. A decade later, Hellenic Mediterranean Lines was created as a separate firm to deal with international trade. The route network stretched from Marseille in the west to Lebanon and Palestine in the east, but enemy attacks in the war

Jahre Line's handsome **Kronprins Harald** departs Oslo for Kiel in the early 1960s. *(Bruce Peter collection)*

With a variety of Italian cars in the foreground, the **Appia** enters Brindisi's inner harbour in the latter 1960s. *(Alan Zamchick)*

Somerfin Lines' initial ferry the **Bilu** (1964) is seen at the beginning of her brief career under the Israeli flag. *(Bruce Peter collection)*

years destroyed the entire HML fleet and it was a case of restarting from scratch, initially with second-hand tonnage.

The 4,458-ton *Egnatia* had 434 berths and accommodated 1,397 passengers. The vehicle deck had space for 130 cars, loaded via the stern. (Given the Mediterranean's small tidal range, linkspans are unnecessary and ferries typically berth stern-in to the quay, dropping anchor to maintain position – a procedure known as a 'Mediterranean moor'.)

The aft section was double height, with space for a handful of lorries or buses. Of the remaining three-quarters of the ship's length, the upper level contained open-plan dormitories with bunk-bedded 'compartments' more akin to couchette railway carriages than to conventional ship interiors – yet ideal for busy summer holiday traffic.

With a service speed of 18 knots, the *Egnatia* proved to be an immediate and enduring success, putting in 35 years' reliable service on the Brindisi-Patras route. The warm Mediterranean climate enabled many passengers to travel quite comfortably in the outdoors Deck Class. First Class meant exactly that: comfortable cabins and well-appointed air-conditioned saloons in which to relax and to enjoy, through large windows, the passing scenery of the rugged Albanian and Greek coasts.

The Italian state-owned contribution to this joint two-ship operation was the *Appia*, delivered in 1961 by the Cantiere Navale Breda SpA shipyard in Venice. Although HML worked year round, the *Appia* was laid up between late October and early March. She had straight hull lines but a transom stern, and a service speed of 17.5 knots. Where the *Egnatia* had dormitories, the *Appia* had blocks of cabins, convertible from day sitting rooms to night sleepers, and the forward-facing observation saloon boasted 200 aircraft-style reclining seats.

As the 'baby boom' generation came of age in the 1960s, it was virtually a right of passage for groups of young adults from northern Europe to go in large numbers on backpacking holidays to the Greek Islands. Hence in summer, the *Egnatia* and the *Appia* were well patronised by students travelling Deck Class, happy to lounge around the swimming pool or sleep beneath the lifeboats.

In spring 1964, Somerfin Lines – an Israeli company founded in 1952 and registered in Geneva – joined the fray with a competing cross-Mediterranean ferry service. The *Bilu*, the first of two large ferries, was introduced on a lengthy 62-hour route from Naples to Piraeus, Limassol and Haifa. Somerfin offered something different from (and arguably more progressive than) Israel's state-owned Zim Lines, in the form of a fortnightly Mediterranean cruise ferry summer service plus short cruises from Miami to Caribbean ports in winter.

Built at Cockerill's shipyard in Hoboken, Belgium, the 6,445-ton *Bilu* was designed to offer economical travel. She was marketed as a 'boatel', carrying up to 524 passengers (berthed in 172 cabins), plus 120 cars and 3 buses (all loaded and discharged via the stern) but no trucks or trailers. Curiously, none of the cabins had windows. Furthermore, there was a night club located in the middle of the cabin deck – hardly the ideal spot for passengers trying to sleep!

The *Bilu*'s usefuless in year-round long-distance ferry operation was obviously restricted by her inability to transport freight in any great quantity and, equally, the lack of outside cabins probably limited her attractiveness as a cruise ship. But as an innovative 'boatel' making a 62-hour, 1,200-mile voyage twice a week between Italy and Israel, the *Bilu* opened the door to new possibilities in motoring holidays and at a price then described by a leading magazine as 'bargain-basement luxury'.

In her Mediterranean summer season, the *Bilu* reportedly transported around 10,000 passengers and 1,000 cars. She then crossed the Atlantic to Miami, arriving in early December 1964, and began a season of 3-day and 4-day cruises to Freeport and Nassau in the Bahamas and to Montego Bay in Jamaica, returning to Mediterranean service in March 1965.

The second of Somerfin Lines' large ferries was the 7,851-ton *Nili*. Similar to the *Bilu* in overall layout, this new ship was somewhat more substantial, constructed in Govan, Glasgow, by the Fairfield Shipbuilding & Engineering Company.

Instead of their original plan to use the *Nili* on a new service between Southampton and Algeciras (in Spain's Costa del Sol), Somerfin initially chartered the ferry to Finnlines in summer 1965 to operate on their Helsinki-Travemünde route.

More significantly, the *Nili* could carry 544 passengers, all berthed, and 120 cars – effectively a passenger liner in miniature. Somerfin Lines also announced their intention to build a further 20,000-ton 'boatel' for 5-day transatlantic service with capacity for 1,000 passengers and 240 cars. And although this intention never progressed beyond an idea – and it was likely that an Atlantic ferry service would have been a failure – the scale of the proposed vessel was a precursor of future ferry design trends for the 1970s and beyond.

NORTH SEA PIONEER

Compared with the relatively tranquil Mediterranean, the North Sea is often stormy – a harsh environment demanding exceptionally robust car ferries capable of operating all year round, as demanded by government contracts to carry the Danish and Norwegian Royal Mail.

The Danish shipping giant DFDS, in particular, had been

The DFDS ferry *England* approaches Esbjerg in the mid-1960s. *(Bruce Peter collection)*

experiencing exponential growth in passenger and vehicle numbers throughout the 1950s and, by the end of the decade, its existing 1940s-vintage Harwich-Esbjerg ships (the *Kronprins Frederik* and the *Kronprinsesse Ingrid*, introduced in 1946 and 1949 respectively) could no longer cope. Hence work began on a new flagship for this fairly lengthy and exposed route.

The newly-appointed Chief Engineer of DFDS, Brian Corner-Walker, oversaw the new vessel's detailed design and construction. Born near Stowmarket, Suffolk, he served in naval destroyers during the Second World War, arriving in Denmark as a naval officer during the city's liberation in May 1945. His civilian employment in Denmark began with the shipbuilders Burmeister & Wain. In 1952 he joined refrigeration specialist Atlas, rising to Chief Engineer.

He took the same title on moving to DFDS in 1963. According to Corner-Walker, the company's long-serving Chairman J.A. Kørbing was justifiably suspicious of the safety and seaworthiness of short-sea car ferries of the kind used in Scandinavian waters at that time. The loss in 1953 of the Irish Sea ferry *Princess Victoria* must also have weighed on his mind. Hence he insisted that the new ship should be essentially a conventional passenger liner with some car capacity. Speed was also essential – maintaining over twenty knots in nearly all weathers – to deliver mail on time. This called for a particularly fine-lined hull configuration, very different from typical ro-ro vessels up to then, a design task undertaken by the DFDS technical staff and the builder, Helsingør Skibsværft.

Delivered in 1964 as the *England*, the new ferry weighed in at 8,221 tons (the world's largest, albeit only briefly) with capacity for 399 passengers (155 First Class and 244 Second, all berthed) and 100 cars. Aesthetically beautiful, she was one of the best-appointed ships of her type.

Her sleek hull was developed from that of the Portuguese-owned liner *Funchal*, a turbine steamer completed at Helsingør in 1963. Where the *England* differed was her engines – two large slow-speed, direct-drive 14,000-bhp Burmeister & Wain diesels, coupled directly to the propeller shafts, delivering a service speed of 21 knots, with reserve power to make up for any time lost in stormy weather so characteristic of the treacherous North Sea. This was basic but well-proven

technology – robust engines of the type fitted singly to the 'deep-sea' cargo liners of DFDS. They were less prone to the fatigue resulting from constant operation in harsh conditions, when propellers could come out of the water with consequent sudden drops in resistance. Having found a formula that had worked well since the 1930s, DFDS saw no advantage in changing to more complicated installations of paired medium-speed engines and gearboxes.

The choice of these so-called 'cathedral' engines for the *England* had implications for the layout of her car deck, as the machinery casing protruded more than two decks above the waterline. Thus the car deck was relatively high up in the hull with a substantial freeboard below, meaning that special ramps were required. And as it was just one deck high, it could only accommodate private cars and, at a squeeze, caravans. Trucks and buses were out of the question.

As with the *Kronprins Harald*, the *England* was a side-loader with hatches in the starboard bow and stern quarters (Chairman Kørbing would never have countenanced the fitting of a 'dangerous' bow visor). Altogether, there were only four vehicle lanes, outboard of which were broad casings containing both

The *England* offloads cars at Harwich via her bow side hatch. *(Bruce Peter collection)*

The splendid **Empress of Australia** emerges from under Sydney Harbour Bridge in the latter 1960s. *(Ambrose Greenway)*

inside and outside cabins. Below the car deck, forward of the engine room, were refrigerated holds to carry Danish agricultural exports, loaded by cranes through hatches in the forward mooring deck, which lined up with secondary hatches cut into the car deck. Thus the *England* was both a ro-ro ferry – a new type of ship for DFDS – and a general cargo liner, much like her predecessors and early-1960s fleetmates.

The interior design work was by J.A. Kørbing's son Kay, who had planned to follow in his father's footsteps but became an architect instead. His first job was to design the Danish Tourist Office HQ in London's Piccadilly. He went on to receive great acclaim for his designs for the DFDS Copenhagen-Oslo passenger liners *Prinsesse Margrethe* (1957) and *King Olav V* (1961).

Forward on the *England*'s Saloon Deck was the First Class smoking room, the interior form of which followed the curved and slanted shape of the superstructure. It was panelled in teak and, as with all passenger spaces, fully air-conditioned, the ribbed ceilings designed to blow in cool air and extract stale air to keep the space fresh and evenly heated. The furniture was ingeniously laid out to create an inward focus by night with the seating and lighting in the middle forming a circular composition. Around the perimeter, groups of chairs were placed around rectangular tables at each window bay. Kørbing repeated this subtle but effective arrangement on other ships in the ensuing years. To the rear was the First Class dining saloon, with a decorative panel by Arne L. Hansen. In between was a hallway with floor-to-ceiling plate glass bulkheads and doors without frames. On the port side was a copper-panelled cocktail bar adjoining the smoking room, and to starboard was a writing room.

Separating the First and Second Class areas was the galley, which served both restaurants. One deck below were the First Class cabins and shops, and below the car deck was a playroom – the first on a North Sea passenger ship, demonstrating the belief of DFDS that every age should be catered for in offering passengers an enjoyable trip. The *England* had covered promenades on either beam and extensive teak sun-decks. The First Class sun-deck was above the bridge and was sheltered by glazed screens to allow passengers to see the ship docking. But as stormy weather sometimes threw spray right over the ship's superstructure, the space was soon fully enclosed with a glassfibre roof to create a kind of winter garden.

Kørbing devised his own ingenious but simple range of modular cabin furniture, which could be used in various permutations to suit different room shapes.

The *England*'s introduction, less than ten years after British wartime rationing ended, coincided with a concerted effort by the Danish government to promote Denmark's manufactured goods, agricultural exports and tourism to Brits. So it was no coinicidence that the ship's design and appeal brilliantly captured the spirit of modern Denmark.

For middle-class British families with cars, motoring holidays in Denmark became an attractive option. Networks of Kros (roadside inns) and farmhouses enabled families to travel from place to place and enjoy an 'authentically' Danish holiday experience. Denmark was marketed as a friendly country with welcoming people, most of whom spoke good English, and with food, drink and customs not so different from the British way of life. Moreover, it had Tivoli in Copenhagen, Legoland near Esbjerg and countless other family-friendly attractions. Thanks to DFDS, getting there by sea took only around 21 hours on the

The tragically short-lived New Zealand Union Steamship Company ferry **Wahine** is seen when newly completed on the Firth of Clyde, prior to her long delivery voyage. *(Matthew Murtland collection)*

Harwich-Esbjerg route, meaning that holidaymakers could arrive relaxed and refreshed, having enjoyed fresh sea air and ample time to eat, drink and sleep. As DFDS pointed out, "the holiday begins as soon as you step onboard."

On 4th June 1964, the *England* left Harwich on her maiden trip to Esbjerg. Within only a short time of her being in service, delighted DFDS directors quickly turned their attention to building a larger sister ship. In the interim, a number of other significant overnight car-carrying passenger liners were delivered to various owners around the world.

FERRIES DOWN UNDER

In the mid-1960s, the world's largest ferries were operating not in European or American waters, but on the other side of the globe – in New Zealand and Australia. These former dominions of the British Empire had enjoyed considerable investment in both international liner and domestic shipping during the preceding decade. This was thanks not only to traditional London-headquartered shipowners – such as Shaw Savill, Port Line, the P&O Group and its subsidiaries – but also to the establishment of new indigenous operators.

One was ANL (the Australian National Line) which owed its creation to the Australian Coastal Shipping Commission Act of 1956. This legislation governed the carriage of passengers, goods and mail between Australian States, to and from Commonwealth territories and in international trade. ANL was founded in January 1957 and high priority was given to establishing a modern ro-ro ferry service across the Bass Strait between the Australian mainland and Tasmania. Since the mid-1930s the two had been linked by the Clyde-built packet steamer *Taroona*, which was due for replacement.

In September 1959, a new stern-loading car ferry, the 3,964-ton *Princess of Tasmania*, was delivered by the New South Wales Dockyard Co in Newcastle. Designed solely for the 14-hour overnight service from Melbourne to Devonport – one of the world's stormiest short-sea routes – she could carry up to 334 passengers and 142 cars. Power came from two Norwegian-built 9-cylinder Nohab diesels, giving a steady 16-knot service speed. Externally, she somewhat resembled Canadian Pacific's *Princess of Vancouver*.

Inboard, she had cabin berths for half of her passenger complement and reclining seats for the remainder. Breakfast was the only meal served onboard, and there was an American-style cafeteria-diner with 80 seats arranged around 3 U-shaped islands. The *Princess of Tasmania* was a transport ship and nothing more – and remarkably successful to the point that ANL next turned its attention to the creation of a second ferry route to Tasmania, this time from Sydney – a sea voyage of 625 nautical miles, the world's longest ferry route. The new ship built to operate it – the 12,037-ton *Empress of Australia* – would also be the world's largest ferry of the time, as well as the largest Australian-built passenger ship and (unlike the rather austere *Princess of Tasmania*) one of the best-appointed vessels in her class.

In 1962, an order was placed with the Cockatoo Docks & Engineering Company, located on Cockatoo Island in Sydney Harbour. This yard was known principally for building naval vessels but since the Second World War had also constructed several large cargo merchant ships. *Empress of Australia* was altogether a new challenge – a complex ship for which many of the major components were imported, leading to unexpected difficulties. For example, in order to operate as intended the vehicle deck stern door had to be partially dismantled and re-designed. Consequently, by the time the *Empress of Australia* was delivered to ANL in January 1965 the yard had made a substantial loss on the fixed-price contract.

The new ferry's superstructure was carried well forward, her decks arranged in receding layers and suggesting speed and power. As with the *Princess of Tasmania*, she was a stern-loader with the slender forward hull lines of a traditional ocean liner, widening to a beamy 21.5-metre midbody. Propelled by two 10-cylinder MAN diesels, she had an 18-knot service speed, but actually achieved 21.5 knots on trials. Both the vehicle and the passenger decks were arranged around short parallel casings, located amidships. Her vehicle deck space offered several options: up to 90 cars, or a combination of 51 cars and 16 trucks, or up to 160 containers loaded on special flatbeds – the latter a very innovative idea subsequently emulated by the England-Sweden Line on the North Sea.

As her route required two nights at sea, all 250 passengers were berthed (in 92 cabins, which included 4 de luxe suites and 5 superior cabins with en suite facilities; the majority of passengers used communal showers and toilets). Cabins, arranged in blocks and located forward away from the engines, were accessed off parallel main corridors and the lower berths were convertible to settees for daytime use. Public rooms were

The ***Canguro Rosso*** arrives in Genoa after a crossing from Sardinia in the early 1970s. Note the large red kangaroo applied to the hull's topsides beneath the bridge. *(Alistair Deayton collection)*

The **Santa Cruz de Tenerife** motors along the quays in Barcerlona harbour in the early 1970s. *(Bruce Peter collection)*

The French CGT ferry **Fred Scamaroni** (1965), built for services from Marseille to Corsican ports. *(Bruce Peter collection)*

aft and included sitting lounges, dining room, smoking room and children's playroom. In fact, the *Empress of Australia* was the first ferry to introduce such a clear vertical (rather than horizontal) split in the arrangement of her accommodation, though externally this was not visually evident as the cabin blocks were inboard of partially enclosed wrap-around promenade decks which, in traditional ocean liner style, featured expanses of large vertical windows.

Overall, the *Empress of Australia* had an unusually large public room-to-cabin ratio, creating a spacious onboard ambience more akin to a mini ocean liner than any ferry typical of northern Europe. The impression was enhanced by Gwendoline Barr-Brice's very handsome decor, similar to that of the then-recent P&O liner *Oriana* and the Alfred Holt (Blue Funnel) passenger-cargo vessel the *Centaur*.

The ANL services from Melbourne and Sydney to Devonport were marketed as the 'Sea-Road' and proved to be highly popular with passengers and freight hauliers alike. Indeed, freight trade grew so quickly that a third ferry, the *Australian Trader*, was introduced in 1969, with a bias for lorry traffic. Built by the New South Wales Dockyard Co at Newcastle, she used the hull configuration of the *Empress of Australia* but with a much smaller superstructure and an open container deck towards the stern.

But come the 1970s, the expanded 3-ship operation proved to be uneconomic for a variety of reasons. One was wage inflation. Another was rising fuel costs. Then there was the apparent lack of thought given to optimising capacity and onboard revenue of the State-owned ferries. Following a government commission, it was decided to sell the *Princess of Tasmania* and utilise the other two ships more intensively and to switch them between routes.

Not to be outdone by Australia in ferry development, New Zealand introduced an important new vessel of its own – the tragically short-lived 9,110-ton *Wahine*, ordered by the P&O-controlled Union Steamship Company from the Clyde-based Fairfield Shipbuilding & Engineering Company in Glasgow.

The *Wahine* was built for the 14-hour night service across the treacherous Cook Strait between Wellington and Lyttleton. Consequently, she had few public rooms and the majority of her 927 passengers were berthed in cabins. As on the *Empress of Australia*, most cabins were located in the forward half of the superstructure, with public rooms aft. Her stern-loading vehicle deck accommodated up to 200 cars and had a double-height

aft section for commercial vehicles and so-called 'Seafreighter' trailers – tarpaulin-covered pallets mounted on wheeled trailers towed aboard by special tractors. Above was a platform deck which could be lowered from the deckhead to accommodate more cars as necessary during peak holiday times. The single-height mid-body section had cabins above. Forward of this, and accessed by ramps from the main vehicle deck, was an upper mezzanine garage for yet more cars. (This layout bore resemblance to the British Railways steamers of the time, the *Caledonian Princess* and the *Holyhead Ferry I*, on which the dining rooms and galleys 'blocked' the vehicle decks' upper levels amidships.) Designed largely by the Union Steamship Company's own naval architect, William Waters, the *Wahine* was solidly constructed with rakish hull lines, pronounced forward sheer and a high forecastle. As with another recent and prominent P&O-owned liner, the *Oriana*, her bridge and funnel were grouped together just forward of amidships, with the radar mast ahead of the bridge. Although this arrangement gave officers better protection from mountainous head seas, it was never subsequently repeated on a ferry.

Most unusually, Waters opted for turbo-electric engines for the *Wahine* – also the choice of the recently-delivered P&O flagship liner *Canberra*. (P&O had first used this type of propulsion in 1929, for the pioneering *Viceroy of India*.) The *Wahine* also had twin bow-thrust propellers to give her ample manoeuvrability even when working against strong currents.

Operating opposite the smaller *Maori*, which was rebuilt as a stern-loading ferry in 1965, the *Wahine* should have been a great success, but in April 1968, when attempting to enter Wellington Harbour after an exceptionally stormy crossing of the Cook Strait, she ran aground on Barrett's Reef and was severely holed. Conditions were so bad that passengers stayed onboard to await rescue. Eight hours later, the weather had worsened and the stricken *Wahine* capsized, ending up on her side, half submerged – a tragedy which claimed 53 lives. Within weeks, further storms broke the wreck into three sections.

The Union Steamship Company belatedly returned to Fairfields for a replacement ferry, the *Rangatira*. Delivered in 1972, it more or less followed the *Wahine*'s overall design. But the Lyttleton-Wellington service never fully recovered from the *Wahine*'s loss and the consequent blow to public confidence. The shorter and direct Picton to Wellington car and train ferry, operated by New Zealand Railways, become more popular at the expense of the Union Steamship service.

In fact, competition was very much in the air. The advent of the Boeing 737 meant cheaper and more frequent flights between New Zealand's North and South islands, and the *Maori* was withdrawn in 1972 and subsequently sold for scrap. The Lyttleton-Wellington route closed in 1976, after which the *Rangatira* had a nomadic existence as an accommodation ship, firstly for North Sea oil workers in Scotland and later during airport construction in the Falkland Islands. She briefly returned to ferry service across the Adriatic during the early 1990s Balkans War, when every available ship was used between Italy and Greece, avoiding Yugoslavia.

MEDITERRANEAN DEVELOPMENTS

During the 1950s, industrialised northern Italy focused on the manufacture of well-designed and affordable consumer goods. The car industry in particular was highly successful, its stylish models capturing every sector of the market.

However, the state-owned Tirrenia shipping company, which operated domestic routes from Italy's major west coast ports to Sardinia and Sicily, barely acknowledged the increase in car ownership and persisted with commissioning rather traditional small motor passenger liners rather than ro-ro ferries. Consequently, it was left to an independent company – the Società Navi Traghetto (the 'Car Ferry Company'), established in Rome in 1959 – to exploit this new business opportunity after studying other European ferry operations.

In 1964 the company ordered two vessels from the Navalmeccanica di Castellammare di Stabia shipyard. It also concluded that a strong brand identity would distinguish its ferries from Tirrenia's packet liner fleet. The result was the *Canguro* (Italian for kangaroo) brand – a clever marketing ploy. It not only highlighted the way in which the ships could carry motor vehicles in vast garages with bow doors, rather like marsupial mothers and their babies; it also lent itself to the notion of the ships 'hopping' efficiently from port to port. By way of a bonus, *Canguro* was a fresh and fun name, very appropriate to the design-conscious post-war era.

Each ferry had a dark grey-blue hull, featuring large white discs on which kangaroo silhouettes were painted in a colour individual to that particular ship. Another distinguishing characteristic was the funnel design, with ventilation grilles at the front and a large fin to the rear, similar to several Italian deep-sea liners of the period such as the Lloyd Triestino vessels *Guglielmo Marconi* and *Galileo Galilei*.

The first of the new ferries, the 5,223-ton *Canguro Azzurro*

(Blue Kangaroo), commenced her first voyage from Naples to Palermo in March 1965. Next, starting November 1965, was the *Canguro Rosso* (Red Kangaroo), operating from Genoa to Cagliari and Olbia. Each had bow and stern doors and could accommodate up to 110 cars or 48 trucks. Two 10,500 bhp Fiat V-diesels delivered a 19-knot service speed and a low freeboard. Passenger accommodation for up to 700 was spread over two decks of superstructure, comprising cabins, reclining seat lounges, cafeteria, restaurant, bar and smoking saloon. With no class division, the *Canguro* ferries were democratic, modern, economical and notable for their fine appointments – the last word in 1960s Italian shipboard design.

Società Navi Traghetto was delighted with the initial public response to its initiative, and shortly after was taken over by the Bastogi Group, a large banking conglomerate with Rome headquarters and business interests in Sardinia. The group set up a further ferry-operating subsidiary, the Società per Azioni Traghetti Sardi, which traded simply as Traghetti Sardi – Sardinia Ferries in English.

Traghetti Sardi quickly ordered 3 further *Canguro* ferries, of slightly improved design, from Castellammare di Stabia. As the initial pair were a little under-powered, the new ships benefited from bigger 11,900 bhp engines, adding more than a knot to their service speed and making them more competitive with Tirrenia's ships. The *Canguro Verde* was delivered in September 1967, the *Canguro Bianco* in February 1968 and the *Canguro Bruno* in June 1968.

Undoubtedly, the golden *Canguro* era was in the latter 1960s – success which inspired the state-owned incumbent Tirrenia to fight back. It rebuilt its *Regioni* class packet liners into car-ferry format and ordered a new *Poeti* class of large purpose-built car ferries, the design of which was heavily inspired by the *Canguro* series

The *Poeti* class initially had 6 ships, the order shared by various leading Italian yards, partly to create employment and partly to ensure that all 6 would enter service on Tirrenia's important routes to Sardinia, Sicily and North African ports during 1970 and 1971. Each was approximately 6,900 tons and named after a famous Italian poet. The first completed was the *Boccaccio* from the Italcantieri shipyard at Castellammare di Stabia. This was quickly followed by the *Carducci*, the *Pascoli*, the *Leopardi*, the *Petrarca* and the *Manzoni*. Some years later came 2 more – the *Deledda* and the *Verga*.)

While the *Canguro* brand was developing ferry services from the Italian mainland to Sardinia, the Compagnie Génerale

The CGT Mediterranean ferry pioneer was the **Napoléon** of 1959, a vessel whose design was developed from the company's existing packet liners. *(Trevor Jones)*

The **Corse** and her sister, the **Comté de Nice** were built for CGT routes to Corsica and North Africa. *(Bruce Peter collection)*

Transatlantique (French Line) was simultaneously engaged in introducing ro-ro tonnage on its routes from Nice and Marseille to Corsica and Maghreb – formerly French colonies in North Africa. The design of the CGT's first car ferry, the 1959 stern-loading 5,802-ton *Napoléon*, had been developed directly from the company's pre-existing fleet of packet liners and, except at the stern, her hull had insufficient free height for trucks and buses. For their next attempt, in 1965 – the 5,140-ton *Fred Scamaroni* – CGT and its builder, the Forges et Chantiers de la Mediterranée at La Seyne, apparently made a conscious effort to emulate the most up-to-date northern European ferries. Engine power, for example, was typical of that in Scandanavia at the time – four 8-cylinder Pielstick diesels coupled in pairs to the propeller shafts to give a speed of 19.5 knots. The vehicle deck arrangement was similar to the *Canguro*, with capacity for 150 cars. For passengers there were 446 First Class, 284 Second Class and 520 Fourth Class compartments. Apart from these, the ferry's accommodation consisted only of a cafeteria and a terrace bar.

In the following year (1966), CGT took delivery of two further ferries of similar appearance for services from France to Corsica and Algeria – the 4,455-ton *Corse* and the *Comté de Nice*, both built by the Chantiers de Saint Nazaire et de Port de Brouc. Their twin Pielstick diesel engines were routed through side casings to provide a single clear-span vehicle deck.

By the mid-1960s, the Spanish market for domestic ferry services to North Africa, the Balearics and the Canary Islands was dominated by Compagnia Trasmediterránea. Their fleet then consisted mainly of post-war passenger liners, some with limited car capacity. Hence a new-build programme for 6 side-loading ferries was initiated, split between the Union Naval de Levante shipyard at Valencia and the Sociedad Española de Construcción Naval at Bilbao. The initial quartet, introduced in 1966-67, were known as the *Albatros* class and named the *Las Palmas de Gran Canaria*, the *Santa Cruz de Tenerife*, the *Juan March* and the *Ciudad de Compostela*.

Each was a 9,977-ton, 21-knot vessel, powered by the twin 7-cylinder Burmeister & Wain diesels common to the company's fleet. These new ships operated alternately on short ferry trips to the Balearics and much longer voyages to the Canaries, their accommodation necessarily flexible. Berths for longer trips numbered 124 First Class and 376 Tourist Class. When serving the Balearics, the cinema's high-backed seats were used to transport a further 250 in more moderate comfort. The double-height vehicle deck accommodated up to 100 cars and was accessed through side-ports located towards the bow and stern – much as on Jahre Line's *Kronprins Harald* and the DFDS ship *England*. Adjacent were turntables for lorries. The engine room was located two-thirds aft and, rather like on the *Bilu* and the *Nili*, a square-shaped casing blocked the centre vehicle lanes. Forward, refrigerated cargo holds, loaded by electric cranes, enabled carriage of fruit and vegetables to the Spanish mainland.

In designing these vessels, Trasmediterránea and Union Naval de Levante appear to have picked and mixed ideas from a wide variety of recent tonngage. For example, their slender twin exhaust stacks were reminiscent of Holland-America Line's transatlantic liner *Rotterdam* and numerous other large ships, and their observation saloons in streamlined dummy funnel structures were akin to those on Silja Line's *Skandia* and *Nordia* and ferries designed by Knud E. Hansen A/S. Yet, as with the *England*, they retained the slender hull profiles and pronounced sheer of traditional passenger liners.

Inboard features included a First Class restaurant, lounge and cocktail bar, a Second Class cafeteria, a chapel and an outdoor swimming pool. The *Las Palmas de Gran Canaria* and the *Juan March*, built at Bilbao, were more flamboyantly decorated than the Valencia-built *Las Palmas de Gran Canaria* and the *Juan March*. All contained decorative panels reflecting the themes suggested by their names. The *Ciudad de Compostela*, for example, featured a series of golden-toned oil-painted murals depicting the cathedral and churches in the famed Galician town of Compostela.

In 1968-69, two smaller 4,900-ton ferries of similar design – the *Antonio Lazaro* and the *Vicente Puchol* – came from the Union Naval de Levante shipyard to link Malaga with Melilla, a Spanish enclave in Morocco. Until the mid-1980s, when they were superseded by more capacious tonnage, these vessels all did sterling service for Trasmediterránea.

NORTH EUROPEAN PROGRESS

In the mid-1960s, the greatest concentration of large overnight ferries served routes across the Baltic, the Kattegat and the North Sea. In particular, a network of new ferry services was developed from West Germany, whose economy was booming, to southern Scandinavia and further afield to Finland and, subsequently, to Britain.

Introduced in 1962, TT-Linie's 3,843-ton *Nils Holgersson* was

Da-No Linjen's Oslo-Frederikshavn ferry **Holger Danske** (1961) in Oslo Harbour. *(Rickard Sahlsten collection)*

A striking image of TT-Linie's **Peter Pan** (1965) crossing the Southern Baltic. *(Trevor Jones)*

Finnlines' **Hansa Express**, originally ordered by Viking Line for a short-duration service. *(Thomas N. Olesen collection)*

The third member of the series, the Lion Ferry-owned **Prins Hamlet** undergoes trials in the Gulf of Finland. *(Bruce Peter collection)*

the first of the new overnight ferries serving West Germany, and its Hamburg-based shipowner J.A. Reinecke also owned the shipyard (Hanseatiche Werft) which built it. The *Nils Holgersson* design was developed from that of a previous ferry built at the yard, the *Holger Danske*, the delivery voyage of which had been instrumental in the decision to build a new ro-ro port facility at Skandinavienkai. This ferry harbour on the River Trave soon became one of northern Europe's busiest.

Neither *Holger Danske* nor *Nils Holgersson* had much freight capacity due to the limited height of the forward sections of their vehicle decks (where cabins were located above the car lanes) – but her twin 12-cylinder diesels at least gave the *Nils Holgersson* a speed of up to 20 knots, enabling her to make three single trips daily during the hectic summer season. With a pressing need for a new ferry better suited to the service, and the Hanseatiche Werft yard now bankrupt, the TT-Linie ordered a second *Nils Holgersson* from the Lübecker Flenderwerke, slightly further up river from Travemünde. Altogether more substantial, this new 4,385-ton ferry was built to an unusually high standard in terms of the close spacing of the frames and the specification of a high safety margin in seemingly all aspects of the design.

Unlike the stern-loading first *Nils Holgersson,* her successor had a bow door – but, as well as the visor and watertight ramp, there was a third guillotine-type door behind which lowered to the vehicle deck to create an extra barrier. Passenger capacity was 850, with cabins for 350 berths located on Main Deck. Crew quarters were below the vehicle deck, which could take 230 cars and significantly more freight than her predecessor. Accessing crew accommodation from the vehicle deck meant going up a deck and then down two decks via separate staircases – fire and flood prevention measures very unusual in a civilian ro-ro vessel but quite typical in naval craft, suggesting that the *Nils Holgersson* had a secondary potential role for transporting tanks and troops. This was, after all, the height of the Cold War, just 4 years after the Berlin Wall was completed.

At the time of her introduction, the *Nils Holgersson* was the largest ferry on the Baltic Sea and highly praised by passengers for the high standards of her cosily traditional German-style interiors, with polished brass and rich wood panelling. TT-Linie quickly developed a reputation for quality that has been sustained to this day.

In 1967 the *Nils Holgersson* was joined by the *Peter Pan*, almost a sister ship, and the two shuttled back and forth between Travemünde and Trelleborg until the mid-1970s.

Among the most advanced of the new armada of ferries were those plying the 'Hansa Route' – 600 nautical miles between Helsinki and the West German Baltic port of Travemünde. This was a Cold War anomaly whereby Travemünde and Kiel were then the closest accessible western European ports to the Finnish capital. Rostock, Sassnitz, Swinoujscie and Gdynia were all nearer but located behind the Iron Curtain in the Soviet-controlled sector of Europe and thus inaccessible to through traffic.

At conventional service speeds of between 18 and 20 knots, the 2-night Helsinki-Travemünde passage in either direction took 30 to 36 hours. This service was the virtually exclusive domain of Finnlines, which was founded in 1947 as the shipping arm of the government-controlled Enso-Gutzeit forestry products conglomerate, exporting paper and wood pulp to European and American ports. In 1962, Finnlines had speculatively bought a partially-completed car ferry from the Hanseatische Werft in Hamburg, ordered by Rederi AB Vikinglinjen of Mariehamn for short day crossings between Sweden and Finland. But even though she was patently unsuitable for the task, Finnlines put this new ferry, the *Hansa Express*, to work on the lengthy Travemünde-Helsinki route. During her first overhaul, as a stop-gap measure, she was lengthened, pending the commissioning of two much more substantial purpose-built vessels.

The first of these, the 7,821-ton *Finnhansa*, built at Wärtsilä's Helsinki shipyard, should have entered service in the spring of 1965 but was seriously damaged by fire while fitting out in Helsinki, postponing her delivery for a year. To fill the gap, Finnlines chartered the Israeli *Nili* from Somerfin Lines.

On the new vessels, Finnlines pioneered 'Finnflow' – an innovative new handling system for reels of paper which greatly increased loading efficiency, reduced the risk of damage during transit and also utilised spaces below the main vehicle deck ahead of the engine room as cargo holds.

The *Finnhansa* and the *Finnpartner* had two Wärtsilä-Sulzer 8-cylinder diesels, providing a 21-knot service speed. The tops of these penetrated the vehicle deck and a large casing had to be built around them (much as on the *Bilu*, the *Nili* and Compagnia Trasmediterránea's *Albatros* ferries, described earlier in this chapter).

In the superstructure, this had the effect of creating a Y-shaped circulation plan with a single axial corridor in the forward two-thirds of the main cabin deck and two parallel corridors on either side of the casing towards the stern. The cabins extended almost to the forepeak, meaning that it was not possible to fit a lifting bow visor and so, instead, hinged doors were developed, opening outwards and meeting at the stem. This solution also avoided the problem of upward pressure caused by wave action placing a strain on visor locking pins as, instead, waves would tend to force the doors more tightly shut. In addition, there were side-doors with fold-down ramps and outer covers which closed flush with the shell plating.

Further cabins were located on Boat Deck, above the main passenger saloons. Yet, because the spaces beneath the vehicle deck were given over largely to cargo holds for paper reels on flatbeds, rather than to large numbers of economy cabins, the berth capacity of the *Finnhansa* was less than it would otherwise have been. This shortcoming was highlighted by the fact that en route she called at Karlskrona in southern Sweden, picking up large numbers of daytrippers for the short sectors to and from Travemünde, thereby indirectly competing with the Sweden-West Germany services of TT-Linie and Statens Järnvägar. The low berth capacity was to some extent rectified on the *Finnpartner* and subsequently both vessels were retro-fitted with extra upper berths.

The *Finnhansa* and the *Finnpartner* had full-width public rooms, entered from hallways forward and aft of amidships. Off the aft hallway was a casino, a gift shop and a hairdressing salon. At the forward end of the saloon deck was a large à la carte restaurant with a panoramic view ahead. Above, the smoking saloon on Boat Deck offered a similar vista. Towards the stern was a cafeteria and a nightclub, where a spiral open-tread staircase ascended to the aft lounge on Boat Deck. Adjacent was an indoor swimming pool beneath a perspex roof – a miniature version of that on the French transatlantic liner *France* and the Soviet *Ivan Franko* class liners, built in East Germany.

A third vessel of the *Finnhansa* and *Finnpartner* class, the *Prins Hamlet*, was built at the same time that they were but by a different shipyard (Crichton-Vulcan in Turku) and for a different operator – Sweden's Lion Ferry. This company entered an agreement with Wallenius Lines, another Swedish shipping business, to jointly operate a route across the southern North Sea from Harwich to Bremerhaven. To do this they formed a subsidiary company called Wallbon Ship AB. There had been serious West German interest in opening such a route for several years, but the Germans' tentative moves were rebuffed

by the various British ports they approached. The core business of Wallenius Lines was operating car transporter ships and the line had good links with various port authorities around the North Sea, not least in West Germany.

Lion Ferry's 'home market' was in operating medium-sized, high-capacity ferries on fairly short-duration routes from southern Sweden to Denmark and West Germany, the big attraction for passengers being the lure of tax-free onboard shopping all year round. But the North Sea ferry market was very different: highly seasonal, with an almost insatiable demand during brief holiday peaks but slack outside these periods. Lion Ferry's solution was to use the *Prins Hamlet* on the Harwich-Bremerhaven route from May to November and in the winter season as a cruise ship, her absence from the North Sea during these months filled by Thoresen's smaller Channel ferry, the *Viking III*, operating under charter. This arrangement made conmmercial sense because the *Prins Hamlet* had a higher berth capacity than her Finnlines-owned near sisters. Instead of cargo holds beneath the vehicle deck, she had economy cabins, creating a total of 510 berths, plus 48 reclining seats in an observation saloon located at the base of the mast.

The *Prins Hamlet*'s maiden (1966) summer season on the North Sea was so successful that Wallenius subsequently ordered a similar vessel, to be named the *Prins Albert*, for delivery in 1968. To operate it, Wallenius established a West German subsidiary, Wallenius Bremen GmbH, so that the new ship could be registered there and employ West German officers and crew, whose wage demands were lower than those of their Swedish counterparts.

The *Prins Hamlet*'s first winter season as a cruise ship to the Atlantic Islands and the West Indies was also such a hit that Lion Ferry decided to rebuild her, sacrificing vehicle deck space to install more cabins and create a total of 684 berths. Carrying only 400 passengers in considerable comfort, her voyages attracted an increasingly prosperous mainly Swedish middle class who saw them as the ideal alternative to the much more expensive cruises operated by Swedish American Line's ships *Gripsholm* and *Kungsholm*.

The rebuilding of the *Prins Hamlet* to capitalise on the initial success of these cruises had two consequences. Firstly, as she

The **Finnhansa** and **Finnpartner** sail in parallel in this latter-1960s Finnlines publicity photograph. *(Bruce Peter collection)*

Swedish Lloyd's elegant *Saga*, built for the Gothenburg-Tilbury route in 1966, carried palletised containers, with cars in a separate upper garage. *(Bruce Peter collection)*

could now carry sufficient passengers and private cars to satisfy North Sea summer season demand, there was no need for the proposed new partner ferry *Prins Albert* ordered by Wallenius. Secondly, the rebuild reduced the *Prins Hamlet*'s freight capacity to such an extent that she was only marginally profitable in ferry mode.

Wallenius therefore withdrew from the joint operation, and what would have been the *Prins Albert* was modified to become a Caribbean cruise ship, the *Bohème*, as in the opera – a theme Wallenius followed when naming cargo vessels and car transporters. The majority of her vehicle deck space was filled with cabins and she was based in Miami and marketed by Commodore Cruise Line.

In 1967, Wärtsilä's Helsinki shipyard (builders of the *Finnhansa* and the *Finnpartner*) delivered a slightly larger version of both these and the *Prins Hamlet* and the *Bohème* to the Finland Steamship Company (FÅA). This new ship, the *Finlandia*, was to operate a Helsinki-Travemünde service to rival Finnlines', and was faster. Her speed of 22 knots was achieved by four 9-cylinder Sulzer medium-speed diesels, coupled in pairs to twin screws through reduction gearing. She also had a less constricted vehicle deck with space for 321 cars. For the next twenty years, the Wärtsilä Helsinki and Turku shipyards adopted the *Finlandia*'s compact and highly effective machinery and propulsion arrangement as a standard design for ferry and cruise ship construction.

On her two-night passage between Finland and Germany, the *Finlandia* was distinctive for high standards of design and service. Accommodation was exclusively of the cabin variety, albeit with the economy-grade rooms located below the car deck. The 647 passenger berths gave the new FÅA ship almost twice the cabin capacity of her earlier rivals, the *Finnhansa* and the *Finnpartner*, and her spacious and elegant public rooms were designed by Finnish architect Jonas Cedercreutz. Remarkably, a full 7 years after the *Finlandia* entered service, Wärtsilä constructed yet another variation on the design. The

Prinsessan Birgitta sailed between Gothenburg and Travemünde for Swedish owners Rederi AB Ragne, but shared marketing with Sessanlinjen's Gothenburg-Frederikshavn ferries and wore the Sessanlinjen brand prominently on her hull topsides.

Another momentous year in this story of ferry development was 1966. Car ferry services across the northern North Sea from Britain to Sweden and Norway saw the introduction of no less than seven large and well-appointed ferries – initiatives coupled with a general rationalisation of the traditional passenger and cargo trades which, hitherto, had been operated by numerous small (and not so small) companies. In order to afford new ferries, it was often necessary to pool resources and so former rivals began to co-operate for mutual benefit.

One such shotgun wedding between old competitors was the England-Sweden Line, formed as a loose consortium of Ellerman Wilson Line (EWL), the Swedish Lloyd and Stockholm's Rederi AB Svea. It was the vision of Torgeir Christoffersen, a major Swedish Lloyd shareholder. Believing that containerisation represented the future of short-sea shipping, he was determined that Swedish Lloyd should invest heavily in container-carrying ships.

While Swedish Lloyd emphasised comfort and elegance, Ellerman Wilson Line was more of a general cargo business whose vessels also happened to carry limited numbers of passengers. Similarly, Rederi AB Svea's routes from Stockholm to UK ports were also cargo-orientated, although the company had long operated passenger steamers across the Baltic from Sweden to Finland. Consequently, when it came to ordering modern ferries, the majority of Swedish Lloyd's Board wanted a miniature passenger liner capable also of carrying containers, whereas EWL and Svea were less keen to abandon the general cargo element altogether in favour of a purely ro-ro car and freight service.

The intention was that each partner would order a ship, designed and built to similar dimensions and with a like capacity. Both Swedish companies agreed a common approach

Delivered in 1967, Swedish Lloyd's *Patricia* initially proved popular between Southampton and Santander in Spain. *(Ambrose Greenway)*

and, at the insistence of Rederi AB Svea's senior management, sought the expertise of Knud E. Hansen A/S in Copenhagen, who had previously designed numerous ferries for the firm and its subsidiaries. However, in developing the design, Swedish Lloyd in particular proved to be rather traditionalist and repeatedly demanded that innovative aspects of the KEH proposals should be altered – to the extent that the final solution was most atypical of KEH's normal output.

As with the *Wahine*, the new ships were to be stern-loaders with centre casings, and only the aft-most sections of the vehicle decks would have sufficient free height for trucks. The idea was that rather than carrying lorries (which Swedish Lloyd's technical staff argued would unnecessarily heighten their centres of gravity), containers would be loaded on pallets and lashed directly to the vehicle deck – a technique which in various guises had already proven successful for the Atlantic Container Line, as well as on ferries in Australia and New Zealand. However, events were to prove that any benefits were vastly outweighed by increased turnaround times – a total contradiction to the whole ro-ro vessel concept. Furthermore, EWL insisted that the new ships should be fitted with electric cranes and hatches to carry general cargo. Private cars were loaded on a separate upper car deck, via an independent shore-based ramp and side hatches. (Many years later, the segregation of cars from freight was reprised by Norfolkline's three 'D' class ferries on the Dover-Dunkerque route, delivered in 2005-6.)

Swedish Lloyd's *Saga* and Rederi AB Svea's *Svea* were built by Lindholmens Varv in Gothenburg and both were delivered in 1966. They were powered by four 6-cylinder Pielstick diesels, coupled in pairs via gearboxes to each propeller shaft. Service speed was 18 knots – significantly lower than the 22-plus expected of the *England*, the DFDS Esbjerg-Harwich vessel, which had much larger twin B&W engines.

In vessels of only around 9,000 tons, a key problem for designers of ferries for the London-Gothenburg service – which necessitated two nights onboard – was to accommodate cabin berths for all 408 passengers (the somewhat larger *Empress of Australia* only had 250 berths). To achieve it, cabins were placed below the vehicle deck and on two levels above. But probably the most progressive aspect of the design was in specifying one-class ships, so avoiding duplication of public rooms – and this at a time when other established North Sea operators still imposed rigorous class divisions. There was also a belief by some – Swedish Lloyd in particular – that the various age groups and social classes travelling by ferry would naturally segregate themselves. Hence the accommodation on the saloon deck was split along the centreline. To starboard were the most exclusive and luxurious facilities (such as the dining saloon and the cocktail bar), and to port were the cafeteria, nightclub and other more popular attractions.

The *Saga* and the *Svea* were immediately acclaimed for their great elegance; indeed, they were floating showcases for the best in contemporary Swedish shipboard design. The *Saga* was decorated by Gothenburg-based architect Rolf Carlsson, assisted by the fashionable interior designer Astrid Sampe of the Nordiska Kompaniet department store. Like a miniature *Kungsholm*, the vessel featured lustrous woodwork throughout the passenger accommodation, accented with soft furnishings in shades of blue and gold. A few spaces worthy of special mention included the Wasa Dining Room (featuring a stylish wrought-iron bas-relief of the famous warship by Bertil Vallien), in complete contrast to which the Britannia Room evoked the ornate neo-Tudor atmosphere of the Smoking Room of the 1929-built Swedish Lloyd packet steamer *Britannia*, and even featured some of her richly-patinated leather armchairs. This throwback to the 1920s was perhaps the most unexpected space to be found on any ferry of the era, but its 'folksy' style and fine craftsmanship evidently proved popular with passengers. The interiors of the *Svea*, by Eva Ralf, were considerably more modern in character, darker veneers contrasting with brightly-upholstered contemporary furniture.

Seen here leaving Gothenburg on her maiden voyage, the **Tor Anglia** offered a higher speed and lower fares than the vessels of the England-Sweden Line. *(Shippax Archive)*

The EWL contribution to the England-Sweden Line was the *Spero,* completely different from her Swedish running mates except in terms of general dimensions, overall capacity and cargo-handling arrangements. The basic design was the work of the builder, Cammell Laird of Birkenhead, in conjunction with EWL Marine Superintendent Captain R. Taunton. As with the *Svea* and the *Saga*, the *Spero* was a stern-loader – but there the similarity ended.

Externally, the *Spero* was angular with none of the graceful sheer which characterised her Swedish running mates. The arrangement of her public rooms was also different, filling the full width of the superstructure without side arcades. Instead, the saloons were accessed directly from the stair hallways. The interior design, by British architect Charles Bosel, was similarly rather more austere. Although commodious, it lacked the elegant touches of modern Scandinavian furniture and lighting designs.

Just as the England-Sweden Line was planning its three-ship service (regular sailings from Hull to Gothenburg by the *Spero* and the *Svea*, and a weekly return from Tilbury by the *Saga*), rival plans were afoot in Stockholm. Four shipping companies, hitherto almost unknown in the passenger transport business, were set to enter this same market – but using tonnage of much more efficient design. They were Trans-Oil and Bratt-Götha in Gothenburg, Rederi AB Rex in Stockholm and the Dutch firm KNSM, and together they formed a ferry-operating subsidiary called Tor Line AB (Tor being the initials of the main shareholders, Trans-Oil and Rex).

Their intention was to develop a triangular service from Gothenburg to Immingham and Amsterdam. The main drivers behind the project were Rederi AB Rex's owner Ragnar Källström and Bratt-Götha's Managing Director Erik Kekkonius, who had previously assisted the Swedish Bonnier publishing group in setting up their Lion Ferry subsidiary. The Swedish naval architect Åke Törnquist was appointed Project Leader, additionally responsible both for Tor Line's graphic identity and the new ferries' stylish interior design.

From their previous Lion Ferry experience, Kekkonius was familiar with the achievements of Knud E. Hansen A/S in terms of efficient ferry design, and initially he retained them to provide the basic design for Tor Line's new ferries. According to KEH's naval architect Dag Rogne, the first sketches were drawn in a Stockholm park between meetings with Tor Line's directors at Rederi AB Rex's headquarters.

Not surprisingly, Rogne produced a solution which was essentially an enlarged version of the typical KEH short-sea ferry type, then being built in substantial numbers for routes throughout Scandinavia and beyond. In almost every respect, the design was optimised for profitability. For starters, Tor Line's ferries would be faster than those of the England-Sweden Line consortium, four Pielstick diesel engines giving each ship a 24-knot speed and the ability to make more crossings per week. Secondly, the drive-through vehicle decks had sufficient free height to accommodate significant numbers of lorries, freight being an important year-round earner. In summer, platform

The **Tor Hollandia** had a slightly larger superstructure than her elder sister. *(Shippax Archive)*

Fred. Olsen's innovative **Black Prince** arrives at Santa Cruz De Tenerife in the latter 1960s. *(Ambrose Greenway)*

decks could be lowered to increase car capacity.

Although slightly smaller in terms of tonnage than their England-Sweden Line rivals, the Tor Line ships had a much larger passenger capacity of 980, only half of whom were berthed in cabins, the remainder occupying couchettes and aircraft-style reclining seats. Travelling at 24 knots meant that passengers would need to spend only one night onboard, so the cabins were compact in comparison with the commodious style of the big ocean liners replicated by other ferry designers and operators. The combined effect of all these efficiencies and differences added up to a very signifcant commercial advantage: Tor Line was able to undercut England-Sweden Line's fares by a substantial margin.

Even though Tor Line was very satisfied with KEH's initial design work, the company was perturbed to learn that KEH was simultaneously attempting to design ferries for Swedish Lloyd and Rederi AB Svea. Consequently, before an order was placed, KEH was fired and the design work completed by Tor

Line's own technical staff, working with the Lübecker Flenderwerke, which successfully tendered to build the ferries.

The *Tor Anglia*, delivered in March 1966 – almost two months ahead of Swedish Lloyd's Gothenburg-built *Saga* –was a success from the outset and her sister, the *Tor Hollandia*, which was delivered the following year with an enlarged superstructure and consequently increased passenger capacity, was equally well received. Due mainly to sharp competition from Tor Line, the joint England-Sweden Line service failed to live up to expectations. The shorter Hull-Gothenburg route took the most direct hit and in 1968 Rederi AB Svea withdrew the *Svea*, selling her to Swedish Lloyd. Renamed the *Hispania*, she served on their Southampton-Bilbao route.

EWL then withdrew the *Spero*, switching her to a short-lived Hull-Zeebrugge service in 1972. At the same time, Swedish Lloyd's Torgeir Christoffersen sold his substantial shareholding in the company to Broström AB. Thereafter, passenger numbers continued to decline and the Tilbury-Gothenburg route was

The forward-facing Westminster Lounge on the **Jupiter,** which in winter operated as the **Black Watch**. *(Bruce Peter collection)*

The **Black Watch**'s lido is seen in 'winter' mode; in summer, the space was converted into a lounge, while the pool became a store for duty-free goods. *(Bruce Peter collection)*

The **Black Prince** catches evening sunlight as she passes Tynemouth at the commencement of a North Sea crossing to Kristiansand and Oslo. *(Bruce Peter collection)*

finally closed in 1977.

As well as focusing on efficiency, Tor Line also developed much more vivid publicity material than the fustily conservative efforts of the England-Sweden Line. This was a time of sexual liberation. The blonde Swedish female became a cultural icon, and Tor Line were not slow to cash in on the possibility that sex might sell ferry tickets. Fronting all of the Line's publicity was a Swedish glamour model, Kerstin Håkansson, typically photographed in a sleeveless mini-dress and clutching a large model of the ferry. The formula certainly captured the more daring spirit of the era. Moreover, it worked! Very soon, Tor Line brochures were utilising every opportunity to portray scantily-clad Swedish women enjoying the leisurely experience of modern luxury ferry travel. Other Scandinavian ferry operators soon followed suit.

As Tor Line's victory in the battle for the North Sea was also due in part to having more cost-effective ships, efficiency became a mantra for further development in the ferry industry in the ensuing decades. But efficiency came at a price. Towards the end of her maiden season in December 1966, the *Tor Anglia* suffered what could have been a catastrophe. On a stormy crossing from Gothenburg, waves broke open her bow visor. The captain quickly turned the ship around while the crew worked to secure the visor, which on arrival in Immingham was welded shut and only reinstated after the locking pins were greatly strengthened.

During the building of the first of Tor Line's ships, Flenderwerke were also involved in the design and construction of two new vessels for another North Sea ferry operation – one linking the UK and the Netherlands with Norway. Ingenuity was again at a premium due to both the high capital costs of passenger ship construction and the seasonal nature of services to Norway. The two established operators – Oslo-based Fred Olsen Lines and Det Bergenske Dampskips-Selskap, whose HQ was in Bergen – joined forces to design a new and unique type of multi-purpose ferry, capable of fulfilling each operator's distinct requirements. Bergenske's principal North Sea route was from Newcastle to Stavanger and Bergen, whereas Olsen operated in summer from Harwich and Amsterdam to Kristiansand and Oslo. In winter, Olsen also enjoyed the lucrative fruits of importing tomatoes from the Canary Islands to London and Amsterdam. The plan was to build ferries capable of doing the same, and more – serving summer holiday traffic on the North Sea, carrying refrigerated fruit and vegetables in winter and, ideally, offering short cruises to the Canaries for a limited number of passengers.

Olsen's Technical Director, John Johnsen, devised an ingenious solution. As a young man he had worked part-time for MacGregor, the famous designer of ships' watertight doors, hatches and cargo-handling equipment, and his initial role in his Olsen employment was assisting in the rationalisation of cargo handling on the company's deep-sea cargo liners. This led to Fred Olsen Lines pioneering the concept of palletised cargo, carried through hatches in the hulls' topsides by fleets of fork-lift

The British Ellerman Wilson-owned **Spero** linked Hull and Gothenburg. *(Ambrose Greenway)*

The **Blenheim**, a larger half-sister to the **Jupiter**/**Black Watch** and **Black Prince**, was delivered to Fred Olsen in 1970. Clyde-built and flying the British flag, this ferry was not a success and was sold out of the fleet in 1981. *(Bruce Peter collection)*

trucks – faster, safer and more efficient than traditional methods.

As with the England-Sweden Line sisters, the new Fred Olsen and Bergenske vessels were small passenger liners, each of around 9,500 tons, with car decks loaded via stern doors. In winter, these spaces could be laterally subdivided into a series of refrigerated holds by means of retractable bulkheads, and palletes of fruit could be loaded and unloaded by fork-lift truck. Each sister could carry 587 passengers in two classes (some in reclining seats, but most in cabins) and 185 cars when in summer ferry service. During winter, only 350 passengers were carried, all berthed in First Class cabins. Propelled by two compact but powerful 18-cylinder Pielstick diesels, each could travel easily at over 23 knots, giving leeway to make up for storm delays on the North Sea or across the Bay of Biscay.

As the first of the sisters was jointly owned, each company insisted on continuing its own nomenclature. Uniquely, each spring she changed her identity from Fred Olsen's *Black Watch* to Bergen Line's *Jupiter*. After completing her summer season on the Bergen-Stavanger-Newcastle route, she again reverted to *Black Watch*. The second ship, *Black Prince*, was solely owned by Fred Olsen. Delivered in autumn, she joined her sister in the Madeira and Canaries service, running each summer between Kristiansand and Harwich.

The *Jupiter/Black Watch* design was bold and modernistic – a long, sleek and fine-lined hull in grey, topped by a low, streamlined superstructure which extended well forward and aft. The horizontal elongation was further exaggerated by the topmost deck being painted buff to match the funnel. Mounted on the bow, in keeping with a 1930s Olsen tradition, was a bronze figurehead with mosaic-covered wings. Equally distinctive was the shape of the funnel, reputedly inspired by a Viking helmet.

The interior design was entrusted to Oslo-based architects Barstad and Skjaevland – former assistants of arguably Norway's most famous designer, Arnstein Arnerberg, architect of Oslo City Hall and other notable buildings. As on the DFDS *England*, First Class passengers occupied the forward half of the superstructure and Second Class towards the stern, two

dining saloons sandwiching the galley amidships and smoking saloons forward and aft. The First Class saloon was particularly notable – essentially, a miniaturised version of the splendid Garden Lounges on the Norwegian America liners, the *Oslofjord* and the *Bergensfjord*. The space was semi-circular in plan with informal groups of armchairs and settees arranged around a centrally-located dance floor and separated from the outer areas by vertically-slatted screens, creating a series of intimate corners. The Second Class saloon, equally intriguing, was U-shaped and built around the tank for the ship's all-weather swimming pool. During summer the pool was decked over and the lido area filled with reclining seats, the tank becoming a store room for the adjacent duty-free shop. No space was wasted on the ship and conversion from cruise to ferry could be achieved either way in only two days. Contemporary Norwegian artworks from the Olsen family collection adorned the bulkheads throughout.

Cabins were variously located, accommodating 350 berthed passengers in winter cargo/cruise mode (during which only First Class cabins were occupied), and 693 in summer, when compact Second Class cabins and reclining seats were added. The ship's only shortcoming was in being unable to carry lorries in substantial numbers due to lack of free height on the car deck.

The two ships *Jupiter/Black Watch* and the *Black Prince* were immediately successful in their versatile year-round roles as ferry/cargo ship/cruiseliner. In 1968 Olsen ordered a third, this one slightly larger. In the same year, the Line's 1951-built passenger liner *Blenheim* was destroyed by fire and the new ship took her name.

At 10,419 tons the new *Blenheim* could accommodate 1,107 passengers and 300 cars. She was ordered from the John Brown & Co shipyard at Clydebank and, as a British Government subsidy was involved, she flew the British flag. During the summer, the three near-sisters worked on intensive schedules to cope with the holiday traffic to and from Norway. According to Fred Olsen's 1972 brochure, Norway's attractions for holidaymakers included magnificent scenery – fjords, mountains, forests and lakes; good accommodation – hotels, guesthouses and country cottages; fine food – and not 'foreign' enough to take a week of getting used to; friendly people – hospitable, charming and very much akin to the British; and no language problems – virtually everyone could speak English.

On the northern North Sea routes between the UK and Scandinavia, car-carrying liner-type passenger ferries were the best solution to modernisation. But further south, on the shorter crossings to the Netherlands and Belgium, more freight-orientated tonnage was optimal, as the successful Tilbury-Antwerp route operated by Transport Ferry Services was proving. Other passenger and cargo services from Britain to the Low Countries were operated by a wide diversity of small general cargo and passenger ships, run by an almost equal variety of shipowners. Of these, Associated Humber Lines was part of the state-owned British Transport Commission, its tonnage comprising the *Bolton Abbey* (1958) and the *Melrose Abbey* (1959). Their German, Dutch and British competitors were many (Reederi Richard Adler & Söhne of Bremen, A. Kirsten of Hamburg, Phs. Van Ommeren of Rotterdam, Hollandsche Stoomboot Maatschappij of Amsterdam, The General Steam Navigation Company of London and The Tyne-Tees Steam Shipping Company of Newcastle) and in 1964 they all joined forces to launch a new jointly-owned ferry company, North Sea Ferries. Even before new vessels could be ordered for the intended Hull-Rotterdam route, A. Kirsten withdrew from the combine. Shortly afterwards the P&O Group, which already owned Tyne-Tees Shipping, merged it with the recently-acquired General Steam Navigation Company, giving P&O forty-five per cent of the capital (and the entire British share) in North Sea Ferries.

The basic design for the new ferries was devised by H. Vreedenburgh of combine partner Phs. Van Ommeren. Built at Bremerhaven by the AG Weser Seebeckwerft, the 3,692-ton *Norwind* and *Norwave* were the world's first overnight ferries with two double-height vehicle decks, stacked vertically, one atop the other – and this at a time when some recent vessels serving British ports had little or no freight capacity. Cars and trucks drove onboard via bow and stern doors, and large hinged internal ramps could be lowered for access to the upper level, which protruded above the hull. Sloping sections fore and aft denoted where these ramps were located. The lower vehicle deck had three lanes running along the centreline with single lanes between the casings and the shell plating. The upper deck had only three centre lanes, the lifeboat promenades being outboard.

Cabins and reclining chairs for 249 passengers were spread over three decks – two above and one below the vehicle spaces. The main saloon deck had a forward-facing reclining seat lounge, a large cafeteria amidships (breakfast and dinner were included in the North Sea Ferries fare) and a galley located towards the stern. On the deck above were a circular nightclub and cocktail bar aft and eight 'special' cabins with private facilities amidships. The majority of cabins were below the vehicle decks, forward and aft of the engine room, their toilets and washrooms being on the deck below that, between the trim tanks. In summary, the *Norwind* and the *Norwave* were extremely compact ferries, two 14-cylinder Smit & Bolnes diesels giving each a 17-knot service speed, and no corner wasted in what was a very logical configuration.

Within only six months of North Sea Ferries commencing operations, the BTC-owned Associated Humber Lines gave up

The Knud E. Hansen A/S-designed **København** was initially successful in providing an alternative for motorists to DFDS' passenger-orientated Copehagen-Oslo route, but her initial acclaim was short-lived once DFDS responded with new tonnage of its own. *(Bruce Peter collection)*

trying to compete, abandoning the Hull-Rotterdam service and laying up its two 8-year-old passenger-cargo vessels.

Denmark's DFDS was simultaneously planning to introduce a whole flotilla of new ferries, including a second large vessel for the Esbjerg-Harwich route and four ferries for principal overnight services within Scandinavia. Shortly after commissioning the *England* in 1964, the company had experienced an extensive boardroom shake-up when rival Danish shipowners Knud and Ivar Lauritzen conspired surreptitiously to acquire a majority of shares. The dynamic Lauritzen brothers sought to quickly modernise the rather conservative DFDS, which was falling behind recently-established rivals on both its domestic and international passenger routes.

North Sea Ferries' innovative double-deck drive-through ferry **Norwave** rests at her Rotterdam Europoort berth in the early 1970s. *(ShipPax archive)*

Top: The Italian-built Esbjerg-Harwich ferry **Winston Churchill** passes through the Channel on her delivery voyage in 1967. *(Bruce Peter collection)*

Above left: The **Winston Churchill**'s aft-facing Second Class smoking saloon, featuring a glazed rear bulkhead. *(Bruce Peter collection)*

Above right: The First Class dining saloon on the **Winston Churchill**, featuring a tapestry panel by Jens Urup Jensen. *(Bruce Peter collection)*

Right: The DFDS Copenhagen-Aalborg ferry **Trekroner** undergoes sea trials in the Gulf of Genoa in 1970. *(Bruce Peter collection)*

On the home front in Denmark, numerous private sector car ferry operators on the Southern Kattegat were muscling in on long-established DFDS overnight passenger services from Copenhagen to Århus and Aalborg. Also facing stiff competition from an upstart car ferry service (the Norske Københavnlinje – Norwegian Copenhagen Line) was the 'capital cities' link between Copenhagen and Oslo – a DFDS flagship service. This rival service was inaugurated in 1966 by Norwegian shipping entrepreneur Sverre Ditlev-Simonsen, using a car ferry named the *København* – a vessel of 3,611 tons, designed by Knud E. Hansen A/S. As well as duplicating the DFDS operation, the *København* made short calls en route at Brevik and Horten. Another DFDS worry was that although its vessels the *Prinsesse Margrethe* and the *King Olav V*, linking Copenhagen and Oslo, were recently constructed, they were far less modern in concept than their new competitor.

Externally, the *København* was a striking ship, styled with sleek and powerful lines by naval architect Tage Wandborg. Unlike previous KEH-designed ferries of the 1960s, the vehicle deck had a centre casing and so the exhaust uptakes were routed through the rear of an elongated funnel, the forward portion of which contained the ship's 'sky bar'.

All public rooms were on the Main Deck, and aft on the Boat Deck was a small saloon, the remainder given over to cabins. There were more cabins both below and on either side of the car deck, giving in all 400 berths – more than half of the total passenger capacity. But the *København*'s real distinction was her stern-loading vehicle deck. It could take 100 cars – three times as many as either of the DFDS vessels – and had sufficient free height to carry commercial vehicles.

The new DFDS North Sea vessel for the Esbjerg-Harwich route was an enlarged and enhanced version of the popular *England*, with an extra hull deck to allow some freight and commercial vehicles to be loaded via bow and stern doors (which former DFDS Chairman J.A. Kørbing had resisted on safety grounds). The new ferries for overnight services within Scandinavia (Copenhagen-Oslo/Aalborg) were to be rather different in concept and Technical Director Brian Corner-Walker and Chief Naval Architect Kai Modeweg-Hansen were despatched by the DFDS Board on a fact-finding tour to the Mediterranean. The two men examined in detail the passenger facilities of the Brindisi-Corfu-Patras ferries *Egnatia* and *Appia* and also of the *Canguro*-type vessels sailing from Genoa to Olbia in Sardinia. Of particular interest to DFDS was how the various ratios of cabins to couchettes and reclining seats on

these ships worked in practice. In Italy, the two DFDS 'spies' also made contact with various shipyards and discovered that build costs were significantly less than in Scandinavia without any compromise in quuality. Consequently, the winner of the tendering process was an old-established Italian shipbuilder, the Cantieri Navale del Tirreno e Riuniti, located at Riva Trigoso to the south of Genoa on the Tyrrenian Gulf.

DFDS technical staff collaborated with the Italians to design the new North Sea vessel, the new sisters for the Copenhagen-Oslo route and the new Copenhagen-Aalborg ships, in that order. Perhaps inevitably, all five materialised as intriguing mixtures of typical DFDS design features, as previously seen on the *England*, and distinctly Italian solutions.

The latter applied particularly to the hull lines, which resembled those of the most recent Italian 'deep-sea' ocean liners. In the words of naval architect Andrea Ginnante, who joined the yard as the DFDS ships were nearing completion: "In the 1960s Italian shipyards could call on the skills of the world's most innovative and talented naval architects and engineers. At Riva Trigoso, our naval architect was the brilliant Giò Melodia, who helped to refine the very beautiful and efficient hull forms for the DFDS ships. Undoubtedly, he was influenced by Nicolò Costanzi, who designed the legendary *Guglielmo Marconi*, *Galileo Galilei* and *Eugenio C*. Like the great Italian liners of the period, their lines at the bow were like a wineglass – concave at the waterline to cut through the waves efficiently and convex above to maximise the deck space. That elegant shape made these ships very distinctive."

The new 8,657-ton Esbjerg-Harwich vessel was launched in virtually complete condition and named *Winston Churchill* in honour of Britain's late wartime Prime Minister. As with the *England*, her engines were two 10-cylinder B&W diesels and to accommodate them she had a substantial freeboard, the vehicle deck being two decks above the waterline. So at Esbjerg and Harwich it was necessary to construct long ramps with a sufficiently shallow gradient to enable cars, buses and trucks to drive onboard. The ship's capacity was 462 passengers and 180 cars.

During the summer season both the *England* and the *Winston Churchill* sailed exclusively on the Esbjerg-Harwich route, but starting in winter 1966 the *England* also ran winter cruises to the West Indies and West Africa and was fitted with an outdoor swimming pool at the stern and a cinema and gymnasium in the car deck. She carried fewer passengers than in her North Sea service, and in one class only. The cruises

British Rail's 1968 Stranraer-Larne ferry **Antrim Princess**. *(Bruce Peter collection)*

The SMZ's Harwich-Hook of Holland ferry **Koningin Juliana** off Harwich in the early 1970s. *(Bruce Peter collection)*

proved extremely popular with Brits, Danes and Germans – a taste of things to come for DFDS.

As with their predecessors, the new 7,956-ton Copenhagen-Oslo ferries were named the *Kong Olav V* and *Prinsesse Margrethe* and in terms of passenger appointments were on a par with the *Winston Churchill*. The First Class saloons, forward on the Saloon Deck, were particularly outstanding. Kay Kørbing's design featured a forward-located smoking saloon and, to the rear, behind a plate-glass partition, a cocktail bar and a dance floor clad in brass and steel panels. On either side of the bar and dance floor were intimate dining rooms. Aft, the hallways featured open-tread staircases which, thanks to ingenious concealed lighting, appeared to float in front of psychedelic mural panels by renowned Danish pop artist Per Arnoldi. Interiors were typically Kørbing – extensive use of dark hardwood veneers contrasting with bright fabrics for curtains and upholstery. Second Class public rooms were also of high standard. On the decks below was an extensive variety of cabins, plus saloons with colour-coded reclining seats. Deck Class was banished and all 506 passengers could sleep in relative comfort.

As ramps for bow and stern loading had yet to be provided in Copenhagen and Oslo, the *Kong Olav V* and *Prinsesse Margrethe* had only side access doors to their vehicle decks, as for the *England*. Moreover, with cabins and reclining seat lounges in broad casings on either beam, their vehicle capacity was restricted to three lanes along the centreline. A maximum of 100 cars could be carried, using platform decks lowered from the deckhead. On the plus side, the new ferries won immediate acclaim for their stylish design. Indeed, Ditlev-Simonsen's Norske Københavnlinje were unable to compete. With only one vessel offering departures every second day, the service was quickly abandoned.

The 7,672-ton Copenhagen-Aalborg ships of 1969-70 – the *Aalborghus* and the *Trekroner* – were less successful for DFDS. As they sailed mainly during the night, they had few public rooms but a large number of cabins and reclining seat lounges. The new ships were victims of circumstance in that, during the first half of the 1960s, several short ferry routes across the Kattegat from Northern Jylland to Sjælland had opened, and the airline SAS had introduced more regular Copenhagen-Aalborg flights. So the DFDS night-time ferry service was not without competition. The company's plan to introduce calls en route at Helsingborg to attract Swedish passengers – and so enable tax-free sales – was dashed by the authorities' argument that even with a brief stop in Sweden, the route was still essentially domestic and tax-free did not apply. Thus DFDS ceased the service in autumn 1970, only months after introducing the *Trekroner*.

This situation highlighted an important fact: for commercial ferry operators in northern Europe, the sale of tax-free goods was vital to survival. The extra income it created helped to keep ticket prices competitive enough to attract more passengers and expand the market. Ferries were no longer means of simply getting from A to B; they were increasingly important as floating leisure and retail environments, generating crucial income.

Unfortunately for DFDS, their Italian-built vessels were not particularly well suited to this new reality. Their two-class accommodation offered only limited facilities and vehicle decks were constricted on either side by cabins and casings. The engineer had to sit on a stool between the main engines, receiving telegraph signals from the bridge and manually adjusting each motor. The engines, Fiat-built Burmeister & Wain diesels of a basic design, had changed little since the 1930s apart from the increase from 10 to 12 cylinders and the adoption of turbocharging. Moreover, most 1960s ferries had separate air-conditioned engine control rooms but DFDS opted to retain an old-fashioned arrangement established on initial (early 20th-century) motor ships. Maybe this logic was rooted in the fact that some bridge officers did not trust the reliability of automated systems and preferred to send commands by telegraph.

For naval architects, however, another problem was causing anxiety – the potential insecurity of ferries' bow visors. Less than a year after the *Winston Churchill* entered service, her bow visor was broken open by high waves during a stormy crossing from Esbjerg to Harwich (as had happened just a short time previously on the *Tor Anglia*). Former chairman of DFDS, J.A. Kørbing, had questioned the security of lifting bow visors on ferries intended for year-round operation in the treacherous conditions of the northern North Sea. British naval architects Don Ripley and Tony Rogan also had good cause for concern as, at that time, three new drive-through ferries for British Rail were undergoing various stages of construction.

The first of these, the 3,730-ton *Antrim Princess*, was being built at the Hawthorn Leslie shipyard on Tyneside for the Stranraer-Larne route, on which the *Princess Victoria* had been lost in a storm fifteen years earlier. In order to lessen the upward force exerted by high waves hitting the visor, the bow design for this new ferry – and for subsequent drive-through vessels by Rogan and Ripley – was fine-lined, with a more vertical stem than was typical on recent Scandinavian ships. This slightly reduced the area of the vehicle deck, especially as the collision bulkhead and inner ramp were also set well back. (The *Winston Churchill*'s visor mountings were strengthened, after which she suffered no serious storm damage throughout the remainder of her long and notably successful service.)

British Rail's new drive-through *Antrim Princess* was to be the fleet's first large motor ship since the ill-fated *Princess Victoria* – a prospect which did not go down well with one captain who half-jokingly commented to the naval architects, "I believe you are building a deeeeesel ferry… I have no desire to be propelled across the Channel by a series of explosions."

The diesels in question were twin French-built 16-cylinder Pielstickls, giving a service speed of 19.5-knots. With the aid of wind-tunnel testing, Tony Rogan devised a suitable new funnel design, consisting of a broad conical-shaped lower section with an exhaust stack protruding from the top – somewhat akin to a fireman's helmet. In various permutations, this subsequently became a symbol of almost the entire British Rail ferry fleet. (Intriguingly, this solution was not dissimilar from the one designed independently for Cunard's 1969 transtlantic liner the *Queen Elizabeth 2* – or *QE2* as she became universally known.)

The *Antrim Princess* was quickly followed by the 7,359-ton Harwich-Hook of Holland ferry *St George,* built on the Tyne for British Rail by Swan, Hunter & Wigham Richardson. Traditionally, this route was primarily a rail-connected service, but now the need was to carry cars and commercial vehicles in substantial numbers and to make more efficient use of tonnage. British Rail's partners in the service, the Stoomvaart Maatschappij Zeeland, simultaneously ordered a comparable ferry, the 6,682-ton *Koningin Juliana*, built by Cammell Laird of Birkenhead to a variation of the *St George*'s design drawings, modified for the Dutch owner by Knud E. Hansen A/S (but completely atypical of

The forward-facing First Class lounge on the **St George**, designed by Ward & Austin. *(Bruce Peter collection)*

The **St George**'s First Class dining saloon, featuring plate glass dividing screens with tree silhouettes. *(Bruce Peter collection)*

KEH's usual ferry design approach).

As rail passengers remained an important part of the mix on the Harwich-Hook service, both the *St George* and the *Koningin Juliana* inherited the two-class layouts of their packet predecessors and fleetmates. This was entirely practical as the route carried a very diverse clientele – everyone from British squaddies bound for West German barracks and students heading for randy weekends in Amsterdam to football supporters attending European fixtures and significant numbers of business people choosing to travel in comfort and tranquillity.

Unfortunately for the latter, the First Class saloons were aft-located and the *St George*'s four 9-cylinder Ruston & Hornsby diesels were prone to vibrate when the ship was travelling at speed on day crossings, while the shape of her stern caused cavitation. The *Koningin Juliana* was fitted instead with four 9-cylinder MAN engines and, as her stern was one of the aspects modified by Knud E. Hansen A/S, she was less prone to vibration. Less successfully, KEH also specified a more rakish bow visor and, as the the upward force of waves damaged the locking pins, this soon had to be replaced with a design similar to the *St George*. Each ferry could carry 1,200 passengers, with about 600 berthed on night crossings, and up to 220 cars.

British Rail's third and versatile new diesel ferry, the 4,760-ton *Vortigern*, was also built on the Tyne, at the Wallsend shipyard of Swan, Hunter. She was a multi-purpose ship, designed to carry trains, or up to 240 cars, or a mix of cars and commercial vehicles, and up to 1,000 passengers. In summer her route was Dover-Boulogne and in winter Dover-Dunkerque, the latter seeing her operate alongside the French *Saint-Germain*, replacing the ageing 1934-vintage *Hampton Ferry*. The *Vortigern* had an additional upper garage for cars in the aft section, accessed by a ramp which could be lowered to the retractable mezzanine car deck. To cover such a variety of duties she was a complex ship, both technically and in layout. Her public rooms were subdivided into a multitude of small spaces, so that overnight passengers could sleep without too much disturbance. As with the *Antrim Princess*, engine power came from two 16-cylinder Pielstick diesels, these built in the UK by Crossley of Manchester. She was a great success, spawning two subsequent near-sisters – the *Chartres* (1974) and the *Saint Eloi* (1975) – and a true reflection of the accumulated expertise of her designers.

The interior design of British Rail's new generation of drive-through ferries was the work of Ward & Austin, who frequently achieved notably fresh and sleek solutions. They made extensive use of moulded glass fibre, bright laminate finishes,

The British Rail Harwich-Hook of Holland vessel **St George** manoeuvres Harwich Parkeston Quay in the early 1970s. *(Bruce Peter collection)*

Top: British Rail's ***Vortigern*** proved to be a very versatile multi-purpose train, car and freight ferry. Here she is seen at Dover's Western Docks in the 1970s. *(Bruce Peter collection)*

Above left: The ***Vortigern*** is launched at the Swan, Hunter's Wallsend shipyard on the River Tyne on 5 March 1969. *(Matthew Murtland collection)*

Above right: The ***Vortigern***'s Tea Bar, designed by Ward & Austin and featuring Eero Saarinen 'Tulip' chairs. *(Bruce Peter collection)*

Right: The ***St George*** rests at the new ferry terminal at Harwich Parkeston Quay in the early 1970s. *(Bruce Peter collection)*

Silja Line's **Fennia** (1966) was by far the largest and best-appointed ferry in operation between Sweden and Finland, and notable for both her stylish external and interior design. *(Bruce Peter collection)*

built-in furniture and large decorative bas-relief panels by Franta Belsky, David Gentleman and other leading British-based artists and sculptors. Designs were robust – sometimes austere – notably featuring wipe-clean surfaces for easy removal of spilled food and drink.

British Rail's two-class railway-orientated Harwich-Hook of Holland ferry route was unusual, and became increasingly so. Elsewhere in northern Europe, particularly in Scandinavia, the future of overnight voyages belonged to an emerging leisure-orientated type of ferry – vessels appropriately dubbed 'cruiseferries.'

This new generation of vessels was to break away from the traditions of class division and other fixed ideas established and perpetuated by the large packet liners of the previous era. The emphasis shifted from transportation to leisure – offering passengers a broad variety of onboard facilities, available to all.

The realisation dawned that significant income could be generated by open-plan interiors with shops, bars, dining options, cinemas, nightclubs, hairdressing salons and more.

A new Baltic ferry for Silja Line – the 6,178-ton *Fennia*, delivered in 1966 from the Öresundsvarvet in Landskrona – pointed the way ahead. With capacity for up to 1200 passengers and 225 cars, she was the first large purpose-built ferry to sail daily from Stockholm to Mariehamn and Turku, rather than from the remote port of Norrtälje out in the archipelago. This gave her the opportunity to transport large numbers of foot passengers, thus posing a potentially serious threat to the steamer services operated by Silja Line's parent companies – particularly as the *Fennia* offered far better facilities at lower cost. The steamers sailed nightly from Skeppsbronn Quay in the heart of Stockholm, the *Fennia* departing each morning from the Värtahamnen docks, just north of the city's main business district.

While Silja Line's own Board was enthusiastic about its splendid new ferry, the directorates of the parent companies – Finska Ångfartygs Aktiebolaget, Ångfartygs AB Bore and Rederi AB Svea – were less enamoured and, indeed, refused to promote in their brochures the *Fennia*'s 22-hour return cruises to Finland. Silja Line responded by distributing fliers in Stockholm and by inviting prospective passengers to come

onboard on open days (organised by the *Fennia*'s officers and crew) to see the ship's attractions, features and facilties first hand. Her futuristic profile and crisply modern interiors were certainly impressive. Externally, she resembled a miniaturised version of Holland America Line's 1959-built transatlantic liner *Rotterdam*, and the design was a development of that of the smaller *Skandia* and *Nordia*.

Intended for crossings both night and day in the fairly sheltered waters of the archipelago, the hull was quite beamy and the superstructure commodious. The main deck featured cabins and reclining seat saloons. On the deck above were lounges, restaurants and even a hairdressing salon, plus 300 berths for night crossings (as opposed to the mere 136 of the earlier ferries *Skandia* and *Nordia*).

Intriguingly, each superstructure deck was slightly narrower than the one below, creating a slight 'stacked' effect. This offsetting of the vertical framing enhanced longitudinal rigidity, resulting in a more robust overall superstructure and also a weight saving – a design solution unique to Silja Line's ferries of the latter 1960s and early 1970s. In the engine room the *Fennia* had four British-made 9-cylinder Ruston & Hornsby diesels – unique in the Silja Line fleet and rare in Scandinavian ferries in general. But they were short lived, replaced in 1975 by four Atlas-MaK diesels.

The most outstanding aspect of the *Fennia* was her splendid interior design. This was the work of renowned Finnish architect Bengt Lundsten, who believed that the design should act as an elegant backdrop to the passengers, their clothes and movement providing colour. The neutral browns, blues and greys of carpets, curtains and upholstery were accented with boldly-coloured contemporary artworks and with modernist Eero Saarinen 'Tulip' and Arne Jacobsen 'Swan' and 'Egg' chairs in leather, all set against unadorned expanses of matt-varnished wood-veneered panelling.

Below the vehicle deck were further cabins, a cinema, a swimming pool and a sauna bath, and the topmost deck boasted an oval-shaped cocktail bar inside the dummy funnel, with a 360-degree panoramic view across the beautiful archipelago. Aft were extensive sun decks and an outdoor bandstand and dance floor. This combination of food, drink,

Stena Line's beautiful **Stena Germanica** inaugurated the route from Gothenburg to Kiel. *(Bruce Peter collection)*

music and scenery was irresistible, the *Fennia* quickly establishing a loyal following amongst Stockholmers. Moreover, she was also the first Baltic ferry with a walk-in tax-free supermarket – a stroke of commercial enterprise copied by virtually all subsequent Scandinavian ferries serving on international routes. In fact, the *Fennia* (sailing daily from Stockholm to Mariehamn, Turku and return) set the standard for future ferries and put in many years of outstanding service on a number of Baltic routes – and this despite the fact that at one point in her story, due to corporate wranglings, she could so easily have taken a completely different course.

After the *Fennia* had first been introduced, a political tug-of-war was raging between Silja Line's forward-looking management and the traditionally-minded directorates of the firm's parent companies. The latter stubbornly continued to seek to protect their existing (and increasingly obsolescent) steamer routes rather than vigorously embrace the era of the cruise ferry. So although Silja Line's Board apparently wanted to commission further overnight ferries of *Fennia* standards, they were directed instead to build two more ferries of similar size and layout to the *Skandia* and the *Nordia*. Equally remarkable is that serious consideration was given to selling the *Fennia* to Alaska Marine

Highway at the end of the 1968 season. Fortunately for Silja Line the sale fell through and the *Fennia*'s future panned out as already described.

The first of Silja's two new ferries, the 3,514-ton *Botnia*, was built by Wärtsilä in Helsinki and delivered in 1967. To optimise fuel economy when sailing at different speeds on day and night crossings, and to deliver extra power for winter ice-breaking, an unusual engine arrangement was specified – eight small Wärtsilä-Vaasa diesels, four geared to each propeller shaft. Two were located ahead of each gearbox and two behind, on either side of the shaft. The precedent for this arrangement had been set in 1964 by Japanese train ferry the *Tsugaru Maru*, with eight Kawasaki-MAN diesels. In 1970 came the second of the two new ferries, the *Floria*. But it was soon apparent that both were too small to handle the growing traffic for which they had been built, and in 1975 they were sold to Compagnia Trasmediterránea in Spain.

While the *Fennia* and her smaller fleetmates were carrying increasing numbers of Swedes and Finns on short tax-free shopping minicruises across the Baltic, Stena Line was likewise expansive on the Kattegat sea. Sten A. Olsson realised that West Germany's prosperity in the 1960s would create the

The **Fennia**'s smoking saloon with Arne Jacobsen 'Swan' chairs and a white baby grand piano. *(Bruce Peter collection)*

Due to political machinations, Silja line built only one **Fennia**, thereafter reverting to smaller ferries; this was a mistake. The **Botnia** was powered by eight small diesels and was short-lived in the Silja fleet. *(Robert Spark)*

The design of the Alaska Marine Highways flagship **Columbia** was influenced by the high standard of the ex-Stena vessels **Wickersham**. *(Bruce Peter)*

The **Sunward** is seen shortly after transferring to the Caribbean, where she became a very popular cruise ship. *(Bruce Peter collection)*

opportunity to open an overnight ferry service between Gothenburg and Kiel, and then to use the ship intensively in between to make shorter day return trips from Gothenburg to Frederikshavn and from Kiel to Korsør. As with the *Fennia* (in constant circulation between Sweden and Finland), Stena Line's intended business model was to offer lower fares to fill ferries to capacity with shoppers and so keep the fleet in service throughout day and night. This was a world away from British Railways' steamer fleet which, even in the mid-1960s, continued to be timetabled with lengthy layovers between trips.

Another trick of Stena's was to look for shipyards with empty order books, teetering on the brink, and to negotiate tough contracts – sometimes getting two ferries for not much more than the price of one. Such was the case with the new ferry for the Gothenburg-Kiel route, for which a sister ship was also speculatively ordered. Both vessels were constructed by the Langesund Mekaniske Verksted (which had previously built the *Stena Baltica*), but outfitting was completed at another shipyard, the Framnes Mekaniske Verksted at Sandefjord, when the Langesund yard ran out of money.

The new ferries were again designed by Knud E. Hansen A/S, whose styling specialist Tage Wandborg produced a particularly striking silhouette. The Swedish magazine *Svensk Sjöfarts Tidning* declared that the first of these ships, the *Stena Germanica*, was the best-looking new Swedish ship of 1967. Her sister, the *Stena Britannica*, was delivered towards the end of the same year and, as there was insufficient traffic at that time to justify two ships between Gothenburg and Kiel, she served instead as a day ferry on the busy Gothenburg-Frederikshavn route. Two interesting footnotes here: she was less than ideal due to her high proportion of overnight cabins and, allegedly, because of Stena's cheap fares, some of Gothenburg's more enterprising prostitutes took to sailing on her, surreptitiously 'entertaining' their clients in the otherwise deserted cabins!

Inboard, the new ferries' most noteworthy feature was in the engine room – exceptionally powerful (for that time) twin MAN 16-cylinder medium-speed diesels, generating up to 12,891 kW and a fast 23.5-knot service speed. Relatively long and low, these small-cylinder motors differed from the much taller 10-cylinder slow-speed, direct-drive engines on the DFDS *Winston Churchill*, delivered the same year and – at a push – capable of a similar speed.

The vehicle decks of these new Stena Line ferries had three double-height lanes along the centreline between the casings, with single-height outer car lanes on either beam and cabins above. Additional cabins were located forward on Main Deck, amidships on Boat Deck and, as with the earlier Knud E. Hansen A/S-designed overnight ferries, on two levels below the car deck. Architects Rolf Carlsson and Robert Tillberg decorated the very elegant public rooms with fine wood veneers, rich colours and mural panels. The cafeteria was above the dining saloon aft and the same galley served both. The smoking saloon and cocktail bar were forward on Boat Deck. As this was a Stena ship, the most important facility (and certainly the most prominently located) was the large tax-free shop, amidships on the Main Deck and right beside the entrance hallway.

As the funnel was aft, much of the ship's topmost deck was open to passengers and had a solarium with floor-to-ceiling windows and a glassfibre panelled roof to keep out the elements. All in all, passengers had every reason to regard the *Stena Germanica* and the *Stena Britannica* as most enjoyable and attractive ships.

Even so, in April 1968, after only the briefest period of service, the *Stena Britannica* was sold to Alaska Marine Highway to operate between the USA and Alaska. Renamed the *Wickersham*, and unable to comply with US flag specifications due to her European construction, she was registered in Panama and made stops en route in Canadian ports. Having failed to secure the *Fennia* from Silja Line, Alaska Marine Highway must have been very happy to purchase a virtually brand new ferry of such advanced design – and Stena, of course, made a small profit on the deal. In comparison with Alaska Marine Highway's existing ferries (US-built, Method 1-compliant and somewhat austere in terms of passenger amenities), the *Wickersham* was a luxurious ship, more like a small cruise liner. But due to American flag restrictions, she could be no more than a stop-gap measure and, in the early 1970s, AMH returned to its regular ferry designer Philip F. Spaulding for a new American-built flagship incorporating the *Wickersham*'s best features.

Since designing the existing fleet, Spaulding had merged his naval architecture firm with that of his main rival in the Seattle area, George Nickum & Associates, to form Nickum & Spaulding. Nickum's ferry designs consisted of very capacious double-ended, twin-deck craft for Washington State Ferries and, following the merger, Spaulding became involved in this aspect of the enlarged firm's ferry design output.

The new flagship for Alaska Marine Highway, the 3,946-ton

The **Starward** developed the Knud E. Hansen A/S 'sky bar' concept into a multi-storey bar and lido complex. *(Bruce Peter collection)*

Columbia, was built by Lockheed Shipbuilding & Construction Ltd in Seattle and delivered in 1974. She could carry 676 passengers (324 of whom were berthed) and 140 cars, loaded via stern and side ports. Unlike her American-built fleetmates, her interior design was notably luxurious – perhaps again demonstrating the *Wickersham*'s impact on her owner's thinking. Even today, the *Columbia* remains the pride of the Alaska Marine Highway's fleet.

CARIBBEAN CRUISE FERRY PIONEERS

In December 1964, the Israeli Somerfin Lines ferry *Bilu* crossed the Atlantic to Miami to begin a season of three- and four-day cruises to Freeport and Nassau in the Bahamas and to Montego Bay in Jamaica – the first large car ferry to operate in the rapidly-expanding Caribbean cruise market.

A year later her bigger fleetmate, the *Nili*, on charter to Pan American Cruise Lines, followed suit to provide short cruises to Nassau. In September 1966 this operation was taken over by Ted Arison, a Miami-based Israeli émigré freight shipping entrepreneur, who additionally planned to charter the *Bilu* for short cruises from Miami to Montego Bay in Jamaica. A disastrous fire at sea the year before had destroyed the *Yarmouth Castle*, a 1927 vintage cruise ship, and Arison was keen to show that modern ferry travel was the new way to go. Large canvas signs declaring 'I'm only one year old' were hung over the *Nili*'s topsides when in port.

Arison's cruise operations were highly successful, hence the need for two vessels, which he advertised as 'The Fun Ships'. Alas for Arison, the ships' owner, Somerfin, got into serious financial difficulties and the *Bilu* was arrested in Italy before she could cross the Atlantic. Shortly after, on 18th November 1966, the *Nili* was arrested in Miami with cruise passengers onboard, leaving Arison in the unfortunate position of having no shortage of passengers but no ships in which to carry them. The *Nili* remained under arrest in Miami for several months while the legal battle between the ship's owners and creditors went to court.

Meanwhile, on the far side of the Atlantic, another cruise ferry entrepreneur, Knud Kloster, was attempting to establish a service of his own, taking British holidaymakers and their cars south to the sun – from Southampton to Vigo, Lisbon and Gibraltar. Kloster was a director of the Lauritz Kloster Rederi of Oslo, founded in 1906, and he had long been involved in the bulk cargo and tanker trades. The ship to operate the proposed new Southampton service was the 8,666-ton *Sunward*, ordered from the Bergens Mekaniske Verksteder for delivery in 1966.

Designed by Knud E. Hansen A/S, the *Sunward* was essentially a greatly-enlarged version of the typical KEH Scandinavian car ferry, but with significant overnight cabin capacity. This filled an entire deck above the car deck and the majority of Main Deck, where there was also a reception lobby. The public rooms were at Boat Deck level and amidships on Bridge Deck, above which there was a 'skybar'. The ship's interior design was created by Danish architect Mogens Hammer and was similar in style to the DFDS ferry *England*. The main lounge was forward and had a fine view over the bow, and the dining room was aft. Between them was an arcade to starboard and galley space to port. Such innovative open-plan design engendered an atmosphere of spaciousness and allowed passengers to circulate with ease, encouraging them to spend more money in the process. As the 1970s progressed, the starboard arcade became a standard feature of ferry interiors throughout Scandinavia and beyond.

Designed for the sometimes stormy Bay of Biscay, the rather 'stiff' hull lines of the *Sunward* were compensated for by fin stabilisers – well-proven technology – and by a stabilising tank located high in the superstructure. The latter was a novelty, consisting essentially of a large water tank with a hydraulically-operated steel panel to force water in the opposite direction to the ship's natural movement. Some captains found that rather than helping to keep the vessel on an even keel, this tended to make matters worse. Nevertheless, the feature was installed in some subsequent Knud E. Hansen A/S ferry designs of the 1960s and early 1970s, including the *Freeport* and the *Prince of Fundy*.

Christopher Moore, then travel correspondent of the *Manchester Guardian*, wrote that the *Sunward* provided "a high-class if expensive service, amounting to a minicruise and motoring holiday in southern Europe without the drudgery (for some) of driving both ways." But Kloster's enterprise was a failure, doomed by a combination of British government restrictions on currency for foreign travel and the growing diplomatic tension with Spain over the territorial status of Gibraltar.

Meanwhile, in Miami, Ted Arison (whose charter of the *Nili* had come to an abrupt halt with her arrest) discovered that the *Sunward* was available and he persuaded Kloster to operate it out of Miami with Arison's company as sales agents. Marketed under the name Norwegian Caribbean Line (NCL), the *Sunward* was an immediate success, carrying passengers and trailer traffic from Miami to Nassau in the Bahamas, Montego Bay in Jamaica and Port au Prince in Haiti. NCL went from strength to strength.

In June 1967 the Israeli government bought the *Nili* and the *Bilu*, undoubtedly as troop carriers in the event of war. Both ships were transferred to the government-owned 'Kavim' Company and the *Bilu* renamed *Dan*. At the government's request, Zim Lines of Haifa undertook to manage the vessels on a cost-plus basis. But for the time being the *Nili* remained in Miami and was chartered to another cruise entrepreneur, Granger Weston, who owned a hotel in Jamaica. The project also involved F. Leslie Fraser, who in the latter 1950s and early 1960s had operated the vintage coastal liners the *Yarmouth* and the *Evangeline* on short trips to and from Nassau. Weston called his operation Continental Cruise Line and put the *Nili* in service from Miami to Jamaica (Port Antonio and Montego Bay), and although she was marketed as the *Jamaica Queen* the ferry was never officially renamed as such). Initially, Continental Cruise Line offered 'all-inclusive' cruises – an innovation that was short lived.

Meanwhile, Kloster and Arison's Norwegian Caribbean Line decided that more ships were needed to cope with the expansion of the Caribbean cruise market. Two larger (12,940-ton) vessels were ordered, to be built to a Knud E. Hansen A/S design and tailored to satisfy the tastes of American passengers. Built at Bremerhaven by AG Weser Seebeckwerft, each vessel represented a further development of the *Sunward*'s design. The construction process was somewhat unusual – built in two halves and joined together in dry dock. The first ship, the *Starward*, was completed in only twelve months and delivered in November 1968.

The *Starward* could carry up to 540 passengers, berthed in en suite cabins, and 220 cars loaded through the stern, which had a special lifting visor over the ramp to continue the lines of the hull so that, when viewed from aft while at sea, the ship looked more like a liner than a car ferry. Certainly, her all-white colour scheme with blue accents, and streamlined funnels located towards the stern, gave the *Starward* a very distinctive appearance. Below the vehicle deck were two 16-cylinder 8,690 bhp MAN V-diesels, chosen for high power output, relatively low height and 21-knot speed.

Ahead of the funnels was a large sheltered lido area for subathing and a three-storey glazed sun lounge above the bridge. The car and freight deck ran down the middle of the hull with two levels of outside cabins on either side and more cabins on Main Deck above. However, the ship's Scandinavian ferry origins were evident from the cramped layout, the lower berths converting into settees for daytime use – an idea reputedly inspired by the staterooms on South Africa's famous Blue Train.

The *Starward* was constructed and outfitted in accordance with American 'Method 1' fire protection standards, specifying non-combustible materials throughout the passenger and crew accommodation. In Scandinavia the 'Method 2' British approach was more common – using finishes which were not fire-retardant but in conjunction with a sprinkler system. Thus the ambience of the *Starward* differed from the earlier, and very Scandinavian, *Sunward*. The new ship used a lot of laminate, aluminium and glassfibre for furniture and for wall and ceiling finishes, giving a light and fresh feel more akin to a modern hotel.

One of the *Starward*'s most striking onboard features was the Tropicana Garden. Three decks high, and enclosed on three sides by glass with the after end open, it was a remarkable space, developed from the 'skybars' on earlier ferries designed by Knud E. Hansen A/S.

The layout and interior design of the *Starward* reflected the need to generate as much onboard revenue as possible. The largest room, the Venus Lounge, was the focus of the ship's social life, and on the Atlantic Deck was a large shop and other retail and leisure attractions which included a barber's shop, beauty salon, slot machine casino and a large photographic studio, the latter an opportunity for passengers to capture a visual record of their Carribean cruise experience for posterity.

For Norwegian Caribbean Line, the *Starward* was a notable

THE FERRY a drive through history

The cruise and trailer ferry **Freeport**, also designed by Knud E. Hansen A/S, operated between Miami and Freeport, Grand Bahama Island. *(Bruce Peter collection)*

Top: The 1968-built *Gedser* was a day ferry with two decks of public rooms, consisting of bars, lounges, restaurants and a shop. *(Jan Vinter Christiansen collection)*

Above left : The 'Dansk Liljan' restaurant on the *Stena Danica* (1969), designed by Robert Tillberg. *(Bruce Peter collection)*

Above right: The *Stena Danica* reverses away from the quay in Gothenburg in the early 1970s. *(Bruce Peter collection)*

Below: The *Stena Danica* arrives in Gothenburg; Swedish American Line's famous *Kungsholm* is in the floating dock behind. *(Bruce Peter collection)*

A cut-away drawing of the **Stena Danica** showing that within her elegantly-shaped shell, she was compactly planned with two decks of public rooms. *(Bruce Peter collection)*

success. The rival *Nili*, when first introduced in 1968 by Continental Cruise Line, alternated between 5-day Jamaica cruises and 4-day trips to Nassau, but by the summer of 1969 she was serving Nassau only, apparently unable to compete with the *Starward* on the Jamaica run. Then in September 1969, all *Nili* cruises were cancelled and she was laid up in Miami. By this time, the well-organised NCL operation was anticipating the arrival of further new vessels. The *Nili* transferred back to the Mediterranean where both she and the *Bilu* operated as ferries between Israel, Greece, Italy and France.

Kloster and Arison's Norwegian Caribbean Line duly took delivery of its third ship, the *Skyward*, bringing Kloster's investment in the Miami cruise business to over $100 million. When she arrived there in December 1969, the new vessel received a tumultuous welcome and was feted by the Miami Chamber of Commerce for the tourism wealth NCL was bringing to the city. Unlike the *Starward*, the *Skyward* was a dedicated passenger ship without a car deck and consequently

boasted berths for 750. Later, in the mid-1970s, the *Starward* was stripped of her vehicle-carrying capacity and the space was used for further cabins and for a cinema/theatre called 'The Four Vikings'. These new facilities were installed gradually, while the ship was still in service, using prefabricated components.

One further key vessel in the Miami cruise-ferry boom of the latter 1960s was the *Freeport*. Initially jointly owned by US Freight of New York and the Bahamas Development Corporation, she was intended to sail as a ferry-cum-cruise ship to bring passengers from Miami in Florida to Freeport on Grand Bahama Island, the attractions being the island's expanding resorts or simply the chance to enjoy a 24-hour cruise. The *Freeport*'s role for US Freight was carrying trailers and containers.

Built by Orenstein & Koppel und Lübecker Machinenbau of Lübeck, the *Freeport* was delivered in 1968. Compared with the 'tear-drop' shape of the 'first-generation' car ferries of the early- to mid-1960s designed by Knud E. Hansen A/S, she had a

Sessanlinjen's 1969-built **Prinsessan Christina** in Gothenburg harbour. *(Bruce Peter collection)*

The smoking saloon on the **Prinsessan Christina**; both Sessan and Stena Line offered their passengers a high standard of accommodation. *(Bruce Peter collection)*

The forward-facing lounge on the **Prinsessan Christina** could also be booked as a private conference and meeting space. *(Bruce Peter collection)*

more angular and evenly-balanced appearance. Her straight hull lines were angled upwards at the bow, which had an exaggerated rakish profile (but, unlike the *Koningin Juliana*, there was no bow door). At the waterline, a pronounced bulb was fitted to optimise the flow of water around the hull. A large single funnel located aft of amidships featured a flying saucer-shaped smoke deflector, placed at a jaunty angle near the summit. This may have been inspired by the funnel on the liner *Angelina Lauro* (then recently rebuilt), as the *Freeport* designer Tage Wandborg admired Italian passenger ship aesthetics.

In terms of overall size and layout, the vessel was similar to the *Starward*, with cabins on either side of the car deck and on Main Deck. Because the *Freeport* was built for a short-duration shuttle service with outward night crossings and day returns, her cabins were notably compact by American cruise ship standards but she had a wider range of public rooms than the *Starward*, spread over two decks – Saloon Deck and Boat Deck – with superior cabins located forward on both. Her total capacity of 812 passengers and 144 cars was impressive given her relatively compact dimensions. An extra freight deck, on top of the ship's bottom plates forward of the engine room, was accessed through a hatch in the main vehicle deck.

There were two dining saloons with the galley in between on the Saloon Deck and a number of lounges plus a casino above. The *Freeport*'s interiors were very striking, and even psychedelic in places. Created by French designers Pierre and François Lalonde, they were ideal for short-duration party cruises to the Bahamas. As with the *Starward*, there was expansive sun-deck space on tiered decks aft and forward of the funnel on top of the Bridge Deck, where tinted Perspex screens and a semi-enclosed solarium gave some shelter (a feature first seen on the *Kattegat* and repeated in enlarged form on the *Stena Germanica*).

The *Freeport*'s operator was advertised as Freeport Cruise Line and later, when the service was taken over by a subsidiary of the British company Common Bros, it became known as the Bahama Cruise Line. Her service from Miami to Freeport was short-lived. The oil crisis which followed Arab protests at the Yom Kippur War resulted in a sharp rise in fuel prices, and in 1973 the *Freeport* was chartered to the Åland Islands-based Baltic Star Line, a Birka Line subsidiary, and transferred to the Baltic to sail between Stockholm and Helsinki. Later, she returned to the Caribbean and is still sailing today. Now named the *Discovery Sun*, she operates between Florida and Grand Bahama Island – a route similar to her original service.

The **Prince of Fundy** is launched sideways at the Schiffbau Gesellschaft Unterweser yard on 9th February 1970. *(Anders Bergenek collection)*

The **Prince of Fundy** makes her maiden arrival at Yarmouth in Nova Scotia. *(Anders Bergenek collection)*

SECOND-GENERATION SCANDINAVIAN FERRIES

By the late 1960s, traffic volumes on short crossings in Scandanavia had grown to such an extent that the earlier generation of ferries (designed mainly by Knud E. Hansen A/S) were struggling to keep pace with demand. Running costs were also increasing significantly. So operators such as Juelsminde-Kalundborg Linien, Grenaa-Hundested Færgefart and Mols Linien all sought to replace four small ferries with two that were substantially bigger – and they turned again to KEH to design them.

In general, these newer ships were broader and longer than their predecessors, with more lanes for cars and lorries across the beam of their hulls. Vertical services were routed through a slim off-centre casing, with four car lanes to port and three to starboard. Above, sandwiched between the hull and Saloon Deck, was a versatile extra deck of superstructure which could be adapted to meet particular needs – fitted out as public rooms or cabins, or used as an upper car deck.

Typically, ships of the new KEH generation had twin engines (usually with twelve cylinders each) rather than four smaller units, coupled in pairs, as used in earlier designs. The 1960s had seen the design and manufacture of compact, reliable and relatively powerful diesels for ferries advance considerably, particularly in West Germany, where MAN and Pielstick became market leaders. In terms of exterior styling, these vessels took their cue from the *Freeport*, all featuring a single funnel aft of amidships.

The first of this new generation was Ragnar Moltzau's 4,614-ton *Gedser* (1968), sailing between Gedser and Travemünde. Built by the Schiffbau Gesellschaft Unterweser AG in Bremerhaven, she could carry 1,200 passengers and 225 cars – a large increase in vehicle capacity over her 2,494-ton predecessor and namesake of 1963. On both decks of the superstructure were public rooms, notably the commodious duty-free shop. This was amidships, next to the entrance hall, with the bar and lounge fore and aft and the restaurant, galley and cafeteria on the deck above.

In 1969, for Stena Line's Gothenburg-Frederikshavn route, came the broadly similar though somewhat longer 5,537-ton *Stena Danica*, built at close to cost price by the AG Weser Seebeckwerft in Bremerhaven – a reflection of the yard's empty order book at that time. A stirring sight as her sleek, powerful lines and relatively large size motored through Gothenburg Harbour, the *Stena Danica* was arguably one of the best-looking ferries of her type and era, establishing Stena as an increasingly dominant force on the short Sweden-Denmark route.

The ship's interiors, designed by Robert Tillberg, were equally impressive – every bit the equal of the earlier *Stena Germanica* and *Stena Britannica*. KEH specified an entirely fireproof construction in line with the US 'Method 1' protocols employed in designing the Miami-based *Freeport*, *Starward* and *Skyward*. Hence Tillberg was unable to use wood veneer for bulkhead finishes, opting instead for brightly-coloured laminates to give the *Stena Danica* a very fresh appearance. Tillberg also chose modernist furniture (as on Silja Line's much-admired *Fennia*), decorating the Restaurant 'Dansk Liljan' mainly in red and white tones with stylish glassfibre Eero Saarinen 'Tulip' chairs. The ship's large windows gave splendid views ahead and to the sides, filling the interior with light. Towards the stern were tiers of spacious teak-planked sun decks. The impressive 22.5-knot service speed was delivered by two 16-cylinder MAN diesel engines.

Within a few months of the *Stena Danica* entering service, Sessanlinjen responded with its first 'second-generation' ferry – the 5,679-ton *Prinsessan Christina*. Sessan's Managing Director, Ulf Trapp, contributed signifcantly to the design and the ship was built by the Aalborg Værft. As with their existing trio of ferries, the hull's bottom provided a lower vehicle deck. The loading procedure was slow – the deck was accessed by a single lift which took only a handful of cars at a time – but compensated for by a high capacity of 360 cars.

Powering the *Prinsessan Christina* were eight compact Nohab-Polar medium-speed V-diesels, four coupled to each propeller shaft via reduction gearing (much as on Silja Line's

The **Kalle III** of Jydske Færgefart had an extra upper car deck in her lower superstructure. *(Burkhard Schütt collection)*

The Yugoslavian-built Gothenburg-Kiel ferry **Stena Olympica** at her berth in Gothenburg. *(Bruce Peter collection)*

Top: Rederi AB Gotland's attractive near-sisters *Gotland* and *Visby* sail in parallel for an official publicity photograph. *(Bruce Peter collection)*

Above left: The cafeteria on the *Gotland*; typically of 1970s ferries, this features a preponderance of orange. *(Bruce Peter collection)*

Above right: The forward-facing smoking saloon on the *Gotland*. *(Bruce Peter collection)*

Right: Reclining seats in the lounge space above the *Gotland*'s navigation bridge. Here, a restful blue has been chosen, rather than orange. *(Bruce Peter collection)*

Botnia and *Floria*). This offered weight-saving advantages and a commonality of spare parts, enabling the ferry to operate even if one or more engines broke down. Most unusually, the three auxiliary units providing power for onboard services were of the same type as the main engines.

Unlike the *Stena Danica*'s superstructure, the *Prinsessan Christina*'s was built all the way out to the stern, so the best views were aft rather than forward. The decorative schemes also differed. Rather than Stena's Swedish modernism, Sessan preferred a mock-historic look, creating 'aristocratic' or 'folksy' atmospheres, particularly in the ferry's restaurants, split into a number of smallish themed spaces.

The 'Herrgårdsmatsalen' and 'Jydske Kro' restaurants were devised by interior designer Harry Nilsson. The former linked vernacular and rococo elements, aiming to resemble a dining room in a grand Danish country house; the latter evoked the atmosphere of a Danish rural inn. These dining saloons were located amidships to port, with a large cafeteria and a cocktail bar facing the stern. Sessanlinjen's policy of maintaining high standard of cuisine and service meant that dining facilities dominated the *Prinsessan Christina*'s Saloon Deck. Inboard, more than half of the seats (and there were enough to cope with the 1300-passenger capacity) were in the restaurants and cafeteria. Externally, the ferry was rather idiosynchratic – long, low superstructure, boxy stern and funnel design– yet this approach was remarkably prophetic, becoming increasingly commonplace in ferries of the 1970s. In 1971, Aalborg delivered a near-sister ship to Sessanlinjen – the *Prinsessan Désirée*.

The latter 1960s and early 1970s were arguably a golden era for Swedish ferry companies as they cashed in on tax incentives to invest in new tonnage. In 1970, for example, Lion Ferry introduced the 7,993-ton *Prins Oberon* on its Harwich-Bremerhaven route. It was built by the Werft Nobiskrug at Rendsburg and designed by KEH. Hansen also designed Lion Ferry's other new build, the 5,464-ton *Prince of Fundy*, which was ordered from the Schiffbau Gesellschaft Unterweser AG in Bremerhaven as Werft Nobiskrug had no spare capacity.

The intention was that the *Prince of Fundy* would inaugurate a new service far removed from the company's existing Kattegat and Southern Baltic territory – in North America, in fact. The route was between Canada and the USA: more specifically, Yarmouth in Novia Scotia and Portland, Maine. The *Prince of Fundy*'s passenger accommodation was designed in accordance with US 'Method 1' specifications. Two Pielstick 12-cylinder diesels gave a 20-knot service speed, each one-way crossing taking ten hours. This meant that passengers could make a return trip as a 22-hour cruise, in the process enjoying a variety of entertainment: live music for dancing, a casino, tax-free and other shopping, and the Swedish 'smorgasbord' in the restaurant, the generosity of which delighted her mainly American passengers.

During summer, the route was such a success that Lion Ferry quickly sought another vessel to provide morning and evening departures in both directions, but in winter the *Prince of Fundy* had to battle through extreme weather. The Atlantic storms took their toll and the ship's structure began to crack around the window openings. The Swedish officers were not amused to learn that the crew of Canadian National Railways' rival ferry, the *Bluenose* – a ship of far more substantial construction – referred to the *Prince of Fundy* as 'The Matchstick Ship'. Furthermore, the *Prince of Fundy* was fitted with a KEH-designed stabilising tank but no fin stabilisers. In

extreme weather conditions, the tank was not only ineffective – it actually exacerbated the ship's motion, so they stopped using it. Without stabilisation, the *Prince of Fundy* pitched, rolled and corkscrewed her way through the big Atlantic swells.

In 1973, Schiffbau Gesellschaft Unterweser AG delivered the *Saint Patrick*, a near-sister to the *Prince of Fundy*, to the Irish Continental Line – a company set up jointly by Lion Ferry and Irish business interests to operate a service from the Irish Republic to Le Havre in France. To stop them from cracking, this ship had smaller saloon deck windows than her older sister, and was fitted with fin stabilisers.

The yard also built three ferries of comparable design, but with an upper car garage space at Main Deck level where the *Prince of Fundy* and the *Saint Patrick* had most of their cabins. These ships were the 3,999-ton *Travemünde* for Ragnar Moltzau's Gedser-Travemünde service, the 4,371-ton *Djursland II* and the *Kalle III* for Jydsk Færgefart, whose business combined the Juelsminde-Kalundborg and Grenaa-Hundested routes.

With potentially three car decks (when the platform decks were lowered), each could carry over 300 cars and up to 1,500 passengers. Reacting to these developments, DFDS took delivery in 1975 of two similar 'second-generation' vessels from Helsingør Skibsværft for its Mols Linien subsidiary. The 4,898-ton *Mette Mols* and *Maren Mols* each had capacity for 1,500 passengers and up to 420 cars.

FERRIES FROM YUGOSLAVIA

As shipbuilding costs in Northern Europe escalated, enterprising Scandinavian ferry operators discovered that building elsewhere could cut construction costs by almost half – savings first demonstrated by Finnish ferry entrepreneur Gunnar Eklund, whose company, Rederi AB Ålandsfärjan, was headquartered at Mariehamn in the Åland Islands.

In 1959, Eklund and his two business partners, Henning Rundberg and Algot Johansson, pioneered the operation of car ferries across the Baltic Sea. They formed the Rederi AB Vikinglinjen, initially using the former Southern Railway Channel steamer *Dinard*. But a disagreement over business strategy resulted in Eklund leaving to establish his own ferry company. In his search for new tonnage, to compete with the rival Silja Line, he found that Yugoslavia was a source of ferries constructed cheaply but of acceptable quality.

His first order was for the 3,159-ton *Kapella*, built at the Brodogradiliste Titovo shipyard at Kraljevica and delivered in 1967. The 3,930-ton *Marella* arrived from the same yard in 1970. Both operated for Viking Line, a brand introduced in 1966 and owned jointly by Eklund's firm and two others – Rederi AB Sally of Mariehamn and Rederi AB Slite of Stockholm. All three were involved in services from Sweden to Finland, via the Åland Islands, and (as was the case for Silja Line) they were very dependent on income generated by selling tax-free goods.

In contrast, services between Sweden and Gotland, provided mainly by the company Rederi AB Gotland, were domestic transport routes with no tax-free sales. Rederi AB Gotland was founded in 1865 and its vessels had operated from the island ever since. In 1955 the company had acquired its first car ferry – the *Kronprinsessan Ingrid*, which they renamed the *Christofer Polhem* – and in 1962 also purchased Sessan's *Prinsessan Margaretha*, which became the *Thjelvar*.

In 1970 Rederi AB Gotland appointed a new managing director, Eric D. Nilsson, who had helped in the acquisition of

THE FERRY a drive through history

the two ships. By this time the company had commissioned Knud E. Hansen A/S to design substantially larger (6,665-ton) 'second-generation' ferries, capable of making day and night crossings. Ordering two such vessels, each more than three times bigger than her predecessor, was a substantial financial undertaking for Rederi AB Gotland, and building them in Yugoslavia appeared to be the best option. Nilsson duly entered negotiations with the Brodogradiliste Jozo Lozovina Mosor in Trogir – a yard with no previous experience of constructing a modern passenger vessel of any kind, let alone state-of-the-art ferries of the type required – and set about the task of raising the capital to pay for them.

Meanwhile, between commencement of these new builds and their delivery, Stena Line's equally money-conscious owner, Sten A. Olsson, learned from Nilsson that Yugoslavian-built ferries were surprisingly cheap. Olsson calculated that for the cost of two from a Swedish or West German yard, he could buy four from Yugoslavia. Hence the Trogir yard received an order for two new daytime ferries – the 6,333-ton *Stena Danica (III)* and *Stena Jutlandica*, to serve the Gothenburg-Frederikshavn route – and another Yugoslavian yard, Kraljevica, picked up Olsson's order for two new 7,125-ton overnight vessels. The latter, for the Gothenburg-Kiel route, were the *Stena Scandinavica* and the *Stena Olympica* (named to commemorate the 1972 Munich Olympic Games). Stena also bought shares in Rederi AB Gotland to help finance the new builds.

Although at first glance all four Stena ferries looked practically identical, the daytime vessels had wider hulls to carry eight rows of cars or six lanes of trucks and an additional upper garage, filling the Main Deck – space occupied by cabins in the the overnight Gothenburg-Kiel ships. The narrower hulls restricted the number of vehicle lanes to seven, with the casing located off centre – as was the case for the forthcoming new Rederi AB Gotland ferries, the *Visby* and the *Gotland*.

As for power, the new Stena ferries had twin 18-cylinder Swedish made Lindholmen-Pielstick diesels and the Rederi AB Gotland vessels opted for multiple compact medium-speed engines, in keeping with the principles established on Silja Line's *Botnia* and *Floria* and perpetuated by Sessanlinjen's *Prinsessan Christina* and *Prinsessan Désireé*. There was a practical reason for this choice: during the lucrative summer season, the schedule dictated that each ship made four single crossings in each 24-hour period. Hence the decision to fit six medium-speed Nohab-Polar V-diesels, connected in groups of three via gearboxes to each of the propeller shafts, as the optimal solution. For fast fast summer crossings, all six engines would achieve a speed of well over 20 knots; in winter, four or less would suffice.

Stena's new Gothenburg-Kiel overnight ferries (the *Stena Scandinavica* and the *Stena Olympica*) could each carry 1,500 passengers (825 berthed) and 250 cars, compared with 1,800 passengers and up to 425 cars for the *Stena Danica (III)* and the *Stena Jutlandica*, serving the Gothenburg-Frederikshavn route. On the overnight vessels, a significant number of cabins were below the vehicle decks. This arrangement differed from that of the new Rederi AB Gotland ferries, which had all 379 berths on the Main and Boat Decks, the remainder of the passengers being accommodated in reclining seats which filled the 'skybars' above the navigation bridges.

When the naval architects of Knud E. Hansen A/S had first visited Trogir on behalf of Rederi AB Gotland, two things surprised them: almost nobody could speak fluent English, and

the technical language of car ferry design was new to everyone there. Steel construction progressed well, but it became clear that outfitting the ships to the required standard would be too much of a challenge. Tage Wandborg, who was in charge of the project, therefore approached Horst Warnekea, owner of the high-quality precision sheet metal company HW Metalbau in West Germany. Together they developed a modular system for the entire interiors, manufactured to within just a millimetre tolerance for assembly and, carefully wrapped in silk paper for protection, exported to Trogir in containers for installation on the ships. This innovation was so successful that fitting out passenger ships with prefabricated modules became standard practice throughout the shipbuilding industry.

At the Kraljevica yard, the *Stena Olympica* and the *Stena Scandinavica* had interiors (designed by Rolf Carlsson) crafted in situ by the yard's joiners – a skill employed and mastered in the earlier building of the *Kapella* and the *Marella* for Gunnar Eklund's Rederi AB Ålandsfärjan. In general, the Gotland ships were more spacious and with superior appointments, although Stena's vessels were also of a high standard.

All six ferries were notably handsome, boasting smartly-flared bow profiles and big red funnels with 'flying saucer' smoke deflectors at their summits. Each ship had extensive teak-planked sun-decks, creating a cruise-style ambience on summer daytime crossings. However, while the *Visby* was under construction Rederi AB Gotland requested that the design of the *Gotland* should be modified in order to make her suitable for cruising as well as for ferrying. Perhaps this was done to generate extra revenue during the winter season. Thus, while the *Visby* had an aft docking bridge, the *Gotland* was given more extensive sun-decks and even an outdoor swimming pool, just like that on the *Freeport*. The six new vessels were delivered over four years from June 1972 onwards.

THE 'PAPENBURGERS'

After the Baltic success of Gunnar Eklund's Yugoslavian-built *Kapella*, Carl Bertil Myrsten – one of Eklund's partners in the Viking Line consortium – wasted no time in deciding to follow suit with a new ferry of his own and of like capacity.

He intended to give the construction job to the Werft Nobiskrug at Rendsburg, then regarded as one of the most efficient ferry builders in northern Europe, but a full order book sent him to another West German yard – the Jos. L. Meyer Werft at Papenburg.

Located far inland, up the River Ems, the Meyer yard was founded in 1795 and for the best part of two centuries had built small cargo vessels such as sailing barges and steam and motor coasters. The yard's first significant passenger ship was the 1963 Danish Bornholm ferry *Bornholmerpilen* for the Dampskibs-Selskab paa Bornholm af 1866, who two years later took delivery from Meyer of a larger ferry, the *Hammershus*.

Up until 1990, the river's constricted width meant that all ships built at Papenburg were launched sideways into the Ems – a spectacular and somewhat hair-raising operation. In 1969 the yard produced the 3,777-ton *Vikingfjord*, an overnight ferry for a Hamburg-based shipping consortium named the Partenreederei Nordlandfähre K.R. Schmidt-Viking. The service was between Cuxhaven, Stavanger and Bergen, taking West German holidaymakers to Norway's scenic west coast.

Myrsten's new Papenburg ferry was the 4,238-ton *Apollo*. Similar in layout to the *Vikingfjord*, it also bore resemblances to ferries of the late 1960s designed by Knud E. Hansen A/S.

Passenger saloons were full width, there was a restaurant forward on Saloon Deck and a cafeteria amidships, and reclining seat lounges aft. Above, on Boat Deck, were the lounge and night club. Two 12-cylinder Deutz diesels gave the *Apollo* a service speed of approximately 19 knots.

Due to developments in steel technology and the design of bulbous bows, the *Apollo* had the distinction of being the first ice-breaking ferry with a bulb. Her vehicle deck had seven car lanes, split by an off-centre casing, and the total capacity of 260 included the retractable platform decks. Unlike ferries designed by KEH, which had fully-enclosed vehicle decks, the *Apollo*'s shell plating had freeing ports. In open seas with the wind side-on these tended to let in water and trap it along the casing, necessitating a change in course in efforts to drain the ship.

When Carl Bertil Myrsten had showed the plans for his new ferry to Algot Johansson, Chairman of Rederi AB Sally, Johansson decided that he too would order a sister for the Viking Line, as the operation's profits were split between the three companies, based on size and capacity of their vessels. Myrsten himself ordered a second ship, and Johansson bought a further three – a grand total of six ferries to shuttle back and forth between Sweden and Finland.

Johansson's new ferries were financed from profits Rederi AB Sally had earned from operating large oil tankers between the Persian Gulf, Europe and the USA. Indeed, with 35 ships, the company was Finland's largest in terms of the total deadweight capacity of the tanker fleet. The final ferry in the series for Rederi AB Sally was the *Viking 5* – an elongated version of the previous ships, measuring 117.8 metres and powered by two 14-cylinder Smit-Bolnes diesels.

Interior design of the 'Papenburgers' was by Robert Tillberg. The first ferries in the series were rather similar in style to recent ferries from Werft Nobiskrug, with Tillberg merely adding bright Swedish furniture and fabrics to spaces otherwise panelled in dark wood-effect laminate. The later ferries benefited from additional input courtesy of the wives of Rederi AB Sally directors. Great enthusiasts for modern Finnish design, they introduced the latest chairs and textiles. *Viking 5*, for example, featured partitions decorated with panels of Maija Isola's 'Unikko' poppy-patterned wallpaper, creating a fashionable 'flower-power' image.

The initial trio of Meyer Werft-built 'Papenburgers' were so successful on Viking Line's Kapellskär-Mariehamn-Naantali route that in 1974 Rederi AB Sally decided to compete with Silja Line, utilising the *Viking 5* to establish a Stockholm-Helsinki service. While the final 'Papenburgers' were being completed for Rederi AB Slite and Rederi AB Sally, a further three broadly similar examples were under construction for the Caminos y Puentes Federales de Ingresos y Servicios Conexos, of Cabo San Lucas in Mexico. Known as 'Transbordadores', this firm operated ferries between La Paz, Mazatlan, Cabo San Lucas and Puerto Vallarta in the Gulf of California. The *Azteca*, the *Coromuel* and the *Puerto Vallarta* were all delivered between 1973 and 1975.

The third shipowner involved in the Viking Line consortium, Gunnar Eklund, was sceptical of the value of the 'Papenburger' design because he reasoned that having four ferries shuttling between Kapellskär, Mariehamn and Naantali was inefficient: fewer and larger ships could do the same job more effectively. Eklund was intrigued by the latest Stena Line ferries designed by KEH and built in Yugoslavia. Both the *Stena Jutlandica* and the *Stena Danica* had an extra upper car deck, virtually doubling the car capacity of a standard 'Papenburger.' So Eklund recruited KEH to assist in developing a design for a similarly capacious ferry – his new contribution to the Viking Line operation.

Eklund observed, however, that the hulls of the Stena vessels were optimised for speed rather than deadweight capacity, and so his Technical Inspector, Kaj Jansson, worked to develop a

The *Viking 4*, a Viking Line 'Papenburger' owned by Rederi AB Sally and delivered in 1973. Subsequently, she became British Rail's *Earl Granville*, serving the Channel Islands. *(Viking Line)*

solution with fuller hull lines. This resulted in a ferry with a car capacity similar to the Stena ships but also with cabin berths for 330, some adjacent to the upper car deck and others below the main vehicle deck, ahead of the machinery spaces.

The 7,210-ton *Aurella* was built by the J.J. Sietas shipyard in Hamburg and delivered in 1973. Boasting capacities of 1,500 passengers and 420 cars, she was highly effective – much to the consternation of Eklund's partners in the Viking Line consortium, Algot Johansson and Carl Bertil Myrsten, who nicknamed the ship 'Jätten Glufs Glufs' because, like a hungry giant, she gobbled up traffic, leaving less for their own 'Papenburger' ferries to carry.

On the other hand, the *Aurella's* economy-of-scale design allowed Viking Line to lower fares but more than compensate for it through the extra income generated by bigger and better onboard facilities for eating, drinking and shopping. The forward-facing restaurant and cafeteria, stacked one above the other, were particularly attractive features, perpetuated in subsequent Viking Line tonnage.

As time progressed, Werft Nobiskrug at Rendsburg churned out one new ferry after another for routes from southern Sweden to West Germany and Denmark. Competition was intense, with TT-Linie, Trave Line (a subsidiary of Stockholm's Rederi AB Svea), Finnlines and Statens Järnvägar (Swedish State Railways) all vying for business. Trave Line protested that the railway had an unfair advantage, resulting in 1972 in SJ transferring its Sweden-West Germany operations to a subsidiary company, Öresundsbolaget, which ran ferries on the short routes between Sweden and Denmark.

In the following year, Lion Ferry took delivery of its new 7,457-ton *Gustav Vasa* from Werft Nobiskrug (designed by KEH and a near sister to the 1970 *Prins Oberon*) for charter to Öresundsbolaget. But unlike the *Prins Oberon*, the *Gustav* was a drive-through ferry with an additional upper garage at the after end of her superstructure. She was driven by four Stork-Werkspoor diesels, coupled in pairs and designed to burn

The Swedish Lion Ferry-owned **Prins Oberon** operated between Harwich and Bremerhaven. Here, she is seen off Harwich in the mid-1970s. *(Bruce Peter collection)*

cheaper heavy-grade marine bunker fuel which needed to be pre-heated in order to flow properly – bad news for the crew, as their cabins, between the heater tanks and the vehicle deck, became stuffy. This led to trade union protests and to design modifications of the next new ship to join the fleet – the *Nils Dacke*, delivered in 1975. She had a more substantial superstructure, all crew cabins located in an extra deckhouse aft on Bridge Deck, making for far better living and working conditions but requiring the funnel to be heightened so that the exhaust cleared the additional structure.

In fact, Swedish ferries of the mid-1970s led the world in terms of quality of crew quarters, and berthing the entire crew on Bridge Deck became standard practice on later vessels.

In 1973, Werft Nobiskrug also delivered two slightly smaller ferries. One, the *Prinz Hamlet* (note the German spelling) was to the Prinzen Linie Schiffarts GmbH of Hamburg, who initiated a Hamburg-Harwich route, sharing marketing with Lion Ferry's *Prins Oberon* from Bremerhaven. Design of the *Prinz Hamlet* was by the shipyard's own drawing office, but there was a great

The **Gustav Vasa** makes a stirring sight during her sea trials in the early summer of 1973. *(Werft Nobiskrug Rendsburg)*

The Hamburg-Harwich ferry **Prinz Hamlet,** designed and built by Werft Nobiskrug and delivered in 1973. *(Bruce Peter collection)*

The SF-owned Viking Line ferry **Aurella** had a substantially larger car and freight capacity than her fleet mates. *(Krystof Brzoza)*

deal of similarity with KEH-designed ferries of the era.

The other newbuild was the *Europafärjan III*, commissioned by Lion Ferry for the Varberg-Grenaa route from Sweden to Denmark. Where the *Prinz Hamlet* had cabins on Main Deck, the *Europafärjan III* was a day ferry with an upper garage instead, giving a capacity of up to 404 cars. Both ships could carry around 1,100 passengers. The *Europafärjan III* looked particularly striking, her funnel topped by a distinctive circular 'flying saucer'-shaped smoke-deflecting plate. She was also very well appointed inboard. The downside for Lion Ferry was that, like all of its West German-built ferries, she was heavily mortgaged in Deutschmarks. As the 1970s progressed, the Deutschmark gained in value against the Swedish krona and the debt repayments became less affordable, resulting in 1982 in the Bonnier Group (owner of Lion Ferry) ceasing its ferry operations and selling off the remaining fleet. The brand was subsequently purchased and revived by Stena Line.

FRENCH-BUILT IN NANTES

In 1964 Knud E. Hansen A/S worked with the Dubigeon-Normandie shipyard at Nantes, producing hull line plans and calculations for the SNCF car ferries *Villandry* and *Valençay*. These ships established Dubigeon-Normandie as an important builder of ferries and, during the 1970s, a significant number of vessels were constructed here.

Between 1969 and 1971, a variety of owners ordered a series of three large ferries from this Nantes yard, based on the KEH-designed *Freeport*. They were the *Eagle*, the *Massalia* and the *Bolero*, each intended for deployment on lengthy overnight routes.

The new ships' layout was very similar to that of the *Freeport* except that, rather than a lower trailer deck ahead of the engine room, they had two decks of cabins. Externally, an obvious change was the routeing of the exhaust uptakes through twin funnels located towards the stern rather than via a single funnel on the centreline. Moreover, the external detailing, altogether more chunky, was carried out by the builder and lacked the refinement of KEH's own design work.

The first of the trio to be completed was the 11,609-ton *Eagle*, delivered in May 1971 to a newly-formed P&O subsidiary, Southern Ferries. The route was new – from Britain to Portugal and Morocco – sailing between Southampton, Lisbon and Tangier. The Algarve was becoming a popular holiday resort and Morocco emerging as a highly fashionable destination for more adventurous travellers.

The second ferry, the *Massalia*, was built for Paquet Lines, a long-established French Mediterranean shipping line. She entered service later in 1971, on a route from Marseille via Malaga in Spain to Casablanca in Morocco, and differed from the other two ferries, as well as from the *Freeport*, in that her dimensions were more generous and her saloon deck was given over entirely to public rooms rather than cabin blocks being in the forward section.

The *Bolero* followed in 1973, ordered by a consortium of Norwegian shipping interests – Fred Olsen, Fearnley & Eger, Ludwig Mowinckels and R.P. Aukner – whose intention was to introduce a ferry route from the Swedish port town of Södertälje, just south of Stockholm, to Travemünde in West Germany. But when the owners realised that Swedes preferred to drive south to take the short southern Baltic crossings, the idea was dropped and Olsen's partners withdrew from the project, leaving him sole owner of the incomplete vessel. A solution was found: chartering the *Bolero* during summer months to Lion Ferry's Prince of Fundy Line – enabling a two-ship service between Portland, Maine and Bar Harbour – and in winter to Commodore Cruise Lines to operate cruises from Miami in tandem with the *Bohème*. In fact, it was this latter charter which inspired the name *Bolero*. Not only was it in keeping with Commodore's existing style (inherited from the *Bohème*'s owner, Otto Wallenius) but in beginning with B was also in line with Olsen tradition.

At 10,513 tons, the *Bolero* could carry 874 passengers, all berthed, and 250 cars or refrigerated fruit cargo, loaded on pallets. Her mix of cruise-style facilities and the inclusion of an observation lounge above the bridge, with aircraft-style reclining seats, made her effective in both ferry and Caribbean cruise modes.

To begin with the *Eagle* operated successfully from Southampton but, as Britain slipped into recession and bookings declined, she was temporarily laid up during the 1974-75 winter season. Crossing the Bay of Biscay in winter months, particularly in violent stormy weather, could be a somewhat frightening experience and increasing numbers of holidaymakers preferred to fly, which of course saved time. In March, the *Eagle* was back in service, now offering slightly longer itineraries and a call at Algeciras to attract passengers wishing to access Spain's up-and-coming Costa del Sol resorts. But in December 1975 she was sold to Paquet Lines, joining her near-sister the *Massalia* and doubling the size of the French company's ferry fleet. In the mid-1970s, the *Bolero* returned to year-round

European ferry service on routes across the North Sea, the Skagerrak and the Kattegat.

Subsequently, all three near-sisters had very diverse careers, mixing both ferry and cruise operations at various times. In 1990, sailing as the *Scandinavian Star*, the former *Massalia* was destroyed by fire in tragic circumstances when operating between Norway and Denmark. The *Eagle* and the *Bolero*, now named the *Royal Iris* and the *Magic 1* respectively, remain in use as Israeli-owned Mediterranean cruise ships – longevity which, combined with the continuing service of the one-time *Freeport*, is surely a tribute to these ships' excellent design.

Silja Line also seriously considered ordering two further car ferries of the *Eagle/Massalia/Bolero* type to inaugurate a proposed new service between Stockholm and Helsinki. But finance and internal politics dictated that instead, Dubigeon-Normandie were invited to construct somewhat smaller vessels, merging elements of these with aspects of the *Fennia*'s design (for example, stepping the superstructure decks inwards) and of the design of the Wärtsilä-built *Finlandia* (notably, hinged bow doors in preference to a lifting visor). The result: the new 8,020-ton *Aallotar* and *Svea Regina*, which in line with existing Silja Line ferries had ice-breaker rather than bulbous bows.

The interior design was again entrusted largely to Bengt Lundsten, assisted by Annukka Mikkilä. Each vessel could carry 1,000 passengers (439 berthed in cabins) and 170 cars. Forward on the saloon deck was a large lounge and nightclub, a cafeteria was amidships and, towards the stern, were the buffet and à la carte restaurants. All were decorated in vivid colours complemented by fashionable Finnish glassfibre chairs.

Below the car deck were economy cabins, a swimming pool, sauna baths and a disco.

Between ordering and taking delivery of these vessels, the three Silja Line parent companies (FÅA, Bore and Svea) decided to reorganise their steamer and ferry services, creating a structure more akin to that of their increasingly powerful Viking Line rivals. Thus instead of remaining a shipping company in its own right, Silja Line became a marketing brand name and a new logo, depicting a stylised seal's head, was introduced on all publicity material and the ships' hulls.

The *Aallotar* and *Svea Regina* were delivered in February and May 1972 respectively – perfect timing to stimulate spring trade before kicking off the summer service of daily departures in both directions. The initiative was so successful that after only one season Silja's parent companies returned to Dubigeon-Normandie to commission a trio of replacement ferries, each twice the size of the *Aallotar* and *Svea Regina*, for delivery in 1975 – a clear admission that they had been badly mistaken in not building far larger vessels when they had the opportunity.

Ironically, only a year after Silja's overnight ferry service was inaugurated, a rival upstart – the Birka Line of Mariehamn – had started its own Stockholm-Helsinki operation, chartering the *Freeport* which, on arrival in Sweden, became by far the biggest ferry in Baltic service, boasting berths for 812 passengers. Silja's solution to this unwelcome competition? To buy the ship (through Stockholm's Rederi AB Svea, one of Silja's owners) from her American owner for use by Trave Line in the southern Baltic between Helsingborg and Travemünde.

Silja Line's new larger ferries from Dubigeon-Normandie, all

Fred. Olsen's **Bolero**, early in her career when operating for the Prince of Fundy Line between the USA and Nova Scotia. *(Shippax Archive)*

Top: Stockholm in the early 1970s with Silja Line's Finnish-flagged ***Aallotar*** and ***Floria*** at their berths. *(Shippax Archive)*

Above left: P&O Southern Ferries' ***Eagle*** rests at Southampton. *(Bruce Peter collection)*

Above right: The ***Aallotar***'s Swedish-owned sister, the ***Svea Regina***. *(Krystof Brzoza)*

Right: SNCM's large Mediterranean ferry ***Esterel*** approaches Marseille at the commencement of her career. *(Bruce Peter collection)*

delivered in 1975, were the *Svea Corona* (owned by Stockholm's Rederi AB Svea), which entered service in May; the *Wellamo* (owned by FÅA) in September; and the *Bore Star* (owned by Bore) in December. The latter, however, was immediately chartered to Finnlines for use on Mediterranean fly-cruise services from Agadir in Morocco. Following this she operated from the Swedish capital to Turku, whereas her two sisters served Helsinki.

The internal layout of these new ferries marked a significant change in planning. As before, the hull had side-casings containing a large proportion of outside cabins, but in the superstructure there were big differences. Instead of a horizontal cabin and public room layout with whole decks given over to each, as in the existing ferries, the new ships featured blocks of additional cabins filling the forward third, with the public rooms spread out across the aft sections of these decks (as on the *Empress of Australia*).

As with Lion Ferry's *Nils Dacke*, the officers and crew occupied the two topmost decks of the superstructures (which were unusually tall for ferries of the era, though this was to be the shape of things to come). Apart from providing an attractive living environment for off-duty staff, there was also a legal obligation and safety requirement to ensure that all crew on ferries likely to navigate through ice should be accommodated above the waterline to prevent their rest periods being disturbed by the hull breaking through ice floes.

Throughout, the interior design was by Vuokko Laakso, an up-and-coming Finnish architect who favoured strong colours and moulded glassfibre and plastic finishes – a style which gave the new ferries an ambience very much in line with the fashion and taste of their period.

Each could carry 1,200 passengers (674 berthed) and 240 cars – a third more than the vessels they replaced. Four 12-cylinder Pielstick diesels paired up on twin shafts delivered a 21-knot service speed, with plenty of power in reserve for ice-breaking duties. Unlike Viking Line's most recent ferries,

however, the new Silja trio were not fitted with bulbous bows, retaining instead the ice-breaker configurations of existing ships in the fleet. One notably retrograde step was the specification of a lifting bow visor rather than hinged doors. This proved to be a mistake when, during the *Wellamo*'s maiden season, she was heading out from Helsinki in stormy weather and the captain spotted that the visor was lifting slightly each time the ship hit a wave. She was immediately turned back to the safety of Helsinki Harbour and the visor was welded shut, not used again until the locking pins were strengthened.

Building five vessels for Silja Line in only four years made the Dubigeon-Normandie shipyard a leading player in ferry construction and so, when the French Government-owned Mediterranean services to Corsica and north African ports were reorganised in 1976 to form the Société Nationale Maritime Corse-Méditerranée (SNCM), the yard was an obvious contender to build its new fleet. Unlike Silja Line's commercial and rather luxuriously appointed ferries, SNCM's vessels served purely for transport purposes and, being partially-owned by the French Railways, offered two classes of no-frills high-density accommodation.

The *Napoléon* (14,918 tons, 1,844 passengers and 500 cars) was introduced in 1976, mainly to serve Algeria. Three years later came the slightly smaller 12,625-ton *Cyrnos*, primarily for Corsican routes. Both were horizontally arranged with centreline casings and entire decks given over to each class of cabin, but with shared restaurants and cafeterias. Cabin berths and couchettes of the kind found in French sleeper trains were provided for the majority of their passengers – but others could sleep in the ships' very commodious cinemas, where large numbers of high-backed reclining seats were provided. (This practice, using space very efficiently, was subsequently repeated on numerous large Mediterranean ferries.) Mechanically, the two ships were similar to Silja's 1975 deliveries, each having four 12-cylinder Pielstick diesels. Next, in 1981 and 1983 respectively, came the *Esterel* and the *Corse*, both of which put more

The SNCM ferry **Napoléon** was one of a series built at Nantes for the French state-owned operator's routes to Corsica and North Africa. *(Ambrose Greenway)*

emphasis on car and freight capacity than on cabin berths for passengers (up to 2300), most of whom were accommodated in reclining seats or in Deck Class. Car capacity of each ferry was 700, spread over three decks.

THE SPANISH 'CANGUROS'

During the first half of the 1970s, Spanish shipowners took delivery of a number of significant ferries of advanced design. The first of this new armada actually owed their existence to events unfolding in the Italian ferry market. In 1967, faced with slimming profit margins due to government-subsidised competition from Tirrenia on their existing routes from Genoa to Sardinia and Sicily, Traghetti Sardi – one of the joint owners of the Canguro fleet – had decided to open a link between Genoa and Barcelona in Spain, cutting out a potentially long and tiresome drive around the Mediterranean's rugged northern coast. For this purpose, a new company called Canguro Iberia was formed to co-operate with the Sevilla-based shipowner Ybarra y Compagnia. The initial ferry was the *Canguro Verde*, which was closely studied by Ybarra's technical staff and by the Union Naval de Levante shipyard's naval architects.

Some years later, Ybarra ordered the first of a new series of six ferries from Union Naval de Levante, developed from the Italian 'Canguro' design. The Spanish vessels were significantly bigger in all respects, yet retained the Italian idea of using twin V-diesels to maintain a low freeboard while ensuring a high power output (the engines this time being of MAN design, manufactured in Spain by Bazan of Madrid).

The new ferries also had a similarly-shaped aftbody, although the bow configuration was completely different – much more rakish lines and no bow door. Above the main vehicle deck was an additional upper car deck, much as on recent Scandinavian day ferries, giving a total capacity of 240 cars.

The Spanish 'Canguros' were, however, overnight ships with berths for 797 – or around two-thirds of their 1,007-passenger capacities. Aesthetically, they were particularly stylish with sleek lines and distinctive twin funnels, tilted back with gently curving 'ski-slope' frontal aspects and topped by broad smoke-deflecting fins. Their masts, which leaned slightly forward, were similar to that on the recent Cunard transatlantic liner *Queen Elizabeth 2*.

The first ship in the series, the *Canguro Cabo San Sebastian*, was delivered as planned in 1972. But Ybarra's subsequent financial difficulties meant that only one other ferry, the *Canguro Cabo San Jorge* of 1976, was built before they went bankrupt.

Trasmediterranea's *J.J. Sister* shows the obvious influence of Scandinavian design practice of the same era. *(Bruce Peter collection)*

The Spanish 'Canguro'-type ferry *Ciudad de La Palma* (ex *Canguro Cabo San Jorge*) in Trasmediterranea's livery in the early 1980s. *(Bruce Peter collection)*

Anticipating this, the government-controlled Compagnia Trasmediterránea stepped in, partly to ensure continuity of work at the shipyard and also because high-capacity ferries of this type could usefully replace their remaining passenger liners on services to the Balearics. The 'Canguro' class ferries that followed were given traditional Trasmediterránea names – the *Ciudad de Badajoz* (1979), the *Ciudad de Sevilla* (1980), the *Ciudad de Salamanca* (1982) and the *Ciudad de Valencia* (1984). All six 'Canguros' proved to be highly effective, most remaining front-line members of the Trasmediterránea fleet for well over twenty years. In between building 'Canguros', Union Naval de Levante completed four other notable ferries for Spanish services.

Firstly, the *Monte Granada* and the *Monte Toledo* were delivered respectively in 1974 and 1975 to Aznar Line to replace passenger-cargo liners on winter routes from Tilbury and Liverpool to the Canary Islands and on summer routes from Southampton and Amsterdam to Santander. Aznar's existing cargo vessels had a niche following amongst British passengers and it was hoped that the new cruise ferries would build upon this. In their winter role, the vessels competed with Fred Olsen Lines' *Black Watch*, *Black Prince* and *Blenheim*, carrying cruise passengers both ways and, northbound, transporting Spanish fruit exports on their vehicle decks and in refrigerated holds beneath. In summer months, Aznar's ferries went head-to-head with Swedish Lloyd's *Patricia* and *Hispania* and also P&O Southern Ferries' *Eagle*. Thus in the early 1970s the ferry routes from the UK to Spain were somewhat crowded with tonnage.

At the time of their introduction, the 10,851-tons *Monte Granada* and *Monte Toledo* were amongst the largest and best-appointed vessels of their kind, able to carry 774 berthed passengers plus more in reclining seats, as well as 272 cars. A notable feature of the spacious and elegantly-designed accommodation was the lido area, located ahead of the funnel and encased within glazed shelter screens, in the manner of Royal Caribbean's recent cruise ships the *Song of Norway*, the *Nordic Prince* and the *Sun Viking*. Below decks, two MAN-Bazan 12-cylinder V-diesels produced a 21-knot service speed.

Unfortunately for the Aznar Line, its brave initiative to build the vessels was sabotaged by unforeseen circumstances. On one hand, the 1973 oil crisis radically changed the economic model for passenger shipping and plunged western Europe in general – and Britain in particular – into recession. On the other hand, the Aznar Company was closely linked to the government of General Franco, whose death in November 1975 was

A stern-quarter view of the Aznar Line cruise ferry **Monte Toledo**. *(Bruce Peter collection)*

followed by Spain's gradual transition to democracy. In this process, companies associated with his dictatorship came to be increasingly marginalised – including Aznar. In 1977 the *Monte Granada* and the *Monte Toledo*, less than three years old, were sold by Aznar, ironically to another dictatorship – Colonel Gadaffi's Libya. The purchaser was the General National Maritime Transport Co of Tripoli, the vessels – renamed the *Garnata* and the *Toletela* – used on Mediterranean ferry routes from Libya to ports in southern Europe.

The *Monte Granada* and the *Monte Toledo* were followed from Union Naval de Levante by a further pair of ferries of essentially similar design (albeit without vehicle deck refrigeration) for the Compagnia Trasmediterránea's service from Barcelona to the Canary Islands. The 9,120-ton *J.J. Sister* and *Manuel Soto* were 10 metres shorter and slightly broader, but their car and passenger capacities were similar to Aznar's vessels. A notable difference was the swimming pool, located aft, rather than a lido area midships. Stylistically, they seemed indebted to the recent output of KEH, having conical-shaped funnels with large fins at their summits but also displaying elements inherited from previous ferries built by Union Naval de Levante. As with Aznar Line's vessels, they were very well appointed but retained class-divided passenger accommodation, in common with the remainder of the Trasmediterránea fleet. High speed was another characteristic: four 12-cylinder MAN-Bazan V-diesels delivered up to 25 knots.

Union Naval de Levante's long-serving Technical Director, Nicolás Franco Bahamonde, died in 1977, bringing to an end a remarkable thirty-year period in Spanish ferry design. During his tenure, the yard emulated the most fashionable ideas in passenger ship naval architecture from elsewhere in Europe and contributed many fine ships to the Spanish ferry fleet.

FLOATING TIVOLIS

Inspired by the successful cruise ferry operations from Miami

of both Norwegian Caribbean Line and Freeport Cruise Line, the Danish shipping giant DFDS decided to get in on the action with their own version of the formula.

Passenger Director Rudolf Bier had joined the DFDS Board in 1969. A travel agent and pioneer in Denmark of Mediterranean package holidays and fly-cruises in the Caribbean, he initially proposed that the company should operate cruise ferries on routes between Miami, New Orleans and Vera Cruz in Mexico. The DFDS Board then switched its attention to the Mediterranean, with a longer-term ambition to enter the North American market too.

Bier realised that for increasing numbers of car-owning north European holidaymakers, with money to spend, Mediterranean resorts were becoming destinations of choice. He saw that with a little imagination, DFDS could cash in on this growing market by redeploying its two modern Copenhagen-Aalborg ferries – the *Aalborghus* and the *Trekroner* – on routes linking the most popular Mediterranean holiday destinations. His greater vision was that DFDS should develop as a large cruise and car ferry operator, with eight identical ships ('floating Tivolis') offering all kinds of dining options, bars, nightclubs and entertainment.

As prototypes, the *Aalborghus* and the *Trekroner* were transformed in Marseille from black-hulled ferries into the white, cruise-styled *Dana Corona* and *Dana Sirena*. Each sported a new marketing name – DFDS Seaways – painted on the hull topsides in elongated blue letters. The two ships then headed for Genoa and took holidaymakers to Tunis, Alicante, Malaga and Palma. It wasn't long before the new DFDS Seaways identity was adopted by the company's north European passenger routes as well, all ships becoming one class only. Furthermore, on North Sea routes, the introduction of couchette overnight accommodation significantly increased the ships' capacities – and their potential profit yield.

DFDS Seaways was one of several 'snappy' brand names introduced by ferry operators on ships' topsides at this time.

Perhaps the most successful was British Rail's 'Sealink' – a 1972 innovation displayed on their newly-delivered Folkestone-Boulogne ferries the *Hengist* and the *Horsa*, and subsequently applied to all vessels in BR, French SNCF, Dutch SMZ and Belgian RMT fleets.

Busy Bier also initiated development work for his envisioned fleet of eight new cruise ferries to be deployed on routes in northern Europe, the Mediterranean and the Caribbean – an ambitious scheme codenamed the 'Dana Futura Project'.

In 1972, a contract was signed with Aalborg Værft to build the first (and, as events unfolded, the last) ferry of the projected series, named the *Dana Regina*. Shipbuilding in Denmark, with its relatively high labour costs, was an expensive option: at over 101 million kroner (£10 million), the new ship cost more than twice as much as the Italian-built *Winston Churchill* had done just five years earlier. Furthermore, as the Aalborg yard was a rather constricted site, the new ferry (153 metres long, with capacity for 975 passengers and 250 cars) could not be constructed as a single entity. Instead, the main body was built and launched in the conventional manner with the bow section manufactured separately. The two were then welded together in a floating dry dock – a convoluted process.

The *Dana Regina* was primarily intended for year-round North Sea service between Esbjerg and Harwich – a replacement for the *England*, which no longer had sufficient capacity. To provide more volume for passenger cabins and public rooms, the new ferry's superstructure needed to be more substantial, yet maintaining slender fore and aft hull lines and keeping the centre of gravity as low as possible to enhance the sea-keeping characteristics. So to save weight, the two topmost decks, the funnel and mast were built of aluminium alloy with a bi-metallic joint at Boat Deck level. The layout of the superstructure was akin to recent KEH-designed ferries.

As DFDS planned to operate subsequent members of their 'Dana Futura Project' on Mediterranean and Caribbean routes, operational flexibility was important. Thus the vehicle deck of the *Dana Regina* had bow, stern and side doors. The bow doors were of a novel 'clam-shell' design which opened out and to the sides of the hull – preventing the possibility of any repetition of the storm damage which had forced open the *Winston Churchill*'s lifting bow visor back in 1968.

To provide a service speed of 21.5 knots, four 8-cylinder medium-speed Burmeister & Wain engines were installed. With possible Caribbean cruise service in mind, a tropical-sized air conditioning system was specified and the vessel was fitted out with fire-retardant materials, compliant with American 'Method 1' standards, as well as a comprehensive sprinkler system – measures which exceeded the requirements of the forthcoming SOLAS (Safety of Life at Sea) 1974 Convention regarding fire safety.

The exterior silhouette represented a significant change of direction from existing DFDS design practice. Architect Kay Korbing was employed at an early stage to not only design the ship's interiors but also to make suggestions about her external appearance, which he developed from the recent Norwegian America liner *Vistafjord*. As a result, the ship evolved with a tall conical-shaped funnel and a special design of lifeboat davits, mounted to allow unobstructed views from the promenade decks.

Korbing's interior design was inspired in part by a visit in 1969 to Cunard's newly-completed *Queen Elizabeth 2*. For example, the steelwork forming the ship's internal staircases

DFDS Seaways' ***Dana Corona***, rebuilt as a cruise ferry from the Danish domestic overnight vessel ***Trekroner***. *(Bruce Peter collection)*

was colour-coded to help passengers find their way around. The Main Deck was given over entirely to cabins, all with private facilities. In total there were berths for 878 and for a further 22 in couchettes on Boat Deck in a space otherwise earmarked for the ship's hospital when operating in cruise mode.

On the Saloon Deck, above, a wide arcade with lounge seating linked the public rooms. The Codan Restaurant, at the forward end, featured a mural of the sun and moon by Erik Clausen which matched the overall blue and gold colour scheme. This was linked with the Bellevue Lounge, above on Boat Deck, by means of a dramatic open-tread spiral staircase which swept downwards on the port side, allowing passengers to make a grand entrance for dinner.

The Bellevue Lounge was decorated in lilac, red and gold and there were two abstract tapestries by Margrethe Agger on the aft bulkhead. To starboard was a circular dance floor laid in Greenland marble, material also used for the tabletops. Moving aft, the circular Mermaid Bar was clad in lilac leather panels. Towards the stern of the Saloon Deck was the Scandia Coffee Shop, featuring a wavy copper ceiling, leather-upholstered aluminium-framed chairs and a large pointillist mural by Rolf Middelboe. Further aft, the Compass Club discotheque featured floor-to-ceiling windows round three sides and low-slung red stools and chairs by Jan Ekselius.

Delivered in June 1974, the *Dana Regina* was not only the most technically sophisticated ferry yet seen but also the most luxuriously appointed. Indeed, such was her overall quality that she could easily withstand comparison with the finest contemporary passenger ships of any kind. Such luxury, however, came at a price: Kay Korbing was a very good architect but, as far as DFDS were concerned, 'astronomically expensive'. Hence, as the 1970s progressed, there was a growing feeling in the company that however beautiful the result, such expense did not make economic sense. Yet for the builder, Aalborg Værft, the *Dana Regina* was a prestige project – the first passenger ship they had constructed to highest international standards.

Elsewhere in DFDS, all was not well. The company's deep-sea cargo liners were losing money and their smaller ferries were only marginally profitable. The *Dana Corona* and *Dana Sirena* Mediterranean services struggled to compete with the increasing numbers of subsidised ferries introduced by government-owned companies of Italy, France and Spain. Hence for DFDS, building more cruise ferries of the *Dana Regina* standards was out of the question. These difficulties led to

The magnificent **Dana Regina** is towed stern-first from the pool of London following a publicity visit in July 1974. *(Robert Spark collection)*

Rudolf Bier leaving the DFDS Board in 1973. But during his short tenure, DFDS Seaways had become a highly respected and quality brand and he had developed a winning formula for shipboard hospitality on overnight routes.

The main problem for DFDS – a problem common to the entire shipping industry and indeed the global econmoy – was the sudden and exponential rise in the cost of oil. Since the Second World War, oil prices had remained more or less stable at around ten dollars a barrel, but in 1973 this price more than quadrupled when the Arab OPEC oil-producing countries, infuriated by American support for Israel in the Yom Kippur War, slashed oil production in protest. The result was crippling for shipping companies. Orders for new tonnage dried up immediately – but at least those ferry companies already operating larger, economy-of-scale vessels were in a better position than most.

While DFDS built only one *Dana Regina*, the Soviet Union's Black Sea Steamship Company commissioned no less than five cruise ferries from the Wärtsilä shipyard in Turku. The Soviets, with the benefit of their own substantial reserves of oil, gas and coal, were able to cope far better with the oil crisis than were Western countries. Furthermore, for the Communist Party it was a matter of pride to appear to be keeping up with cultural and technological developments in the West. Consequently, in Soviet eyes, large and luxuriously-appointed car ferries needed to be seen on the Black Sea – despite the fact that comparatively few people in the Soviet Union were car owners.

The country to benefit from this unique combination of circumstances was Finland. Since the 1950s, Finnish yards had built ships for the Soviets at favourable rates and must have welcomed with open arms the large order for high-value Russian tonnage which came their way. Much as with Rudolf

Bier's DFDS Seaways concept, the Soviet plan was to use the new vessels interchangeably on domestic Black Sea routes, centred on the Black Sea Steamship Company's home port of Odessa, or on charter to earn hard currency in the cruise markets of the West. The wider Soviet passenger fleet – the biggest in the world by far – was ageing and, sooner or later, modernisation would have to begin. So a design that could satisfy multiple roles would be the ideal solution.

Unlike the rather constricted Aalborg Værft, Wärtsilä's facilities at Turku were well arranged and the five Soviet cruise ferries, each around 16,400 tons, could be quickly constructed and outfitted with deliveries at five-monthly intervals. All were given the names of Soviet republics. The *Belorussiya*, the *Gruziya* and the *Azerbaizhan* were completed in 1975, followed in 1976 by the *Kazakhstan* and the *Kareliya*. Each could carry 1,009 passengers (504 berthed) and 256 cars. Twin Wärtsilä-built Pielstick diesels ensured a 21-knot service speed.

The design was most clearly influenced by Wärtsilä's recent building of two series of cruise ships for the Norwegian-owned Royal Caribbean and Royal Viking Line consortia – although the Soviet cruise ferries had straighter lines and bluffer bow profiles. Wärtsilä's cruise liners had been designed jointly with KEH, and it would appear that the layout of the earlier KEH-designed *Freeport* was also an influence, although the exterior aesthetics of the new ferries displayed a distinctly Soviet 'space age' quality, particularly evident in the design of their funnels.

As with the *Freeport*, these new cruise ferries had broad casings containing cabins on each side of their vehicle decks, which featured bow, stern and side doors. The construction was robust, the frames closely spaced for extra stiffening (so that in times of war they could be deployed to carry troops, tanks and other heavy military vehicles). Above was a deck comprising almost entirely of cabins, with the main Saloon Deck above. The latter was a similar arrangement to Royal Caribbean's cruise ships, with lounges forward and aft and a large dining room amidships.

The Soviet cruise ferries were robust, economical and popular, more often finding lucrative niches at the budget end of the cruise industry than operating on Black Sea ferry routes. At the time of going to press, all five remain extant although their original Soviet owners might have been distressed to learn that several nowadays are used as casino junket ships.

The apotheosis of the 1970s cruise ferry is represented by the 15,650-ton *Tor Britannia* and the *Tor Scandinavia*, constructed for Tor Line's North Sea routes from Gothenburg to Immingham, Felixstowe and Amsterdam and delivered in 1975 and 1976 respectively. At that time, they were the world's biggest, fastest and most sumptuously-appointed ferries yet seen – but they too entered service at a difficult time with a deep recession in Britain and fuel prices standing at around $45 a barrel, a situation which worsened when the Iran-Iraq war began in 1980. Back in 1972, when Tor Line had first approached KEH to begin design work for these vessels, the prognosis for the shipping industry looked very different, with continued strong growth expected in all sectors.

Only a year after the advent of Tor Line's 'first generation' of ferries in 1966, the company's original founders, Trans-Oil and Rex, had been taken over by new owners – the mighty Swedish shipping conglomerate Salénrederiena – which was also heavily involved in shipbuilding (owning the Götaverken yard in Gothenburg), reefer shipping and the oil tanker trade (for which they it was building a fleet of very large crude carriers – VLCCs). It was evidently bullish about the future, continuing to invest heavily in new tonnage for various subsidiaries, but new ferries for Tor Line were regarded as a particularly prestigious project.

As Immingham on the Humber estuary was to be a port of call for these ships, their breadth was constricted by the size of the tidal lock and, to compensate, they were over 182 metres long. To maintain Tor Line's desired 26-knot maximum speed, their hulls had very fine lines and a powerful set of four 12-cylinder Pielstick PC3 diesels was installed, geared in pairs to each propeller shaft and together generating 45,600 bhp.

The vehicle deck could accommodate up to 420 cars. It was arranged around a narrow centre casing, cars entering via one of two wide stern doors and exiting either via a hatch in the bow quarter or by making a U-turn around the casing to drive off aft on its other side. The superstructure layout, however, was similar to the *Freeport*, the *Eagle*, the *Bolero* and the 1975 Silja Line sisters, with a cabin deck and public rooms filling the aft two-thirds of the two decks above, and more cabins filling their forward sections.

KEH produced the basic design but all subsequent development was carried out by Tor Line's Technical Director, Lars Wikander, who appointed an ex-Swedish Lloyd engineer, Thomas Wigforss, as Project Manager. The superstructure as actually constructed was similar to the original KEH basic design but with the Boat Deck promenade continuing unbroken around the front and extra blocks of cabins added. In order to fit silencers to the engines it was necessary to greatly increase the height of the funnel, but this reduced the ships' deadweight capacities.

When tenders were invited for building the ships, the Dubigeon-Normandie yard in Nantes seemed the likely winner, but a full order book there resulted in the job going to the Lübecker Flenderwerke.

As delivered, the *Tor Britannia* and *Tor Scandinavia* exhibited a mixture of KEH design traits (such as the tiered afterdecks, reminiscent of recent tonnage for Stena Line) and Tor Line's own ideas. In common with the *Nils Dacke* and the new Silja ferries, a major priority was ensuring the comfort of the crew, all accommodated in the two topmost decks of the superstructure – the ships' most attractive areas. The architect given the task of co-ordinating the overall interior design was Kay Kørbing, whose work in 1973 on the America Line cruise ship the *Vistafjord* had greatly impressed Tor Line's senior management. The Dane was also invited to design the restaurants and cabins for these new ships. His work, very refined and elegant, contrasted with the bright colours favoured by the Finnish interior designer Vuokko Laakso, whose contribution was to design the nightclub, discotheque and casino on Boat Deck and the sauna below the vehicle deck. To further enrich the ships' interiors, notable contemporary Scandinavian artists and sculptors were commissioned (at a cost of 1.5 million Swedish

The Soviet Black Sea Steamship Company cruise ferry **Kazakhstan**, one of five built in Finland for Black Sea routes but more commonly used as cruise ships in the Western market. (*Bruce Peter collection*)

The ***Tor Britannia*** shows off her striking lines and bold livery shortly after completion in 1975. *(ShipPax Archive)*

kronor) to decorate the public rooms, and school children from Britain, Sweden and Holland were invited to make drawings to frame and display in cabins. As for passenger comforts, there were berths for all 1,507.

Although intended first and foremost for North Sea routes, the 'Tor' ships featured outdoor lido areas with sheltering glass screens on their topmost decks, forward of the funnel – facilities rarely used in daily service but in marketing terms invaluable in helping to promote Tor Line. In fact, only *Tor Scandinavia* ever left the North Sea to sail in sunnier climes (on early 1980s winter charters to the Middle and Far East to promote Dutch goods and trade). But it was on their regular North Sea service that the 'Tor' sisters eventually proved to be outstanding successes, subsequently used on a variety of routes linking Britain, Denmark, Sweden and The Netherlands.

In the mid-1970s, when the ships were introduced, one of the most popular TV shows in America was the soap opera *The Love Boat*, produced by Aaron Spelling and filmed onboard Princess Cruises' *Pacific Princess* and *Island Princess* as they sailed from Los Angeles and San Francisco to Acapulco and other 'exotic' destinations. The show persuaded Middle America that cruising was a romantic and affordable holiday option for 'ordinary people', and is credited with kick-starting the subsequent boom in the American mass-market cruise industry.

Tor Line persuaded the BBC to ape the idea with a similar TV drama, to be shot onboard the *Tor Britannia* and the *Tor Scandinavia*. The result was *Triangle*, which hit the airwaves fronted by the glamorous young Irish actress Kate O'Mara, starring as the Purser. But as an enticing and exotic background, the North Sea somehow lacked the appeal of sun-kissed California, and *Triangle* soon sank out of sight.

Despite the fact that the *Tor Britannia* and the *Tor Scandinavia* impressed many who travelled on them, the latter 1970s proved to be a bleak period for Tor Line's parent company, Salénrederierna. It was hit hard by two major problems. The first was unexpectedly high bunker prices, which

seriously reduced the ferries' profitability. The second was that having over-invested in the oil tanker and reefer markets, which subsequently collapsed, the company was heavily burdened with debt. To try to alleviate matters, Tor Line was sold to DFDS in 1981 – but it didn't prevent Salénrederierna from going bankrupt in 1984.

DFDS was expanding rapidly at the time, taking over one ferry operator after another and – at last – making serious attempts to establish its long-proposed cruise ferry business in North America. The plan for this new operation was to move the *Tor Britannia* to the Caribbean, but in a last-minute change of heart she resumed North Sea service with her sister. Both ferries served DFDS well until (in 2003 and 2006) they were sold to the Italian Moby Lines, which they still serve on routes between the Italian mainland and Sardinian ports.

The ***Tor Britannia***'s a la carte restaurant offered panoramic views over the ship's stern. The sculptures of dancing teenagers are by Axel Olsson. *(Bruce Peter collection)*

CHAPTER SIX

'Large Block Principle' Design and the Jumbo Ferry

The term jumbo ferry was first applied to Washington State Ferries' double-ended 3,246-ton vessels the *Walla Walla* and the *Spokane*, designed by Nickum & Spaulding, built by Todd's Shipyard in Seattle and introduced between Seattle and Winslow (on Bainbridge Island) in 1973.

The trend towards larger car ferries had been ongoing since the 1930s. In the post-war era the number of ferry ports also increased substantially but in many instances their limited facilities and dimensions could not cope with vessels much longer than those of the 1960s generation, the majority of which measured between 90 and 140 metres. So if the size of port installations could not be significantly enhanced to accommodate bigger ferries, then the vessels themselves needed to become taller rather than longer and, to offset their consequently raised centres of gravity, broader.

A second major influence on ferry design development was the huge increase in shipbuilding and operating costs. To be profitable, it was no longer enough for ferries to be primarily regarded as a pleasurable and leisurely way to travel. What was needed was an enormous leap in perception – seeing and designing ferries as floating revenue centres, utilising every last square metre of superstructure and deck space to generate income.

These evolutionary trends and demands were best exemplified by four new ferries constructed in West Germany for delivery in 1974: TT-Linie's 12,528-ton *Peter Pan* and *Nils Holgersson*, built by Werft Nobiskrug at Rendsburg, and North Sea Ferries' 12,988-ton *Norland* and *Norstar*, built by AG Weser Seebeckwerft in Bremerhaven. All were approximately 150 metres long, but their widths varied – 23.5 metres in the case of the TT-Linie twins and 25 metres for North Sea Ferries, the latter being the maximum able to fit through the lock at the entrance to Hull Docks, where NSF vessels berthed. In comparison, the 1967 Wärtsilä-built *Finlandia* was pretty much the same in length but only a little over 20 metres wide.

The extra metres translated into extra freight lanes on the vehicle decks, the dimensions optimised by squared-off transom sterns and rather bluff bow lines, mitigated to an extent by pronounced bulbous bows. Above, the superstructures extended well forward and aft, resuling in bow and stern decks of unprecedented shortness. On the TT ships, the twin 16-cylinder diesels were of Pielstick design, and those on the NSF vessels were Stork-Werkspoor units.

There the similarities ended. The *Peter Pan* and the *Nils Holgersson* were drive-through ferries, intended for intensive 24-hour operation between Travemünde and Trelleborg, a route of 6-8 hours duration, whereas North Sea Ferries offerered only night crossings between Hull and Rotterdam. The *Norland* and the *Norstar* spent daylight hours in port – ample time to handle freight trailers. To cut costs only a stern door was fitted, although there were three double-height vehicle decks, stacked one above the other. The engine room was located aft and the space forward used for trailers. These extensive freight decks were great earners for NSF coffers and really came into their own in 1982, when the *Norland* was on charter to Britain's Ministry of Defence, carrying military equipment and troops to and from the South Atlantic during the Falklands War.

In all four vessels the superstructures had horizontal layouts. The *Norland* and the *Norstar* had cabin berths for 1,072 of the maximum 1,243 passengers, and a large buffet restaurant and a lounge, bar and shop reflected NSF's all - inclusive policy. In comparison, the *Peter Pan* and the *Nils Holgersson* had more of a mix of cabins and public rooms, in keeping with their dual usage as night and day ferries. So effective were these TT-Linie vessels that DFDS bought the design drawings from Werft Nobiskrug and modified them as the basis for a further new ferry for the Esbjerg-Harwich route – the 14,399-ton *Dana Anglia* – built by Aalborg Værft and delivered in 1978.

The new *Dana Anglia* and the existing *Dana Regina* were very different in appearance. The *Dana Anglia* was fractionally shorter, but broader by four metres and much more four-square

The **Peter Pan** shows off her rather bluff hull lines as she leaves Travemünde, bound for Trelleborg. *(Burkhard Schutt collection)*

North Sea Ferries Dutch-flagged **Norstar** in Hull in the mid-1970s. *(Bruce Peter collection)*

Two cut-away drawings enabling a comparison between North Sea Ferries' first-and second-generation ferries. *(Bruce Peter collection)*

in silhouette. Furthermore, she could carry 1,370 passengers and 470 cars, as opposed to the 1,065 and 300 of the *Dana Regina*. The *Dana Anglia*'s most significant new initiative was a large and well-equipped office from which the entire vessel was managed as an autonomous business unit – a first for a passenger ship.

Concurrently with TT-Linie's commissioning of the *Peter Pan* and the *Nils Holgersson* from Werft Nobiskrug, Stena Line worked with naval architects Knud E. Hansen A/S on the next, and more extreme, phase of jumbo ferry design development. Shipowner Sten A. Olson believed that ships were beautiful only on the balance sheet and instructed KEH to establish the maximum achievable capacity for a ferry with similar hull dimensions to those of the existing vessels in the Stena fleet. The big challenge was to extend the accommodation to the stern – effectively, on top of the propellors, where vibration was a problem. The eventual solution proved to be a twin-skeg stern design. This helped to dissipate unwanted cavitational forces, improving propulsion and enabling passenger accommodation to be built directly above.

This ingenious design development gave rise to the box-shaped 5,426-ton *Stena Nordica*, *Stena Normandica*, *Stena Nautica* and *Marine Atlantica*, built by Rickmers Werft in Bremerhaven and delivered in 1974-75. This quartet was intended principally for the lucrative charter market, from which Stena earned a great deal of income during the 1970s. What these ships lacked in looks they made up for in capacity, each accommodating 1,460 passengers and 500 cars.

Stena and KEH then set about optimising the capacities of Stena's existing ferries. In 1976-77, the three-year-old Yugoslavian-built Gothenburg-Frederikshavn day ferries *Stena Danica* and *Stena Jutlandica* were radically rebuilt at the Wilton-

Fijenoord shipyard at Schiedam in the Netherlands. Their superstructures were cut away and jacked up while steelwork for a new deck was inserted to make their upper car decks double height so that commercial vehicles could be loaded on two levels. To mitigate the resultant raised centre of gravity, sponson tanks were welded on to each side of the hull at the waterline.

During the latter 1970s, KEH carried out significant ferry rebuilding work to increase capacity – usually with results that aesthetically were unappealing. While the previously good-looking *Stena Danica* and *Stena Jutlandica* were visually impaired, the rebuilding of DFDS's Copenhagen-Oslo vessels the *Kong Olav V* and the *Prinsesse Margrethe*, with superstructures built out to their sterns to accommodate more cabins, not only ruined their looks but also reduced deadweight capacities. The fact that such alterations were acceptable to shipowners demonstrates that the culture of the shipping industry had changed; all that mattered was the bottom line.

THE REMARKABLE SEARUNNER CLASS

The idea that ships could be designed from the outset with the possibility of future enlargement was a novel one – and Stena Line's ro-ro freight ferry division pioneered it. In the early to mid 1970s, Stena built a succession of classes of freightferry for the charter market, mainly following the 'superstructure forward, machinery aft' layout of the early 1960s. Stena and naval architect Dag Rogne of KEH noted that a ferry with both engines and superstructure towards the stern would be simpler to maintain, and that the midbody could be cut in two more easily for lengthening without disturbing the machinery spaces. Ro-ro freighters with this layout were a first credited to Italian shipowner Aldo Grimaldi, whose Grandi Traghetti ('Big Ferries')

DFDS **Dana Anglia** was built to a design developed from TT-Linie's **Peter Pan** and **Nils Holgersson**. Weight was saved by fitting inflatable rafts rather than lifeboats. *(Bruce Peter collection)*

The **Stena Nordica**, one of four jumbo ferries whose superstructures were built all the way aft to optimise capacity. *(Bruce Peter collection)*

commenced operations in 1970 using the purpose-built *Freccia Rossa* and *Freccia Blu*.

Stena's design was known as the 'Searunner' class and eleven ships were ordered in two batches from Hyundai Shipbuilding & Heavy Industry at Ulsan in South Korea for delivery between 1977 and 1978. This was another first – European ferries built in the Far East, Hyundai impressing with their very large and efficient organisation. Propelled by twin 12-cylinder Pielstick V-diesels, the ferries had an 18-knot service speed and, as delivered, could accommodate 1,650 lane metres of freight. Shortly after, several were lengthened, enclosed shelterdecks added to expand their lane metres, with sponsors increasing deadweight capacities. Three were even given passenger accommodation in prefabricated modules on top of their enclosed shelterdecks. The Searunner design was an immediate and enduring success, some still surviving in Stena's fleet today.

TOWNSEND THORESEN BECOMES MARKET LEADER

In British waters the railway fleets, trading under the Sealink brand, faced serious competitor in 1968 when Townsend's Dover Strait ferries were merged with those of Thoresen on the western English Channel. Three years later, the combined Townsend Thoresen purchased Atlantic Steam Navigation as

Townsend Thoresen's **Free Enterprise V** makes a dramatic sight as she crosses the Dover Strait on a windy day. *(FotoFlite)*

part of the privatisation of road services by Edward Heath's government, giving the company additional freight-orientated routes on the Irish Sea and southern North Sea, increasing their status to that of a very large and powerful ferry operator.

Even before this consolidation, both Townsend and Thoresen had expansion plans. The former had continued a vigorous newbuild programme of five more 'Free Enterprise' ferries from Werf Gusto for Dover Strait routes for delivery from 1969 onwards. These circa 5,000-ton vessels proved very effective and so the British and Belgian partners in Sealink sought to emulate certain aspects of their layout in their own subsequent newbuilds. Unlike Townsend's first three 'Free Enterprise' ferries, the vehicle decks had short casings and the centre lanes were not lowered, allowing more space for commercial vehicles to manoeuvre.

A feature that remained unique to Townsend Thoresen ferries from the *Free Enterprise IV* onwards was triple-screw propulsion, maintainting a high service speed with only a single rudder, as it was thought easier to adjust the pitch of the KaMeWa propellers to improve manoeuvring in port. But experience of the *Free Enterprise IV* in service showed that when the centre engine was out of use, this benefit was to some extent negated as it reduced the effectiveness of the outboard propellers. From the *Free Enterprise V* on, all Townsend Thoresen ferries had naval XK hubs on their centre propellers and consequently were much more manoeuvrable.

Prior to its merger with Townsend, Thoresen was also planning a new generation of ferries to replace the original 'Vikings' from Southampton to Le Havre and Cherbourg. Designed by James Ayers and built by Aalborg Værft between 1975 and 1976, the 6,387-ton *Viking Venturer*, *Viking Voyager*, *Viking Valiant* and *Viking Viscount* shared many features with the 'Free Enterprise' series, including triple-screw propulsion. All had a distinctly angular appearance as Ayers knew from experience that replacing flat plates damaged when attempting to berth in fog or gusting winds was easier than replacing those with double curvatures.

As well as coping with increased passenger bookings, Townsend Thoresen enjoyed a leap in freight traffic on the Dover Strait, initially chartering the new 2,444-ton ro-ro cargo ferry *Stena Sailer* in 1973. This vessel provided a design formula for Townsend Thoresen's own freighter fleet, designed by James Ayers. The 4,236-ton *European Gateway*, *European Enterprise*, *European Clearway* and *European Trader* of 1975-78 were the first Dover Strait ferries with two double-height freight decks,

The **Viking Venturer**, one of four 'Super Viking' ferries built in Aalborg for operation on the Western Channel and between Felixtowe and Zeebrugge. *(Bruce Peter collection)*

each ship having 1,000 lane metres. Their construction began a successful relationship between Townsend Thoresen and the Schichau Unterweser shipyard in Bremerhaven, who built all of their subsequent vessels.

Throughout the 1970s, British Rail and SNCF lost market share as they continued to use 1960s tonnage with far less freight capacity than Townsend Thoresen's fleet. In 1976, British Rail's naval architects Tony Rogan and Don Ripley began design work on a new double-deck ro-ro ferry type which was intended to be a standard design for Sealink's short-sea routes to France and Ireland. Apart from having a substantial deadweight capacity, these ferries also needed the ability to load at single- and double-deck linkspans.

British Rail ordered four examples of the type from Harland & Wolff's Belfast shipyard – the 6,630-ton *Galloway Princess* for service between Stranraer and Larne, the 7,197-ton *St David* (Fishguard-Rosslare) and the 7,003-ton *St Anselm* and *St Christopher* for Dover-Calais, which had become Sealink's premier Channel ferry route. Compared with railway-owned ferries of the past, the high-density passenger accommodation for over 1,000 occupied only a small proportion of the ships' superstructures, and the 744 lane metres for freight was unprecedented in a railway context. Shortly after, SNCF ordered a large new Dover-Calais ferry from the Ateliers et Chantiers du Havre to operate alongside British Rail's forthcoming sisters.

British Rail ordered the new ferries in May 1979 and Townsend Thoresen responded urgently to this unexpected threat. Given the prospect of further competion from hovercraft

The 'Spirit' class ferry **Herald of Free Enterprise** powers across the Dover Strait. In 1987, this vessel sank off Zeebrugge due to her officers and crew carelessly putting to sea with the bow doors open. *(Bruce Peter collection)*

Sealink's **St Anselm**, one of four high-capacity car and freight ferries built in Belfast for British Rail's Dover Strait and Irish Sea routes. *(Bruce Peter collection)*

A cut-away drawing of British Rail's Dover-Calais ferry **St Anselm**: note the vast internal ramps between the upper and lower vehicle decks. *(Bruce Peter collection)*

and the Channel Tunnel, Ayers argued that the best solution was to construct three fast, identical 8,000-ton double-deck ferries, each able to make five trips a day.

In designing a new generation of Dover Strait ferries, Ayers used his extensive knowledge and experience of his previous ships to produce a highly original and imaginative design solution: combining high speed with a high deadweight capacity to achieve crossings in only 75 minutes – 15 minutes less than ' Sealink's. As with the most recent 'Free Enterprise' class, triple-screw propulsion was specified, three Sulzer diesels providing a 24-knot service speed. Each vessel had capacity for 1,300 passengers and 350 cars.

To enhance stability, the centre of gravity was kept low partly by reducing the freeboard amidships and partly by narrowing the superstructure and stowing the lifeboats in recesses on either side of the upper vehicle deck. This arrangement was also believed to be safer as there was only a three-deck drop to the water and so aircraft-style evacuation chutes could be used. As the Dover Strait has a large tidal range, all existing ferries had pronounced tumblehome (inward sloping topsides) from the belting upwards to prevent their superstructures from fouling shore facilities as, when tied up with a rising tide, they heeled over towards the quay. On the new design, the tumblehome began at mezzanine deck height, half-way up the hull topsides. Above the upper vehicle deck, the superstructure widened out to maximise the saloon deck area, then narrowed again for the officers' accommodation on the topmost decks. This entirely practical design gave the ferries a uniquely dynamic and sculptural appearance, enhanced by chunkily-proportioned masts and twin funnels. Another design innovation was the 'neat-stow' bow and stern doors. Ayers also considered it essential that in shape and livery, Townsend Thoresen's ferries should look very different from those of Sealink – a goal he most certainly achieved.

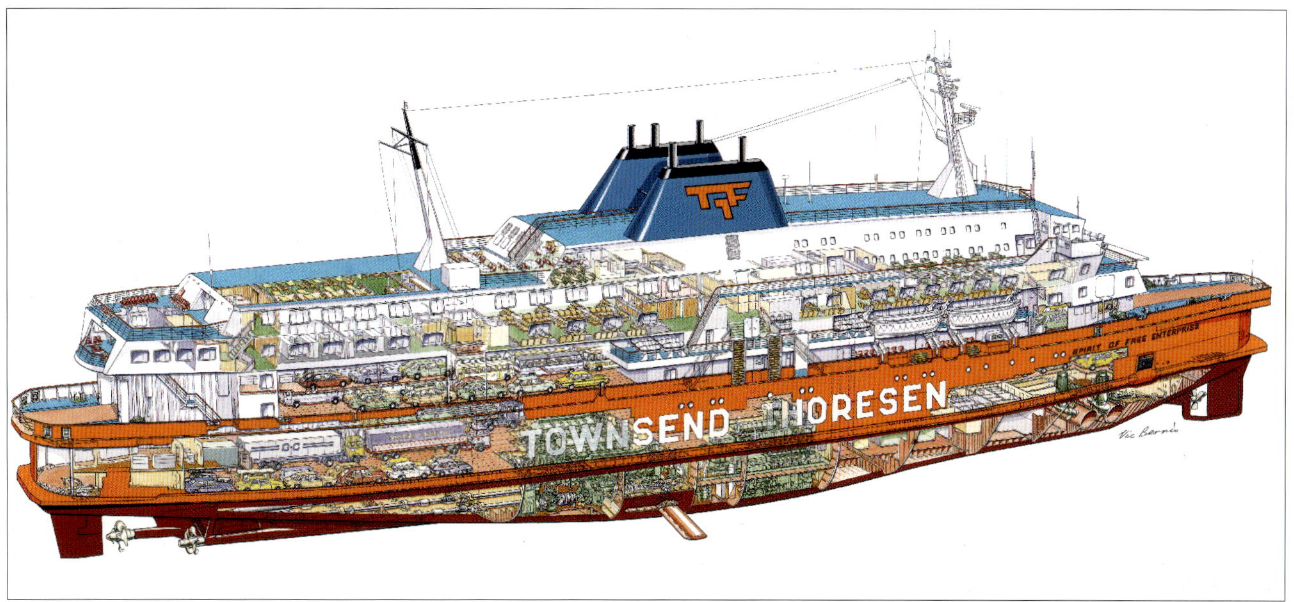

A similar cut-away drawing of Townsend Thoresen's rival **Spirit of Free Enterprise**. *(James Ayers collection)*

Townsend Thoresen was fortunate that Bremerhaven-based builders Schichau Unterweser were able to build each ferry in only a year. The first, the *Spirit of Free Enterprise*, was completed in January 1980, nine months ahead of British Rail's *St Anselm*. The *Herald of Free Enterprise* and the *Pride of Free Enterprise* followed shortly after.

Having claimed the record for the fastest Dover-Calais crossing by conventional ferry (55 minutes, 19th January 1980), Townsend Thoresen marketed the route as its 'Blue Riband Service.' Once Sealink introduced the much-delayed *St Anselm* and *St Christopher*, these and SNCF's new *Côte d'Azur* were branded 'Flagship Service' and competition between the two companies became intense. However, shortly after Sealink's new vessels arrived, Margaret Thatcher's government announced that British Rail's shipping services would be privatised as a top priority. This marked the beginning of the end for state-owned ferry operation.

THE DEVELOPMENT OF 'LARGE BLOCK PRINCIPLE' DESIGN

In the second half of the 1970s, a trend for so-called 'large block principle' design emerged in ferry newbuilds. In practical terms this concept translated as splitting passenger accommodation into a series of multi-deck 'blocks' containing the cabins, public rooms and service spaces, as opposed to the standard 'layered' solution, with entire decks given over either to cabins or to saloons. Typically, cabin blocks were situated in the forward half of the superstructure, as far removed as possible from engine noise and vibration, and public rooms located towards the stern, usuually with separate lounge and restaurant decks and hallways in between. In a 1970s jumbo ferry, however, cabin blocks were more akin to hotels than to traditional passenger ships, though this achieved further efficiency savings on both the accommodation and catering aspects of overnight ferry operation.

THE REMARKABLE FINNJET

Undoubtedly, one of the most outstanding and sophisticated ferries of the 1970s was the Enso-Gutzeit-owned *Finnjet*. Quite apart from her gas-turbine propulsion system and much higher service speed, the *Finnjet* set a whole new standard for passenger accommodation and service. Since the *Finnhansa* and *Finnpartner* had entered service between Helsinki and Travemünde in the mid-1960s, sea traffic between these ports had grown rapidly and it was anticipated that by 1978 passenger volume would leap from 40,000 a year to 200,000 – a five-fold increase.

Finnlines and its builders, Wärtsilä, proposed four design alternatives for new ships codenamed the *Finnhansa II*, the *Finnslow*, the *Finn-Midi* and the *Finnjet*. *Finnhansa II* was a larger version of the existing ships, while the higher-capacity *Finnslow* represented the status quo option for retaining the existing two-night voyage duration. The *Finn-Midi* approach was for a considerably faster 26-knot diesel-powered ship, capable of reducing the round trip time to three days. With no significant increase in size over the *Finnhansa II* and *Finnslow* alternatives, additional space needed for larger and more powerful machinery would be gained at the expense of reducing passenger and vehicle capacities.

The *Finnjet* approach ultimately adopted was for an altogether larger and faster ship, around three times as big as the existing ferries and with a service speed of 30.5 knots – much like a transatlantic liner. As implied by the name *Finnjet*,

The *Finnjet* is off Helsinki early in her career. Her bold hull graphics complement the overall design. *(Krystof Brzoza)*

the engines would be aviation-type gas turbines, propulsion successfully introduced in merchant shipping on the 1967 American freighter *Admiral William M Callaghan*. Gas turbines were compact and light in comparison with steam or diesel machinery of similar performance.

Those chosen for the *Finnjet* were twin Pratt & Whitney FT4C-1 DLF engines. The 8,300 rpm turbine speed was stepped down through three-stage reduction gearing to the 171 rpm turn of the ship's twin controllable-pitch propellers. This machinery, along with five auxiliary diesel generator sets and other equipment, was housed two-thirds aft, beneath the drive-through vehicle deck.

Apart from following the ideals of large block principle design, the *Finnjet*'s layout was also modularised, though without recourse to prefabrication in her construction. Naval architect Kai Levander, who led Wärtsilä's Project Department, was appointed Project Manager and Chief Naval Architect for the *Finnjet*. He started by determining the volume of space needed to fulfil the ship's capacity and service requirements and drew this as a block with the hull lines and other details therafter. In essence, he created the hotel and garage first and then fitted the ship – with its hydrodynamic requirements, machinery and other supporting services – around these.

The result was a large slab-sided vessel with absolutely flat decks and a very straightforward internal layout – a practical solution, as between sailings there would be just two hours in which to clean and service the passenger accommodation.

The slender hull form was designed with a waterline length of 200 metres and bulbous forefoot at the bow, developed to yield the 30.5-knot service speed with a minimum propulsion power of 55 megawatts (75,000 bhp). Yet, as models of the ship were extensively tested for both summer and winter navigating conditions prior to construction, the designers apparently realised that, contrary to traditional liner design practice, streamlining of the superstructure was unnecessary as air resistance is of far less significance than the hull's performance in water. The fluid superstructure lines of such iconic liners as the *Normandie*, the Cunard *Queens* and the *United States* were devised to give a tangible impression of their great speed – at least in the eyes of the travelling public. The *Finnjet*'s rectilinear massing made a compelling impression of power and strength.

Considering the possibilities of noise and vibration from the engines and propellers at 30 knots, particularly in the shallower waters off Travemünde, all cabins for passengers and crew needed to be located in the ship's quieter forward half.

A cut-away drawing of the *Finnjet*, showing the absolute segregation between cabins in her forward half and public rooms towards her stern. *(Bruce Peter collection)*

Spacious full-width central lobbies on the three principal passenger decks provided absolute separation between the sleeping and public areas forward and aft, and also served not only as a sound barrier to the hotel block but also as mustering spaces for disembarkation at voyage's end.

Cabin categories were limited to only three standard types – luxury en suite, smaller twin-berth cabins and economy-grade rooms with four fixed berths. The vehicle deck was a straight-sided double-height tunnel running 212 metres from bow to stern. A hoistable upper platform deck, fitted in sections, made it possible to carry a mix of commercial vehicles and up to 350 cars.

With the sailing schedule dictating a two-hour turnaround, the ship's design had to include provision at both ports for getting up to 1,500 passengers ashore and onboard – not to mention provisions, housekeeping and bunkering. Double-decker glass-enclosed boarding bridges with wide internal stairways helped to speed the movement of passengers.

Finnlines, owned ultimately by the Finnish government, wanted the *Finnjet* to be something of a 'ship of state', demonstrating to the world the ingenuity of Finnish industry, technology and shipbuilding, as well as showcasing the nation's mastery of architecture and design. Everyone involved knew that the *Finnjet* had the potential to greatly influence the future of passenger ship design, and to assert a very high reputation for Finland and Finnish shipbuilding throughout the world. Yet, at the same time, Kai Levander wanted to avoid creating anything too highbrow or elitist. Unusually for a naval architect, he placed particular emphasis on the sociology of ferries and cruise ships, studying and speculating on how they are consumed and experienced by the paying customers – passengers.

Wärtsilä's rather austere original external styling proposal was reworked by the prominent Finnish pop artist Kimmo Kaivanto to give her a distinctive identity. A key element of this was Kaivanto's 'hands across the sea' motif, visualising the hull as a pair of cupped human hands with the fingers forming the ship's bow and the upturned thumbs representing the side-by-side funnels. The traditional Finnlines hull colours, funnel style and insignia were dropped altogether in favour of a bolder midnight blue for the hull and funnels, which were also given a more robust shape reflecting the imposing mass of the superstructure. The name *Finnjet* appeared in huge two-deck-high bold white letters two-thirds aft.

The *Finnjet*'s interiors received a full architectural and graphic design treatment from prominent and progressive modern Finnish designers Sistem Oy, Antti and Vuokko Nurmesniemi and Vuokko Laakso. Sistem designed the multi-function conference facilities, nightclub, discotheque, the Sky Bar's upper gallery, hairdressing salon, children's playroom and sauna area. In addition to onboard signage, husband-and-wife team Antti and Vuokko Nurmesniemi were responsible for the main restaurant, shops, cabins and all linking areas such as the corridors, stairways and deck lobbies. Antti Nurmesniemi was best known for furniture and lighting fixtures produced by Artek,

The *Finnjet*'s Pub Maritime, designed by Vuokko Laakso. *(Shippax Archive)*

The buffet restaurant on the *Finnjet* typified the elegant interior design found throughout the vessel. *(Shippax Archive)*

SMZ's 1978-built Hook of Holland-Harwich ferry **Prinses Beatrix** was a forerunner to Knud E. Hansen jumbo ferries of the 1980s. *(Bruce Peter collection)*

The Knud E. Hansen A/S-designed Rederi AB Gotland jumbo ferry **Visby**. *(Trevor Jones)*

and his wife Vuokko was a glass, ceramic and textile designer. The *Finnjet*'s pub, grill restaurant, aperitif bar and particularly the large main lounge were designed by Vuokko Laakso. Located on the topmost deck was the Sky Bar – a bright and airy lounge and café. Above was a clerestory, enclosing a long seating gallery and gving a spectacular panorama from a height of 25 metres above the sea.

The *Finnjet*'s onboard hotel-style conference facilities were among the first of their kind on any ship and featured a large central auditorium with a stage and projection booth, spaces that divided into smaller meeting and reception rooms, and a small break-out lounge and bar. The auditorium could serve alternatively as a cinema and the auxiliary areas as additional lounges with airline-style seating to increase capacity on summer peak-season.

As far as possible, Finnish-made fixtures, fittings and other items (including Marimekko uniforms for female staff) showcased the nation's design expertise. Paintings and other works were commissioned for the interiors, one of which was a mural by Kimmo Kaivanto entitled 'Pictures of Finland' and stood three decks high in the main stair tower.

Perhaps more than any other ferry, the *Finnjet* was a proud and effective national ambassador, entering service in May 1977 to great public acclaim. But as fuel prices continued to rise, and winter service brought its own special problems, it is unlikely that she was ever entirely commercially successful.

Following the fall of the Berlin Wall in November 1989, the reunification of Germany, the ultimate dissolution of the Soviet Union in 1990, and German and Polish ports nearer to Helsinki once again opening to through traffic, the whole rationale for a ship of the *Finnjet*'s size and speed changed. The *Finnjet* spent increasing time on short booze cruises from Helsinki to Tallinn and became somewhat down at heel. Withdrawn from Baltic service in April 2004, she was sold for scrap at Alang in India in 2008.

THE FIRST SWEDISH JUMBOS

Towards the end of the 1970s, the Swedish ferry operators Sessanlinjen, Rederi AB Gotland and Rederi AB Sally (a member of the Viking Line consortium) each ordered two jumbo ferries for operation on its respective routes – Gothenburg-Frederikshavn, Nynäshamn–Visby (on Gotland), and Stockholm-Helsinki. All six ferries exemplified variations on 'large block principle' design. During the ensuing decade, the boom in leisure and consumerism, known in Sweden as the 'champagne economy', inspired a spate of new ferries, beginning in

Scandinavia and spreading throughout northern Europe and beyond.

Under pressure from the Swedish government to help keep the ailing Öresundsvarvet Shipyard at Landskrona in business, Rederi AB Gotland ordered two ferries, each almost 15,000 tons and designed by KEH. The bow configuration was very bluff with convex lines above the water to maximise the internal volume and a long upward-pointing bulb below to improve the flow of water around the hull. In order to alleviate the problem of severe aftbody cavitation, as experienced by the 1978-built Dutch Stoomvaart Maatschappij Zeeland Harwich-Hook of Holland ferry *Prinses Beatrix*, which had a similarly bluff bow and squared-off transom stern, the hull of the new ferry (to be named the *Visby*) had a twin-keg stern and an innovative 'duck-tail' sponson. This lengthened and stiffened her aftbody at the waterline, adding extra buoyancy and increasing her deadweight capacity. Fuel economy was also improved and the transmission of vibrations into the upperworks was reduced.

Naval architect Dag Rogne, who with colleague Poul Erik Rasmussen came up with this solution, revealed the inspiration behind it. They were enjoying a lunchtime sandwich in Churchill Park in Copenhagen and, feeding bread to the ducks, noticed that when a duck wants to paddle quickly, it pushes its tail feathers down into the water to increase the length of its body at and below the waterline. So the 'duck-tail' sponson was born – and worked, the hull projecting out beyond the stern to give a longer, sleeker, stronger and more buoyant form in the water.

Within the *Visby*'s hull was a cavernous double-height vehicle

Sessanlinjen's jumbo ferry **Kronprinsessan Victoria** was designed in Aalborg, but built in Sweden due to government subsidies. The cascading windows towards her stern indicate the location of her show lounge. *(Rickard Sahlsten collection)*

Upon delivery in 1983, the **Stena Danica** could claim to be the world's largest day ferry. Here she is en route across the Kattegat in the early 1990s. *(Bruce Peter)*

deck, entered via a large door in the middle of the stern. An extra deck for cars, sandwiched between this and the superstructure, was accessed by means of two smaller doors on either side and by internal ramps, so that cars and commercial vehicles were entirely separated. The superstructure extended all the way aft, with three decks of cabins and a large reclining-seat lounge. Car capacity was 515, with berths for 1,142 of the maximum 2,000 passengers.

As the Gotland service was a domestic link with no tax-free sales, the extra attractions found on the majority of large Scandinavian overnight ferries were missing. Facilities comprised a cinema, sauna, two large cafeteria-restaurants and a lounge bar.

The original contract price for the *Visby* was 165 million Swedish kronor but the final figure was close to 400 million. Little wonder that the venture was soon being described as the biggest gamble in Swedish shipbuilding history. It also failed in its prime objective of securing a long-term future for Öresundsvarvet. The *Visby* was finally delivered to Rederi AB Gotland in October 1980, five months behind schedule by which time the company was having second thoughts about the need for two ships. Hence the second of the new sisters was chartered out, firstly in the Gulf of Bothnia as the *Wasa Star* and later as the fourth of Larvik-Frederikshavn Fergen's ferries to be named the *Peter Wessel*.

For Sessanlinjen's new jumbo ferries it was a different prospect altogether, built for a high-density cross-Kattegat service in which tax-free shopping was the big attraction. Aalborg Værft produced a design which was perhaps the era's most visionary. Of similar tonnage to the Gotland jumbos, each could carry 2,100 passengers and 700 cars and had two double-height vehicle decks, the upper levels accessed by large hoistable ramps. The triangular void space above the aft ramp was put to ingenious use by inserting a vast tiered show lounge, Las Vegas style, with a stage, bandstand and dance floor – the prototype for similar attractions on numerous cruise ships that followed. To the rear was a cocktail bar, the large windows

overlooking the ship's wake. Unusually for daytime services, en suite cabins with berths for 400 were in the forward superstructure.

Simultaneously, Sessan's aggressive rival on the Gothenburg-Frederikshavn route, Stena Line, was building a pair of its own jumbo ferries, developed by the Technical Department in collaboration with KEH. The new *Stena Danica* and *Stena Jutlandica* claimed to be the world's largest daytime ferries. The capacity of each was 2,300 passengers and 630 cars, the latter loaded through bow and stern doors at the lower level and through side-doors to port into a full-height upper vehicle deck – an arrangement successful on their predecessors. The main limit on the jumbos' size was the suspension bridge across the mouth of Gothenburg's inner harbour, which they cleared by a margin of just a few metres.

The Chantiers du Nord shipyard at Dunkerque in France tendered the lowest construction bid, but due to delays neither entered service until 1983. Stena meanwhile, fearing that Sessanlinjen might gain a big advantage if its Swedish-built jumbo ferries entered service first, took Sessan over in 1981 via a successful hostile bid. Sessan's *Kronprinsessan Victoria* entered service between Gothenburg and Frederikshavn as planned, but work on the *Prinsessan Birgitta* was suspended while Stena's own jumbos were introduced instead. Sessan's ferries had a 'cabins forward, public rooms aft' vertical block subdivision, but the Stena ferries had only a small number of cabin berths below their vehicle decks and two entire decks given over to revenue-generating attractions.

KEH's original Stena ferries design drawings show that twin-skeg sterns and duck-tail sponsons were specified, as for the *Visby* and the *Wasa Star*. But their French builders were so sceptical that a twin-skeg would significantly increase the ships' speed that Stena opted for the yard's cheaper solution – with the result that the ships vibrated quite markedly in their after sections. Yet for their time they were technically sophisticated, equipped with onboard computers and a great deal of other technology, including CCTV cameras to enable officers on the bridge to see the stern when negotiating quays and linkspans, and to monitor the car deck and engine room. Although such technology is now standard for all European ferries, Stena Line was the first to use it.

In the Baltic, Viking Line and Silja Line were locked in fierce competition between Stockholm, Helsinki and Turku. Each company ordered a pair of large superferries for delivery from Wärtsilä in 1980-81, the Viking ferries to be built in Helsinki and Silja's newbuilds at Wärtsilä's Turku yard.

Kai Levander had a key role in the design and build of the Viking Line ships (the *Viking Saga* and the *Viking Song*), which effectively were shorter and broader-beamed versions of the *Finnjet*, with conventional diesel propulsion and a 20-knots service speed for the 15-hour overnight crossing between the Finnish and Swedish capitals. Unlike the *Finnjet*, they had two double-height trailer decks, stacked one above the other, and sectional hoistable platforms above the upper trailer decks, thus giving these 13,900-ton ships a remarkably high vehicle capacity of 60 trucks or 540 cars.

This was in line with the aims of Rederi AB Sally, which had ordered these Viking Line ships and was focused on maximising income from the vehicle decks by catering in the most flexible way possible for seasonal demand: a mix of cars and commercials in spring and autumn, cars in peak summer and predominantly commercials in winter.

To achieve this, Kai Lavendar had studied the double vehicle deck layout of the *Norstar* and the *Norland* (North Sea Ferries 1974) and of the forthcoming *Spirit of Free Enterprise* (Townsend Thoresen) and *Kronprinsessan Victoria* (Sessanlinjen). Starting with the car decks, he then designed the *Viking Saga* and the *Viking Song* around them. In doing so, he and his colleagues overcame several complex technical difficulties, and additional model testing of the hull was needed to address the concerns of navigating the Baltic in winter ice.

The planning of the rival Silja ferries, the 25,680-ton *Finlandia* and *Silvia Regina*, was handled by an altogether separate technical team at Wärtsilä's Turku yard. Their objective was to do something conceptually different from Viking's ships,

retaining a unique identity and style of service. Silja opted for a more conventional length-to-beam ratio with a single drive-through vehicle deck and hoistable platforms arranged around a centreline casing. A traditional horizontal accommodation plan was favoured, with public rooms and hotel areas relegated to separate decks rather than fore and aft.

The ferries' bow profiles were most unusual, with a very pronounced knuckle-joint immediately above the waterline, slightly increasing the vehicle deck's area – but at the cost of comfort and, possibly, safety. Although this design was proven on a short and sheltered route, the Stockholm-Helsinki service is relatively lengthy, two-thirds of its distance through open water. Consequently, Silja's ferries slammed, rolled and corkscrewed alarmingly in the autumn gales, and during their first refits extensive surgery was carried out to modify the bow profiles.

The facilities of the new Silja ships were innovative, emphasis given to a single large combined dining and entertainment complex, occupying the entire forward part of the superstructure's upper decks, where passengers could spend the whole evening. Both the Viking and Silja sisters were equipped for fully-containerised stores handling, using a 3-metre half-length container unit designed for the purpose.

While the *Viking Saga* and the *Viking Song* were considered the more technically advanced for their twin-skeg hulls, double trailer decks and *Finnjet*-style modularised planning, the horizontal layout of public spaces on the *Finlandia* and the *Silvia Regina* had a more profound influence on subsequent Baltic ferry design. Apart from the basic differences in overall layout between these two pairs of ships, each pair was unique architecturally. The *Viking Saga* and *Viking Song* interiors, designed by Vuokko Laakso, followed a contemporary Scandinavian aesthetic, with clean forms and bright colours. The interiors of the *Finlandia* and the *Silvia Regina* were created by a cadre of Finnish architects, led by Ilmo Isakainen and Vuokko Laakso. Their cruise-inspired approach was especially prevalent in Laakso's handling of the co-joined Maxim À La Carte and Terrass Buffet, where a festive Las Vegas cabaret aesthetic was created through the lavish use of marble and

Viking Line's Stockholm-Helsinki jumbo ferry **Viking Song**. *(Viking Line)*

Silja Line's *Finlandia* undergoes sea trials in thick ice in the Gulf of Finland. Her bow design proved less than effective in rough seas and quickly required substantial rebuilding. *(Shippax archive)*

mirror mosaic, illuminated stained-glass and other such decorative flourishes.

A third ferry for Rederi AB Sally's contribution to Viking Line was the 15,566-ton *Viking Sally*, built by the Jos L. Meyer shipyard in Papenburg, West Germany, for the Stockholm-Mariehamn-Turku route. As with other recent Baltic ferries, her hull had a very fulsome profile with a knuckle-joint above the waterline at the bow. As there was a long bulbous bow below, a ramp of substantial length was needed to reach the linkspans, and as this was not hinged, an extra housing was needed within the top of the bow visor to enclose its outer end while the ship was underway – a mistake which had tragic consequences when the ferry sank in a storm while sailing as the *Estonia*. The *Viking Sally*'s loss clearly demonstrated that large commercially-owned ferries of the 1980s were designed to stretch such safety regulations as existed to the absolute limit, at the expense of building in substantial safety margins.

On the southern North Sea, West Germany's TT-Linie acquired the hitherto Danish-owned (Ole Lauritzen) ferry route from Sheerness to Vlissingen – a strong competitor to Sealink's long-established Harwich-Hook of Holland link. Olau's new owners designed two new ferries – the 14,990-ton *Olau Hollandia* and *Olau Britannia* – which were delivered by AG Weser Seebeckwerft in Bremerhaven in 1981. Aesthetically, they bore similarities to the *Norland* and the *Norstar*, but in layout

and capacity had more in common with the *Viking Sally*.

Designed for an eight-hour English Channel service, they provided high standards of comfort but were geared more to transport than to mini-cruising, although attractions included sauna and indoor swimming complexes. Furthermore, while the *Olau Hollandia*, delivered first, was rather dark and Germanic in character, with sombre wood-effect veneer throughout, the subsequent *Olau Britannia* was completely different, with far brighter colours and more diverse finishes emulating the latest Baltic vessels.

Another notable large 1981 ferry was the 16,332-ton *Prinsesse Ragnhild*, built at Howaldtswerke-Deutsche Werft for Jahre Line's overnight service between Kiel and Oslo. Rather than follow the trend for a *Finnjet*-style modular layout, the owners opted to perpetuate the route's existing two-class offer. Facilities in each class were considerably expanded to include a First Class restaurant, First Class cabins and suites, bars, lounges, cafetaria, tourist cabins and an airline-style overnight lounge with reclining seats. Interior design was by Arkitektfirma H.G. Finne & Co A/S of Oslo.

With a cargo capacity of 43 eighteen-metre trailers on her main drive-through deck, the *Prinsesse Ragnhild* could carry a mix of commercial traffic and private cars or a maximum of 600 cars only using the hoistable platform deck and ramp-accessed holds for cars at two levels beneath the trailer deck.

THE *SCANDINAVIA*

Lest the American mass cruise industry should have forgotten its origins from 1960s-generation car-passenger ships such as the *Nili* and the *Sunward*, in the early 1980s the two species seemed destined to converge again. Bruce Nierenberg, the youthful former Executive Vice-President of Norwegian Caribbean Line, convinced J. Lauritzen, the parent company of DFDS, to back a venture to open a New York-Bahamas-Florida cruise-ferry route .

The idea was to build a deep-sea ferry to operate between New York and Freeport, from where smaller ferries would run a feeder service to take passengers to their Florida destinations. This would negate the legislation which prohibited passengers from travelling directly between American ports aboard foreign-flag ships. Trips on the *Finnjet* were already being successfully promoted in the United States as part of longer European package holidays. Silja's new *Finlandia* and *Silvia Regina* were likewise amply capable of meeting American expectations for en suite bathrooms, abundant hot water for showers, power points

The Rederi AB Slite-owned Viking Line ferry *Viking Sally*, built by Meyer Werft at Papenburg. *(Krystof Brzoza)*

Jahre Line's handsome 1981-built Oslo-Kiel ferry *Prinsesse Ragnhild* lies at her berth in Kiel. *(Trevor Jones)*

for hairdryers and shavers, ship-to-shore 'phone service and plenty of crushed ice in the drinks. If Americans could be persuaded to take their cars with them on a ferry instead of heading for the freeways, it would be job done.

Branded as Scandinavian World Cruises, a subsidiary of DFDS, the new venture tested the waters with the 26,748-ton *Scandinavia*, which entered service in October 1982. Designed by KEH and built in France by the Dubigeon-Normandie yard in Nantes, her design was influenced by the modular layout and vertical segregation of cabins and public rooms of the *Visby* and by the overall superstructure configuration of the *Tor Britannia* and *Tor Scandinavia*, constructed a decade earlier.

The *Scandinavia*'s two-and-a-half-day passage over the 950 nautical miles between New York and Freeport took her round North Carolina's infamous Cape Hattaras, where frequent storms can whip up the shallow waters into long swells and cause severe pitching motion. The great Atlantic liners were built with long hulls to cope with such sea conditions, but the *Scandinavia*'s dimensions were restricted by the tight confines of Freeport's relatively small harbour to a length of 185 metres, 27 metres beam and a draught of not more than 6.58 metres.

A little longer and slightly narrower than Silja's *Finlandia* and *Silvia Regina*, the *Scandinavia* had to cater in every way for passengers remaining onboard for several days. This meant serving three meals a day in the large main restaurant, and providing other services and facilities such as the spacious enclosed pool and lido with adjoining bar and café.

Unusually for a ferry of her era, DFDS reverted to twin Alsthom Atlantique-built B&W slow-speed diesels to power the *Scandinavia*, as similar engines had proven their worth in the rigours of Atlantic service on the company's cargo liner fleet. With hoistable sectional upper platforms, her car deck could accommodate 376 American-sized automobiles (in a space that would take 550 European cars!).

Passenger accommodation and facilities were arranged *Finnjet*-style. These included the Windows of the World dining room (named after the prestigious top-floor restaurant in New

The giant DFDS-owned Scandinavian World Cruises flagship ***Scandinavia*** arrives at Nassau during September 1982. *(Bruce Peter collection)*

York's World Trade Centre), the main Broadway and Blue Riband show lounges, Galaxy nightclub and discotheque.

Accommodation comprised 470 standard cabins, 25 large staterooms and two de luxe suites. The *Scandinavia*'s interior design was by Robert Tillberg.

Operationally, the *Scandinavia* differed considerably from the *Finlandia* and the *Silvia Regina* in that a larger crew of 354 was needed for about the same number of passengers – mostly to provide the expected higher standards of cruise ship service in areas such as the hotel, catering, laundry and housekeeping. Consequently, far more space was needed beneath the vehicle deck to store and handle provisions and the ship's laundry.

The *Scandinavia* entered service in October 1982, sailing on a five-day rolling schedule with an evening departure from New York, arrival in Freeport the third morning, departure early afternoon the same day and arrival back in New York mid-afternoon on the fifth day. The feeder services from Freeport to Miami and Port Canaveral were handled by the former *Blenheim* and *Caribe*, refurbished and renamed the *Scandinavian Sea* and the *Scandinavian Sun*. On days between feeder services, these

North Sea Ferries' 'third generation' ferry ***Norsea*** undergoes trials off the Isle of Arran in April 1987. *(ShipPax archive)*

TT-Line's 1986-built jumbo ferry **Peter Pan** off Travemunde shortly after entering service. *(Bruce Peter collection)*

ships ran day excursions to Freeport from their respective base ports in Florida, carrying mainly gamblers attracted by the extensive onboard casino facilities.

The initial response to Scandinavian World Cruises and the *Scandinavia* was positive – enthusiastic even – but ultimately the whole venture failed. One of the major reasons was difficulties in maintaining the *Scandinavia*'s sailing schedule because of delays caused by frequent storms and high winds off Cape Hattaras. Not only did the ship often arrive in New York after midnight, but sometimes needing substantial repairs to severe bow plating damage. Passengers bound for Florida were unhappy having to switch from one ship to another in Freeport

merely to get around the foreign-flag legislation. But perhaps the greatest problem was that highway travel is part of the American way of life and, for many heading south to the sun, the road trip is all part of the holiday adventure.

By the end of November 1983, the *Scandinavia* had returned to Europe for overnight service between Copenhagen and Oslo. DFDS lost so much money through Scandinavian World Cruises that the venture almost drove the company to bankruptcy. In 1985, to reduce the debt, the *Scandinavia* was sold. After a varied career and much rebuilding, she is still in service today – as Thomson Cruises' *Island Escape*.

Two generations of Olau ferries at Sheerness in October 1989: the new **Olau Hollandia** has just been delivered from her builder while her smaller 1981-vintage namesake lies at the berth behind. *(FotoFlite)*

Bulky but businesslike, the **Koningin Beatrix** ploughs through the North Sea. *(FotoFlite)*

The Rembrandt a la carte restaurant on the **Koningin Beatrix**, designed by H.G. Finne of Oslo. *(Miles Cowsill)*

THE MID-EIGHTIES GENERATION

The mid-1980s saw a further leap in the size of ferries – on paper at least. In 1984 the rules governing the gross tonnage calculation of ships' volumes were changed to include additional partially-enclosed spaces. So ferries delivered during the second half of the decade apparently increased in size by up to 20%, even if their dimensions were little different from earlier vessels.

By mid-decade, the large Baltic block-principle ferry had progressed, 30-40,000 tons virtually standard for short-sea passenger and vehicle transport in northern Europe. New ships of this type entered service for TT-Line, Stoomvaart Maatschappij Zeeland (SMZ), North Sea Ferries and domestic Canadian operator Marine Atlantic, with *Finnjet*-style modularised accommodation plans and various vehicle-deck arrangements tailored to suit the individual needs and preferences of each owner.

TT-Line's 31,356-ton jumbos *Peter Pan* and *Nils Holgersson* were delivered by Seebeckwerft in 1986-87 for the Trelleborg-Travemünde service and each had two double-height vehicle decks arranged around a centre casing, the upper deck flanked by single rows of outer cabins for passengers.

SMZ's 31,189-ton *Koningin Beatrix* was built to modified plans for the overnight Sealink service between the Hook of Holland and Harwich. She had three decks of public rooms and dining facilities were served by a single galley. First Class lounges were on Boat Deck.

Compared with ships such as these, North Sea Ferries' 1970s jumbo ferries the *Norstar* and the *Norland* were already comparatively small and becoming dated against the standards of newer tonnage. P&O, the joint company's British partner, therefore initiated a fleet modernisation programme. In 1985 two new jumbo ferries were ordered for the overnight Hull-Rotterdam service, one to be owned by P&O and the other by its Dutch partner Nedlloyd.

The construction of the P&O-owned *Norsea* was entrusted to Govan Shipbuilders on the Clyde in the hope that it would help to revitalise the yard's former status as a builder of passenger ships. It had been anticipated that the Nedlloyd vessel the *Norsun* would be built by van der Giessen-de Noord in the Netherlands, but the Dutch government's refusal to subsidise it saw the order go instead to the Yokohama yard of Nippon Kokan (NKK) in Japan.

KEH was commissioned to handle the technical design for the *Norsea*, much of the work adopted for the *Norsun*. These new North Sea Ferries ships were to be large and operationally flexible vessels, comparable with other recent examples such as the latest SMZ and TT-Line tonnage. But achieving the necessary size and capacities presented a unique design challenge as the ships had to be narrow enough to pass through the Port of Hull's 25.9-metre-wide King George Tidal Lock. Furthermore, a small draught was necessary due to the need for safe navigation in the shallow waters off England's North Sea coast. The 31,727-ton *Norsea* had an overall length of 179 metres and a beam of 25.38 metres, allowing a clearance of only 270 millimetres to either side for passage through the lock.

Operationally, the *Norsea* and the *Norsun* had a strong emphasis on freight traffic, qualifying them as precursors to the subsequent breed of ro-pax ships. The overnight passage between Hull and Rotterdam (197 nautical miles) took 14 hours, at a speed of 18.5 knots eastbound and, compensating for the hour's difference between the UK and European time zone, at 16.5 knots westbound.

Remarkably close relatives of the *Norsea* and the *Norsun* were the domestic Canadian ferries the *Caribou* and the *Joseph and Clara Smallwood*, designed by KEH and built by Davie Shipbuilding in Lauzon, Québec. Like those of North Sea Ferries they were double-decker ships but constructed for year-round service in often inhospitable and stormy waters, and with a greater emphasis on freight transport. Completed in 1986 and 1989 respectively, they continue to maintain a government-mandated lifeline link across the Cabot Strait between the mainland port of North Sydney in Nova Scotia and Port aux Basques on the island of Newfoundland.

The ships were ordered for the Atlantic Marine Highway services of CN Marine, originally part of Canadian National Railways and later established as a separate Crown Corporation named Marine Atlantic. While their overall dimensions and tonnage are similar to the *Norsea* and the *Norsun*, they are functionally quite different. Classified by Lloyd's as +100A1 Baltic Ice 1A Super +LMC, the *Caribou* and the *Joseph and Clara Smallwood* have the ice-breaking capacity needed during the winter and spring months. Unlike a true ice-breaker, the hull form has a modified twin-skeg stern arrangement with bulbous forefoot. During the *Caribou*'s trials in the St. Lawrence River in early 1986, she encountered an up-bound freighter stuck in the ice and altered course to cut the ship free, continuing on her way with the freighter following in the channel cut by the *Caribou*.

Top: The ferry square on DSB's *Peder Paars* was three decks high and naturally illuminated through a large roof light. *(Bruce Peter collection)*

Above left: The cafeteria on the *Peder Paars*, featuring Arne Jacobsen and Hans J. Wegner furniture and murals by Susanne Ussing. *(Bruce Peter collection)*

Above right: The *Peder Paars'* business lounge was notably stylish with Borge Mogensen chairs and Poul Henningsen lighting. *(Bruce Peter collection)*

Right: On large ferries, graphic design is important to prevent passengers from feeling disorientated. DSB's *Peder Paars* was an exemple of best practice. *(Bruce Peter collection)*

Århus-Kalundborg ferries of different generations in Århus harbour: the **Prinsesse Anne-Marie** of 1960 is dwarfed by the new **Peder Paars**. *(Bruce Peter collection)*

DSB JUMBO FERRIES

In Denmark, domestic ferry services continued to be split between the state railway, Danske Statsbaner (DSB), and private sector operators, and it was DSB which made the largest investment in new jumbo ferry tonnage for routes across the Great Belt. Such investment helped to stave off the closure of some of Denmark's struggling shipyards – in particular, those at Nakskov and Helsingør – and there was also a real need for more commodious train-carrying tonnage, particularly to cover the crowded Nyborg-Korsør route. Since the mid-1970s, DSB had followed West Germany's lead in operating hourly inter-city trains between Denmark's principal cities, creating the need for an intensive ferry timetable operated by three large vessels. As train lengths increased, the existing Great Belt fleet struggled to cope.

DSB's Great Belt train ferry **Kronprins Frederik** is seen off Korsør in 1994. By then, her funnel had been heightened so as not to pollute the town. *(Bruce Peter)*

The answer was to design a trio of new jumbo train ferries for delivery in 1981 – the 10,600-ton *Dronning Ingrid*, *Kronprins Frederik* and *Prins Joachim*. The basic design work was carried out by KEH, although the result was atypical of the firm's usual ferry output, with DSB's own architects and technical staff making a significant contribution. Able to load and unload simultaneously on two tracks via its bows, each ship had train deck space for 18 Eurofima 26.4-metre West German inter-city coaches on four tracks within the ship, although in reality these ferries carried DSB's own slightly shorter B-type coaches, which formed the bulk of DSB's Inter-city rakes. The *Dronning Ingrid*, *Kronprins Frederik* and *Prins Joachim* were notably successful, not least because of their elegant and modern interiors, designed by Kay Kørbing and complemented by artworks created by a variety of contemporary Danish artists.

DSB planned to build further similarly large ferries – but deciding where best to deploy them was affected by wider political issues. While DSB wanted new double-ended ferries for the Rødby-Puttgarten service across the southern Baltic, it was decided instead to build more conventional jumbo vessels to replace ageing 1960s tonnage on the Århus-Kalundborg route, where such ferries might relieve some of the car traffic between Halsskov and Knudshoved.

The 19,763-ton *Peder Paars* and *Niels Klim* were designed by the Danish firm Dwinger Marine Consult and built by Nakskov Skibsværft. While the fulsome hull configuration was typical of 1980s jumbo car ferries, such as the *Visby* and the latest Stena vessels, the ships' silhouettes and passenger spaces were largely developed from the high standards set by the three *Dronning Ingrid*-class Great Belt ships. Each had a main trailer deck with space for 30 eighteen-metre trailers and a fixed upper

Townsend Thoresen's mighty 'Chunnel Beater' **Pride of Dover** shortly after delivery, and following their take-over, featuring P&O's funnel livery. *(James Ayers collection)*

car deck accommodating 152 (or 331 in peak season, when no commercial traffic was carried) For DSB, passengers continued to be an important element and each ferry could carry up to 2,000. As previously, the ships' interiors were designed by Kay Kørbing.

In addition to cafeterias, restaurants, bistro, children's playrooms, video cinema, reading room, First Class lounge and various other lounge and seating areas, onboard facilities catered for passengers who wanted to work while at sea. The 74 'office cabins' located beneath the car deck each had a workspace, desk lighting and a typewriter. The twin beds and en suite toilets also enabled conference delegates to use these cabins for overnight stays.

The *Peder Paars* and the *Niels Klim* were two of the most impressive (and expensive) ferries built during the 1980s boom, but they were also 'white elephants'. Freight capacity was insufficient and at only 17.5 knots they were too slow. When the Danish government finally decided to build a fixed link across the Great Belt, DSB was pressured in 1990 to sell the ferries to finance the construction of new tonnage elsewhere. The *Peder Paars* went first to Stena Line, as the *Stena Invicta*, and later to Color Line as the *Color Viking*. The *Niels Klim* continues to sail with Stena as the *Stena Nautica*. Both vessels were virtually gutted by their new owners and, in many regards, downgraded to better suit the commercial demands of their new routes. When new, these ferries represented the apotheosis of public sector ferry design – but the future lay elsewhere.

THE 'CHUNNEL BEATERS'

From the moment in July 1985 when it was announced that a rail tunnel would be built beneath the Dover Strait, Townsend Thoresen and the then recently-privatised Sealink British Ferries began planning their responses.

Townsend Thoresen's solution was to develop a pair of 26,443-ton 'Chunnel Beaters' – large, double-deck triple-screw ferries, each to carry up to 2,260 passengers and 650 cars, and to a design evolved from its successful 'Spirit' class. Sealink British Ferries, owned by Sea Containers, opted against building anew and in 1988 purchased two large freight ferries, the *Tzarevetz* and the *Trapezitza*, from the Bulgarian company So

Mejdunaroden Automobile Transport. SBF's plan was to convert these ships, built in 1980, into multi-purpose Dover-Calais ferries.

Townsend Thoresen's new ferries were built by the Schichau Unterweser shipyard in Bremerhaven. While the first, the *Pride of Dover*, was nearing completion, the *Herald of Free Enterprise* was deputising on the Dover-Zeebrugge service. On the evening of 6th March 1987, with her bow doors open, she left the ferry berth in Zeebrugge and headed out to sea. There was a high tide and she was trimmed downwards at the bow, and as her speed increased she began to scoop up increasing amounts of water into the vehicle deck. Almost thirty minutes after departure, she became critically unstable and capsized, sinking too quickly for her life-saving appliances to be used. Of the 573 passengers onboard, 193 drowned.

At the public enquiry into the sinking, it was revealed that Townsend Thoresen ferries not infrequently put to sea with their vehicle deck doors open. Moreover, when the 'Spirit' class vessels had been constructed, the company's senior management (in order to save £25,000 per ship) vetoed the installation of sufficiently powerful trim pumps – equipment

The spacious forward-facing Motorists' Lounge on Sealink British Ferries' **Fantasia**, designed by Warren Platner. *(Shippax Archive)*

Seen here crunching through winter ice off Stockholm, Viking Line's *Mariella* has proven to be an enduring success and remains on her original route from Stockholm to Helsinki. *(Bruce Peter)*

Sealink British Ferries' **Fantasia**, showing the large sponsons fitted to improve her survivability in the event of an accident. *(William Mayes)*

which would have ensured that the ferries sailed on an even keel. The enquiry further revealed that Townsend Thoresen captains had a poor understanding of the deadweight capacity of these vessels and, although the bow doors were visible from the ends of the bridge wings, there were no indicator lights on the bridge consoles to show whether or not the doors had been closed. Other failings became apparent too, such as the bosun sleeping in his cabin on the night of the tragedy when he should have been supervising the implementation of correct security procedures on the vehicle deck prior to departure. Overall, the public enquiry revealed a culture of sloppiness permeating Townsend Thoresen's operations. Shortly before the disaster, the company had been purchased by P&O and a management upheaval followed.

Twenty-three years after the *Herald of Free Enterprise* disaster, one of her sisters, the former *Pride of Free Enterprise*, remains in operation across the Channel between Ramsgate and Oostende as the TransEuropa Ferries' *Oleander*, and the *Pride of Dover* and the *Pride of Calais* (the final designs of this class by naval architect James Ayres) continue to give sterling service for P&O between Dover and Calais, one of the world's most intensive and competitive ferry routes. The passage of time has proven Ayres' ferry designs to be enduringly successful.

While the Zeebrugge disaster enquiry was progressing, Sealink British Ferries' naval architects Tony Rogan and Don Ripley (senior members of the team working for Sea Containers) were planning the *Tzarevetz* and *Trapezitza* conversions to be carried out by the Lloyd Werft shipyard in Bremerhaven – complex work which took nine months for each ship.

With passenger accommodation designed by American architect and interior designer Warren Platner, the first of Sealink's two new-look ferries entered service in March 1990 with the decidedly untraditional name the *Fantasia*. Her sister meanwhile was transferred to Sealink's French partner on the route, the SNCF subsidiary Societé Proprietaires des Navires, and was introduced that July as the *Fiesta*.

FREEDOM OF CHOICE

As the North Sea and TT-Line ferries of the mid-1980s were entering service, Silja and Viking Lines were already progressing their next round of newbuilds for the Finland-Sweden market, to be constructed by the Wärtsilä yards – Silja's 33,829-ton *Svea* and *Wellamo* in Helsinki, and Viking's 37,899-ton *Mariella* and *Olympia* in Turku.

The Silja ships aimed to deliver *Finlandia* and *Silvia Regina* standards of service on the shorter Stockholm-Turku route. The *Mariella* and the *Olympia*, replacing the *Viking Saga* and the *Viking Song* only five years after their introduction, would do the same on Viking's Stockholm-Helsinki operation. Compared with Silja, the Viking tradition was for smaller ships delivering a less expensive and more basic service, but to stay competitive the time had come to up the stakes – particularly as the economic boom in Sweden and Finland meant that many travellers had higher expectations than ever.

Both pairs of ships followed an overall layout derived from the *Finlandia* and the *Silvia Regina* – a horizontal rather than vertical delineation of public and private facilities and a conventional single drive-through vehicle deck with hoistable platforms. The challenge of designing the key public areas of the Silja ships, in a manner similar to those of the line's Stockholm-Helsinki vessels, fell to architect Lennart Janson.

For the Viking Line interiors, Robert Tillberg was briefed to achieve a style closely resembling that of recent North American cruise ships. As the *Mariella* and the *Olympia* were to serve the emerging and lucrative mini-cruise and onboard conference markets, the owners sought to emulate the higher design standards of Silja's latest ships and to create cruise-style appeal with a tempting choice of restaurants, lounges and entertainment. The business and conferencing facilities were to rival those of the newer Stockholm and Helsinki hotels.

Furthermore, Viking wanted to create empathy between passengers and the natural environment as the ferries sailed through the beautiful archipelago – hence the large windows completely surrounding the saloon decks. Along with public

The ***Silja Symphony*** brought a completely new approach to ferry and cruise ship design as most of her cabins and public rooms were accessed off an internal mall. Externally, the ferry was notably stylish, thanks largely to an ingenious livery application. *(Bruce Peter)*

rooms accessed from a side arcade, these were to become a distinguishing feature of all subsequent Viking Line tonnage.

For Robert Tillberg the *Mariella* and *Olympia* were significant reference ships for his later design work. The transatlantic swagger of both Viking ferries grabbed passengers from the moment they boarded into a vast marble-lined reception lobby with red carpeting, a mirrored ceiling, polished brass trimmings and a glass sculpture in an atrium which rose through three decks.

With features such as casinos, show lounges, discotheques, children's playrooms and extensive business and conference suites, Baltic ferry culture was advancing ever more in the direction of leisure cruising. By 1986 Stockholm, Helsinki and Turku were all served year round by nightly sailings aboard the world's largest and most modern ferries. Two-night minicruises became increasingly popular – particularly as the terminals were near the city centres and cruises could be enjoyed on the spur of the moment, economies of scale making fares easily affordable. By the mid-1990s, the number of Baltic minicruises and day trips enjoyed annually by Finns alone was around ten million – double the country's population.

Ferries with cruise facilities of the type first introduced by the *Svea* and the *Mariella* tend to be referred to as 'third generation' – developments of the jumbos and superferries of the *Finnjet* type and of the smaller car ferries of the 1950s and 1960s. As naval architect Kai Levander has expressed, each generation reflects the changing times and needs of the people that the ships were built to serve, and is therefore an important chapter in transport and social history.

Viking Line's *Mariella* and *Olympia* effectively became the lead ships of a generation of similar newbuilds, all delivered in the comparatively short timeframe of about five years. These included the 34,384-ton *Amorella* and *Isabella* (1988-89) for SF Line's Stockholm-Mariehamn-Turku service, plus three additional

Viking Line ships from Wärtsilä. The Finnish newbuilds comprised the 40,012-ton *Athena* and *Kalypso* (1989-90) to serve the Stockholm-Mariehamn route for Rederi AB Slite, and the 46,398-ton *Cinderella* (1989) for SF-Line's three-times-a-week Helsinki–Stockholm service and overnight excursion to Tallinn.

From the latter 1980s onwards, greater attention was paid to the external aesthetics of Baltic ferries in order to emulate the image and appeal of Caribbean cruise ships.

INTROVERT AND EXTROVERT

Compared with Viking Line's impressive new late 1980s armada, Silja's fleet from earlier in the decade already appeared obsolescent. Clearly, to regain and hold its supremacy on the Baltic, Silja needed to do something spectacular. The *Finlandia* and the *Silvia Regina* had already been refitted and the idea of

Viking Line's innovative Swedish-flagged ***Athena*** was designed with extensive glazing to allow passengers to enjoy panoramic views of passing archipelago scenery. *(Bruce Peter collection)*

lengthening them was mooted as a means of giving both a new competitive edge.

Kai Levander and his colleagues in the Project Department of Wärtsilä's Helsinki shipyard had other ideas though, thinking more in terms of a radically different approach to designing a new generation of cruise ferries. Concepts they had toyed with in the 1980s included proposals for catamaran and large monohull ships. One of these ideas was called 'Ferry 85' – a Baltic cruise ferry with wider superstructures that offered the possibility of innovative arrangements of the passenger spaces.

With an earlier concept for the AOC (All Outside Cruise) ship having been successfully realised in the trendsetting *Royal Princess*, Silja was persuaded to take a bold new step forward and put itself decisively ahead of the Viking Line fleet.

Hence Levander and Silja's naval architect Harri Kulovaara started work on two new 58,000-ton 'ferries of tomorrow', featuring a wide variety of spectacular amenities. The project was developed in great secrecy, those people involved obliged to sign non-disclosure agreements.

To put a fresh perspective on the Silja brief, Stockholm firm FFNS Arkitekter – a practice with extensive experience in designing shopping malls and other large commercial projects ashore – was commissioned to develop an overall architectural design concept.

The idea was to design virtually all of the public areas around a unifying central open space – an arcade, five decks high, extending right through the centreline of each ship beneath a linear glazed roof vault, similar to famous arcades ashore (such as Milan's cruciform Galleria Vitorio Emanuele II, Hamburg's Hansaviertal Passage and Canada's vast Eaton Centre shopping mall in Toronto). The proposals also suggested using traditional shipbuilding materials such as painted steel, brass, canvas and sailcloth, and teak planking for floors and stair-treads.

The mall's location was at the base of the superstructure, on

Part of the **Silja Serenade**'s five-deck-high internal atrium. Over the years, the shops, bars and restaurants have changed according to demand. *(Bruce Peter collection)*

Deck 7, where its wide centreline promenade would form a pedestrian high street, lined with shops, cafés and other services on both sides, and four strata of cabins above with windows facing inboard to give occupants a 'street view'. In essence this brought about a change from extrovert to introvert planning – from looking outwards to the passing vistas of the archipelagos to looking inwards and becoming absorbed in the onboard milieu being played out in the mall.

In addition to the various speciality restaurants, bars, cafés and shops arranged along the mall's length, other onboard

Silja Line's **Wellamo**, delivered early in 1986 for service between Stockholm and Turku. Notable design improvements since Silja's earlier jumbo ferries included, for example, more slender bow lines and an attractively streamlined forward superstructure. *(William Mayes)*

Viking Line's Yugoslavian-built Stockholm-Turku ferries **Amorella** and **Isabella** meet at Mariehamn in winter ice. The small Kapellskär-Mariehamn shuttle ferry **Ålandsfärjan** lies at her berth. *(Viking Line)*

attractions included the main à la carte restaurant, tax-free supermarket, smorgasbord dining room, conference centre, show lounge, nightclub, intimate observation lounge and, contained within thick glazing that maintained tropical temperatures, an indoor spa and fitness complex with Roman baths, jaccuzis and pools with chutes and water flumes. Externally, the ferries were styled by Helsinki-based architects Windell & Riikanen.

The two new ferries were named the *Silja Serenade* and the *Silja Symphony*. The former made her service debut to great acclaim on the Stockholm-Helsinki route in November 1990, her near-identical sister following eighteen months later. While these ships were an immediate hit with passengers, some industry pundits argued that rather than being universal trendsetters they served only the needs of the niche Sweden-Finland market and would be less adaptable to routes demanding smaller ships.

Cruise lines, and indeed the cruise industry, tend not to admit to being attracted by ferry innovations as they regard their own aspirations to be somewhat loftier than those of short-sea operators. Yet the show lounge with terraced seating and a cascading row of windows introduced onboard Sessanlinjen's *Kronprinsessan Victoria* was adopted by Carnival Cruises in its 1981 *Tropicale* and in its three *holiday* class ships later in the 1980s. Royal Caribbean Lines also showed the influence of Silja's malls in the design of its Royal Promenade linear atrium plans for the Line's 'Voyager of the Seas' class ships. Almost fifteen years after the introduction of Silja's acclaimed sisters, the promenade concept was seen again in the design of Norwegian Color Line's 75,027-ton ferry the *Color Fantasy*, likewise built in Turku.

Silja rivals Viking Line were especially critical of the *Silja Serenade* and the *Silja Symphony*, feeling it was a mistake to turn the focus away from the natural beauty of the Stockholm and Åland archipelagos and putting it on the commercial milieu

of onboard malls. In 1989 Viking had already launched its own innovative 'ship of tomorrow' design project, codenamed *Futurella*. Rather than trying to upstage the 'wow' factor of the Silja malls, Viking chose to give its passengers an enhanced visual experience of the archipelagos from wrap-around bands of floor-to-ceiling windows completely surrounding two full decks. These gave panoramic close-up views from dining tables, cafés, lounges, deck lobbies and promenade spaces. On either side and around the stern, the windows were angled outwards beyond the ship's sides to give expanded panoramas of sea and sky. Furthermore, the entire superstructure, styled by Per Manfredsson, was characterised by sweeping curves. While the panorama is enjoyed at its best on summer passages when there is only a brief twilight between late evening sunset and early morning sunrise, the winter experience – completely in darkness – has its own fascination, with periodic glimpses of lighthouses and passing ships.

Viking Line's new flagship was designed as a larger and more sophisticated rendition of the *Athena* and the *Kalypso* – 25 metres longer, three metres wider and with an additional deck in the superstructure. Within these increased dimensions, the total passenger capacity was more than doubled from 1,742 in 573 rooms to 3,738 in 1,194 cabins and suites, including six de luxe suites with private saunas. Car capacity was, however, reduced from 620 to 400.

At the stern was the Ocean Club – a vast nightclub which claimed to be the longest ever shipboard bar, and at the time of her completion this ship probably also boasted the best conference and business facilities afloat. The only major inside public space was the 564-seat Theatre Moulin Rouge, presenting theatrical and musical shows as part of the mini-cruise experience. Most of the interiors were designed by Per Manfredsson.

Due to the 1990 insolvency of the Wärtsilä shipyards, the

The **Silja Europa** (1993) was the final Baltic ferry planned during the 1980s boom. She was ordered by Viking Line's Swedish partner, Rederi AB Slite, but due to financial problems she was delivered instead to the rival, Silja Line. *(Bruce Peter)*

new ferry – to be named the *Europa* – was built by Meyer Werft in Germany, delivery scheduled for early 1993 for service on the Stockholm-Helsinki route. But in the face of a deep recession in Sweden and much of western Europe, Viking Line's Swedish partner Rederi AB Slite, which ordered the ship, was also forced into bankruptcy despite the fact that its operations were profitable and assets valuable. Very quickly, the *Europa* was chartered instead to Silja Line and delivered as the *Silja Europa*. With the bankruptcy of Rederi AB Slite, Viking Line lost all of its Swedish-owned ferries and came under the sole control of the Eklund-owned SF Line, based in Mariehamn and sailing largely under the Finnish flag.

The *Silja Europa* and sister ships the *Silja Serenade* and the *Silja Symphony* ended the Silja-Viking Line spiral of competitive new building. At approximately 60,000-tons, and with capacity for more than 2,000 passengers, each set the ultimate economy-of-scale limits for vessels of this type.

The latter 1980s and early 1990s were the golden age of tax-free shopping ferry criuises. Unfortunately, however, safety concerns returned to haunt the industry only seven years after the *Herald of Free Enterprise*'s loss when, on the evening of 28th September 1994, the Baltic ferry *Estonia* (ex *Viking Sally*) foundered in a storm. Bound for Stockholm, she left Tallinn with 989 passengers and crew and encountered a severe gale in the Gulf of Finland. The vessel's port bow quarter took the full force of the waves which repeatedly battered the bow visor and strained the locking pins. It is believed that in the first few hours of the voyage, during which the ship was running at about 16 knots, the locking pins suffered metal fatigue and failed sequentially. Consequently, the visor came loose and began to move from side to side.

On the *Estonia* – and indeed on other Baltic ferries of the early 1980s – the watertight inner bow door, which doubled as a car loading ramp, protruded into a housing at the top of the visor. According to the official accident investigation, the failure of the locking pins and movement of the visor caused the bow ramp to lever open, slowly at first but faster with every wave. Not long after, the visor was ripped off and as it no longer enclosed the top of the ramp, the ramp was pulled open, leaving the ship at the mercy of the elements. The car deck began to flood with water and, as more waves prised the ramp further open, the ingress worsened.

Once the officers on the bridge became aware of their dire situation, they could do nothing other than send a frantic Mayday call for assistance. Only minutes later, other ferries in the vicinity picked up a final distress call from the Estonia's agitated and frightened Third Mate: "Really bad, it looks really bad here now." There was no further contact from the ship.

Both the *Mariella* and the *Silja Europa* raced to the *Estonia's* last known position – the *Mariella* arriving within twenty minutes – but it was too late. The *Estonia* had capsized, taking 851 passengers and crew with her. Passengers disembarking at Stockholm when the *Mariella* arrived some twelve hours late described how they had joined forces with the crew to search for survivors, taking up positions on the ship's deck and peering into the darkness for signs of life.

It was subsequently revealed that since 1974 there had been five instances of Baltic ferries' bow doors breaking open, although prior to the *Estonia* disaster there had been no previous fatalities on the Baltic routes. But in a wider context, ferries were viewed as worryingly disaster-prone. In each case where a total loss was due to flooding, the accident happened so quickly that the ship's life-saving equipment was of no use. The *Estonia* vanished in twelve minutes from the first Mayday call. The *Herald of Free Enterprise* capsized in 2 minutes 35 seconds.

Brittany Ferries' **Bretagne** brought Baltic-style cruise ferry standards to the Channel when introduced between Plymouth and Santander in 1989. *(Miles Cowsill)*

The *Estonia*'s loss brought about a significant decline in business for all Baltic ferry operators and, pending the imposition of new design and operational regulations to improve ferry safety, no further new vessels were ordered between the *Silja Europa* in 1993 and the *Romantika* in 2002. In the interim a great deal of research work was undertaken and pressure placed upon the maritime safety authorities to produce a new set of rules governing ferry safety.

Shortly after the *Estonia* disaster, the International Maritime Organisation (IMO) convened a panel of experts to develop new global safety rules for ro-ro ferries, and the European Union responded with its own initiative to develop new regulations for all vessels sailing to and from EU ports. However, for the seven countries around the Baltic and North Sea, this was not enough, especially as southern European nations such as Greece argued that ships sailing in Mediterranean waters should be exempted

due to the more temperate weather – a posture which proved to be misguided by the subsequent loss of the *Express Samina* off Paros in September 2000.

At a summit in Stockholm in 1996, an agreement to insist on additional stability rules for all ferries operating in the Baltic and North Sea regions was ratified. Labelled the 'Stockholm Agreement', it was later adopted by all seafaring EU countries. As a result, all existing ferries were individually assessed for damage survivability and, during the ensuing five years, each was retro-fitted with either external sponsons or flood control doors across the car decks. These alterations were intended to provide extra buoyancy or to prevent floodwater spreading and causing free surface effect. In addition, all ferries were fitted with a third inner watertight door behind the existing ramps and visors.

In the Baltic, where ferries have ice-breaking capabilities, the

The spacious arcade on the **Bretagne**, linking her main public rooms. *(Miles Cowsill)*

The **Bretagne**'s a la carte restaurant; throughout, her interior design is by the French firm AIA. *(Miles Cowsill)*

favoured solution was to fit flood control doors across the car decks and, at the stern, duck-tail sponsons to add extra buoyancy. Side-sponsons were favoured on ferries sailing from British ports, where there was no need to maintain an ice-breaking hull configuration at and below the waterline.

In addition to these physical alterations, much thought was given to improving crew training and operational systems, known as the International Safety Management Code or ISM. Since the *Estonia* tragedy, the ferry industry in northern Europe has been transformed for the better. Ferry companies have become much more professional and safety conscious, with crew emergency training and vessel maintenance now very high on the agenda.

IN THE WAKE OF THE BALTIC GIANTS

The great size and spectacular design of the 1980s Baltic ferries attracted worldwide attention, and ambitious Channel and Mediterranean operators sought to emulate the quality and comfort enjoyed by passengers travelling between Sweden and Finland.

On the Western Channel, Brittany Ferries (founded in 1973 by Breton farming interests to protect their agricultural exports to Britain) had grown exponentially to a point where, in 1986, the company ordered a new flagship for its Plymouth-Santander service to northern Spain, to be built by Chantiers de l'Atlantique at St Nazaire.

Named the *Bretagne*, the new 24,534-ton ferry was the largest and most impressive yet seen on the Western Channel. The vessel's design was a three-way joint effort among the owner, Finnish naval architects Deltamarin and French interior designers Architectes Ingéneurs Associes (AIA). Headed by Bernard Bidault, this firm was best known for hospital design but it took to ferry interior design with great enthusiasm and today is the leading French specialist in ship interiors.

As the new *Bretagne* was intended to operate primarily on the relatively lengthy Plymouth-Santander route across the Bay of Biscay, it was imperative that she had superior sea-keeping qualities and a great deal of testing was carried out on prototype models to achieve the optimum hull form. This had a slender entry and sweeping lines to just forward of amidships. Below the water, there was a ram-shaped bulb and the forepeak was built up, more in the manner of a traditional ocean liner than the rather bluff configurations favoured for the majority of large ferries at that time. (It is instructive to compare this solution with, say, the Baltic superferry *Mariella*). Four Wärtsilä diesels gave a 21-knot service speed, with a margin of extra power to make up for lost time in the event of adverse weather. The vehicle deck filled the width of the hull with a centre casing. Above, the passenger accommodation was spread over superstructure's uppermost three decks.

Cabins filled nearly all of Deck 7 and the forward part of Deck 8. With some extra cabins below the vehicle decks, no less than 2,056 passengers could be accommodated, 1,146 of whom were berthed. Facilities and attractions included self-service and à la carte restaurants, café, cocktail bar, shop and a show lounge. Throughout were murals by Alexander Goudie, a Scottish artist living in Brittany, and these were so appreciated by passengers that Goudie was asked to work on subsequent Brittany Ferries ships until his death in 2004. Sailing south to the sun, the *Bretagne* also featured expansive sun decks and a lido bar. In terms of aesthetics she was a highly distinctive ship both outboard and inboard. Strips of panoramic windows enhanced

SNCM's cruise ferry **Napoleon Bonaparte** enters Marseille harbour at the end of an overnight voyage from Bastia on Corsica. *(Bruce Peter)*

THE FERRY a drive through history

the bright and spacious atmosphere.

Shortly after the *Bretagne* entered service in 1988 to considerable acclaim, Brittany Ferries began work on two further new vessels – each highly innovative. The 20,133-ton *Barfleur* was to be a ro-pax vessel for the company's 'no frills' subsidiary Truckline, operating between Poole and Cherbourg. The 27,541-ton *Normandie* (a name evocative of both a region and the legendary French transatlantic liner) was to be a high-capacity jumbo ferry to serve the Portsmouth-Caen route. Both ships were ordered from Kvaerner Masa-Yards in Finland, following on from the completion there of the *Silja Serenade* and the *Silja Symphony*.

On the Portsmouth-Caen route, three single crossings are made in each 24-hour period – two fast sailings by day and a slower one at night. As a considerable amount of freight is carried, the *Normandie* needed to combine the qualities of three ships in one – an overnight cruise ferry, a daytime ferry and a ro-ro freighter.

The solution was to design a ship with two freight decks and cabins in the side-casings at the upper level, much as TT-Line's *Nils Holgersson* and *Peter Pan*. As with the *Bretagne*, three decks of superstructure were given over to passenger spaces, linked by the ship's most remarkable feature – a single continuous diagonal staircase, descending through a circular void between all three decks. Around this were the Purser's bureau, seating areas and various shops, creating a bustling open-plan heart. The general arrangement was otherwise similar to that of the *Bretagne*, albeit with more reclining-seat lounges and a large shop forward of the entrance hallway on the main deck.

With cabins to be made up for night crossings and a great deal of food and drink to cater for throughout the day, careful attention was paid to the design of the *Normandie*'s 'hidden' servicing, and Brittany Ferries again benefited from Kvaerner Masa's accumulated design expertise. The specification of a containerised system to load and unload catering and hotel supplies directly to the galley and linen stores enabled a very quick turnaround of the *Normandie* so that she could spend at least twenty of every twenty-four hours at sea.

MEDITTERANEAN CRUISE FERRIES

With spacious arcades and numerous large windows, the *Bretagne* and the *Normandie* reflect distinctly extrovert design, influenced by Viking Line's mid-1980s tonnage. Developing this approach further was a third French cruise ferry, SNCM's

La Superba of Grandi Navi Veloci arrives in Genoa at the end of a daytime crossing from Palermo in Sicily. *(Bruce Peter)*

44,307-ton *Napoléon Bonaparte*, delivered in 1996 by Chantiers de l'Atlantique for services from Marseille and Nice to Bastia (Corsica). Unusually, her public rooms were all located on the upper three superstructure decks, encased by expanses of glazing in a way resembling the topmost decks of Royal Caribbean's Chantiers de l'Atlantique-built cruise liners such as the *Sovereign of the Seas*. Above the bridge was an impressive double-level show lounge, aft of which a seven-deck atrium plunged down to the ship's reception and cabin areas. The restaurants were aft but – most importantly on a Mediterranean ferry – a large lido area was located amidships, sheltered by tinted glass screens. At the base of the twin funnels was a nightclub, placed in a large glazed pod, overhanging the ship's sides and in a style similar to the lounges of Royal Caribbean's cruise ship the *Viking Crown* and the nightclubs on the *Silja Serenade* and the *Silja Symphony*. In order to emulate the style of Baltic ferries, the French government-owned SNCM approached Robert Tillberg to carry out much of the interior design, in a manner similar to his recent projects for Viking Line and the Caribbean cruise industry, featuring numerous chandeliers and generous expanses of marble.

Unlike Brittany Ferries' ships, the *Napoléon Bonaparte* enjoys fairly relaxed turnarounds and, typically of Mediterranean ferries, has only single-level loading. Yet her vehicle deck, filling the entire width of the hull, has capacity for 708 cars. Nearly all of her 2,462 passengers are berthed in cabins, and travellers to Corsica get there in considerable comfort. Yet despite Tillberg's best efforts, the ambience of a state-owned ferry such as this is very different from commercial operations in northern Europe. The individual public rooms tend to have restricted opening times negotiated with the French maritime unions, whereas on Baltic ferries virtually the entire ship is open throughout the voyage to maximise revenue. Moreover, as Mediterranean passengers tend not to consume alcohol with anything like the abandon of northern Europeans, the mood onboard is usually very sedate.

Come the 1990s, Italy too began constructing large cruise ferries for western Mediterranean services. The leading

entrepreneur was the veteran shipowner Aldo Grimaldi, whose Grandi Traghetti freight ferry business was established in 1970, connecting the Italian mainland to Sicily and North African ports. His ferries the *Freccia Blu* and the *Freccia Rosso* had been lengthened and rebuilt with enlarged superstructures, each to carry over 1,000 passengers, but as demand remained strong Grimaldi decided to take drastic action. In 1992 he founded a new company called Grandi Navi Veloci ('Big Fast Ships') to operate a fleet of state-of-the-art cruise ferries. He wanted to emulate ferry design developments in northern Europe but also sought to bring a distinctly Italian cruise liner style to his country's domestic and international short-sea routes. His idea was to provide the best-appointed ships to transport cars and a substantial amount of freight together and at considerable speed. He ordered the initial ships for his new fleet from the Nuovi Cantieri Apuania di Marina di Carrara in early 1993 and 1994.

As with the *Norsea* and the *Norsun*, Grandi Navi Veloci's vessels were to be stern-loaders with two vehicle decks and further capacity in a lower hold. Yet more car lanes were provided below that. Above the vehicle decks were three decks of passenger accommodation, designed by leading Italian ship interior specialists Studio DeJorio of Genoa. Their approach involved the ostentatious use of large expanses of marble and large spaces for passengers to see and to be seen. Their main saloon decks, as those of Costa Line's cruise ships the *Costa Allegra* and the *Costa Marina*, were lofty and arranged largely in open plan, with terraced seating in places. Aft, under a retractable glazed roof, was a lido area with a pool and Jacuzzis.

Externally the new ships' chiselled Lamborghini-like styling was striking, making them instantly recognisable when seen passing by at speed. Appropriately, these initial Grandi Navi Veloci vessels were named the *Majestic* (32,746 tons) and the *Splendid* (38,109 tons, reflecting her longer midbody). Three more ferries followed – the 25,186-ton *Fantastic* (1996) and the 39,739-ton sisters *Excellent* (1998) and *Excelsior* (1999), both very similar to the *Splendid*. All five served on a network of routes centred on Genoa and Civitavecchia, to Palermo, Barcelona, Malta and Olbia (Sardinia).

Flushed with success, Grimaldi went on to order two more even larger cruise ferries, also from the Nuovi Cantieri Apuania di Marina di Carrara, for delivery in 2002 and 2003 – the 50,400-ton *La Superba* and *La Suprema*. Again, interior design was by Studio DeJorio, who conceived what must rank as two of the world's most glamorous, capacious and fastest ferries. Each accommodates up to 3,000 passengers (2,148 berthed in comfortable cabins) and 719 cars, and has a top speed of 28 knots. Moreover, their interiors are spectacular.

Passengers board via the stern and reach the main reception lobby via escalators and a broad corridor. The lobby resembles a very grand hotel, with vast expanses of white marble and a long, curved counter. This impressive styling continues in an open-plan piazza with seating, surrounded by a piano bar, photo-gallery and gift shops. An even grander atrium boasts curved staircases, glass lifts and walls clad in faceted mirrors. The main entertainment facilities include a very large terraced show lounge, an observation lounge, cinema, conference suite, cruise-style lido buffet and a top-deck circular nightclub with panoramic windows. This standard is mantained throughout and the ships are operated with considerable panache, typically sharing sailings from Genoa to Olbia and Palermo.

While Aldo Grimaldi's flamboyance in investing in seven cruise ferries within a decade certainly attracted attention, it became clear over time that vessels of this kind were far from ideal for the majority of Mediterranean routes. There was no demand for such extensive passenger facilities, and freight was the real year-round revenue earner – especially as the EU's expansion and further development of a single trade zone brought about a significant increase in lorry traffic.

To build such remarkable ships, Aldo Grimaldi had borrowed

One of the impressive internal atria onboard *La Suprema*. (Bruce Peter)

substantial sums and, although the Grandi Navi Veloci operation made significant profits (57 million euro in 2003), they were not enough to repay the 350-million euro debt. In 2004, in a bitter-sweet solution for the fiercely independent and pro-Italian Grimaldi, London-based investment fund Permira came to the rescue by buying 80% of Grandi Navi Veloci's shares.

In an enlarged and deregulated Europe, the future of ferry services on the majority of routes lay not with cruise ferries but with a different type of vessel – one with more freight capacity and fewer passenger facilities. 'Ro-pax' ferries had arrived.

The restaurant on *La Suprema*, designed by the Italian interior architects Studio De Jorio. (*Bruce Peter*)

THE FERRY a drive through history

One of the most impressive daytime ferries of the current generation, Color Line's **Superspeed I** was styled externally and within by Finn Falkum-Hansen. Here she is seen in rough weather off Hirtshals. *(Søren Lund Hviid)*

CHAPTER SEVEN

'Motorways of the Sea' and the Ro-Pax Ferry

As the European Union grew, its central axis politically, economically and culturally was a belt of relatively prosperous, densely-populated industrial areas stretching from England's West Midlands through to London, the Home Counties, the Benelux countries, northern France, Germany's Rhine and Ruhr valleys, Austria, Switzerland and northern Italy.

Known to planners as the 'golden melon' (or 'golden banana'), this belt became the subject of a long-term policy to shorten journey times to its key cities by investing in transport infrastructure. Hence France created the TGV network, and in Scandinavia new rail bridges and tunnels were built across the Great Belt, the Sound and the Fehmarn Belt.

For Greece, which joined the EU in 1981, the problem of getting closer to the heart of Europe could be best solved by enhancing the 'sea bridge' across the Adriatic. The route from Brindisi to Igoumenitsa and Patras was served well into the 1990s by ageing pioneer ferries the *Egnatia* and the *Appia*, supplemented by a motley but fascinating collection of second-hand tonnage. Although Greek shipowners were adept at converting and rebuilding old vessels, by the mid-1970s they had found Japan to be a valuable source of 'used' ferries.

These included the 11,880-ton *Ishakari* (1974) and *Daisetsu* (1975), built by the Naikai Zosen KK shipyard at Setoda. Each had two freight decks with passenger accommodation above. In 1990 and 1987 respectively, they were bought by Greek owners and became Minoan Lines' the *Erotokritos* and ANEK Lines' the *Lato.* Their 22-knot service speeds, provided by twin Mitsubishi-built MAN diesels, and their generous capacity of 1,550 lane metres for freight made them useful carriers of agricultural

The **Superfast Vi** and Minoan Lines' **Europa Palace** pass at speed off Ancona. *(Bruce Peter)*

exports from Crete, where their owners were headquartered, and across the Adriatic from Greece to Italy. These vessels, and numerous similar examples bought from Japan, provided the basic design formula for the first of a new generation of purpose-built Greek-owned ferries for both the Adriatic routes and the domestic Piraeus-Crete link.

During the 1990s, the ending of the Cold War and subsequent collapse of Communist regimes in the former Warsaw Pact countries, along with the disintegration of Yugoslavia, gave ferry services across the Adriatic a further

The **Superfast I** (right) and **Superfast III** lie at Patras during Easter 2000. *(Bruce Peter)*

Top: The *Superfast IX* leaves Rosyth for Zeebrugge during her brief tenure on the North sea route from Scotland to Belgium. *(Bruce Peter)*

Above left: *Superfast XII* passes the rocky coast of the Greek coast on her way from Patras to Igoumenitsa. *(Bruce Peter)*

Above right: Minoan Lines' Norwegian-built *Pasiphae Palace* approaches Igoumenitsa in June 2008. *(Bruce Peter)*

Right: The *Pasiphae Palace*'s a la carte restaurant, designed by Finn Falkum-Hansen. *(Bruce Peter)*

Blue Star Ferries' **Blue Star Ithaki** on her way from island to island in the Aegean in September 2009. *(Bruce Peter)*

boost. In the latter case, traditional overland routes through the Balkans were closed and lorries heading east had to cross by ferry from Italian ports to Igoumenitsa in Greece. Hence to provide extra capacity, Greek ferry companies acquired as much used tonnage as possible and numerous new operators appeared on the scene.

In 1989 respected Greek shipowner Pericles Panagopoulos, seeing the potential in Adriatic ferry services, sold his successful Royal Cruise Line and purchased shares in established Greek ferry company Strintzis Lines. in 1993 he deveoped a new ferry brand, Superfast, to operate fast 20-hour crossings on the 504-nautical-mile route between Ancona, on northern Italy's Adriatic coast, and the Greek mainland port of Patras.

Two ships were purpose-built for this service – the 23,663-ton *Superfast I* and *Superfast II*, constructed by Schichau Seebeckwerft in Bremerhaven, Germany. Their overall structure was based on the yard's earlier ro-ro freighters the *Nils Dacke* and the *Robin Hood* (TT-Line, 1988-89) and the *Pride of Burgundy* (P&O, 1993). The 25.5-knot service speed was achieved by four powerful Wärtsilä Sulzer 12-cylinder diesels, and the hull had a particularly fine-lined bow configuration above the waterline, the underwater form derived from that of the *Olau Hollandia* and *Olau Britannia* (1986-87).

Knud E. Hansen A/S, which had worked successfully for Royal Cruise Line, was appointed as consulting naval architects to help refine the general arrangement of the passenger accommodation and to give the ferries a unique external identity. A striking bright red and white Superfast livery was created which, along with a streamlined funnel design and the word 'Superfast' emblazoned on the hull topsides in a slick font, suggested speed and modernity and immediately set the new vessels apart from the majority of existing Greek-flag ferry tonnage. Panagopoulos himself assumed a highly active role in the design and building processes, delegating interior design to

Oslo-based architects Yran & Storbraaten.

The majority of the hull and superstructure volume on the Superfast vessels was given over to two vast freight decks with 1,850 lane metres, arranged around centre casings. Above were three passenger decks to accommodate everyone from budget-conscious backpackers to tourists and truck drivers.

In the warm Mediterranean climate, sleeping in a caravan or mobile home on the vehicle deck was an accepted way of travelling cheaply, and the Superfast design incorporated circular openings to allow fresh air to ventilte these spaces, with electric sockets and communal toilets and washing facilities provided adjacent.

Other more conventional passenger accommodation included airliner-type reclining seats, three-tier couchette-style upholstered berths (with sleeping bags or bedding available), and separate single-occupancy cabins for commercial drivers. All other cabins were outfitted to a very high standard. As the Superfast concept was all about speedy and comfortable travel, there were few entertainment facilities.

From the outset the Superfast operation was a great success and Panagopoulos ordered a further ten vessels (for delivery between 1995 and 2003), not only to expand his Adriatic operations but to introduce three north European routes. The 29,067-ton *Superfast III* and *IV* were built in Turku, Finland, by Kvaerner Masa to an improved design with a more sleek forward superstructure and interiors by Greek firm AMK Design (which was subsequently responsible for all Superfast newbuilds and numerous other Greek ferries and cruise ships). The *Superfast V* and *VI* came from Howaldtswerke Deutsche Werft in Kiel and had a higher service speed of 28 knots in order to include a stop at Igoumenitsa in north-west Greece within the established Ancona-to-Patras voyage time. The 30,285-ton *Superfast VII* to *Superfast X* were also built in Kiel.

Operations expanded into the Baltic, with new services to

Top: ANEK Lines' *Hellenic Spirit* arrives at Igoumenitsa in June 2008. *(Bruce Peter)*

Above left: The arcade on the *Hellenic Spirit*, linking the ferry's main public rooms. *(Bruce Peter)*

Above right: The *Hellenic Spirit*'s a la carte restaurant; as with Minoan Lines' Norwegian-built ferries, this is the work of Finn Falkum-Hansen. *(Bruce Peter)*

Right: The *Hellenic Spirit*'s forward-facing lounge. *(Bruce Peter)*

Minoan Lines' Italian-built **Olympia Palace** rests at Ancona between fast crossings of the Adriatic to Greece. *(Bruce Peter)*

the German port of Rostock from Södertälje in Sweden and Hanko in Finland. But as the Sweden route was a flop, the ferries were quickly redeployed to open a new route from Rosyth in Scotland to Zeebrugge in Belgium.

Two final vessels, the 30,902-ton *Superfast XI* and *XII*, were delivered in 2002 by Flender Werft's yard in Lübeck, again for the Ancona-Patras service, and replacing the original *Superfast I* and *II*.

Superfast was the first of several Greek ferry companies to invest heavily in new tonnage during the boom years of the 1990s, aided by willing Greek banks. Only two months after the *Superfast I* made her April 1995 maiden voyage, the Cretan ferry operator Minoan Lines introduced the first of its own ro-pax ferries on cross-Adriatic routes (from Venice and Ancona to Patras) and on the Aegean (from Piraeus to Heraklion on Crete). The 28,417-ton *Aretousa* was built at Bruce's Shipyard in Landskrona, Sweden, and outfitted near Trondheim in Norway by Fosen Mekaniske Verksted. The same yard built the 30,010-ton *Ikarus* and *Pasiphae* in 1997 and 1998. All followed a design formula similar to Superfast's vessels, albeit with arguably superior layouts of passenger accommodation. Externally and inboard, these vessels and three subsequent Fosen-built ro-paxes for other Mediterranean operators (Compagnie Tunisienne de Navigation's 32,298-ton *Carthage*, delivered in 1999 for services from Tunis to Marseille and Genoa, and ANEK Lines' 32,694-ton *Olympic Champion* and *Hellenic Spirit* for the Ancona-Igoumenitsa-Patras route) were characteristic of the external and interior design input of Norwegian architect Finn Falkum-Hansen.

Responsible for the interiors of Jahre Line's *Prinsesse Ragnhild* and *Kronprins Harald*, and SMZ's *Koningin Beatrix*, his designs for Mediterranean ro-pax ferries were notably striking, the *Carthage* and the ANEK sisters distinguished by curvaceous forward superstructures, parabola-shaped funnels and matching downward sweeps of the shelter screens surrounding their aft

sun-decks. Inboard, they were much more luxurious than the Superfasts, with expensive-looking finishes and large tinted circular windows.

As well as ordering in Norway, Minoan Lines commissioned Fincantieri in Italy to build a class of four additional ro-pax ferries – the 37,482-ton *Knossos Palace* and *Festos Palace* for the Piraeus-Heraklion route and the 36,825-ton *Olympia Palace* and *Europa Palace* for the Adriatic, where competition with Superfast and ANEK Lines was intense. With a service speed of 31 knots, the *Knossos Palace* and the *Festos Palace* cut the passage time over the 174 nautical miles between Heraklion and Piraeus from eleven to six hours. Measuring 214 metres long and 26.4 wide, these greyhounds of the Aegean and the Adriatic came close to the Finnjet's overall dimensions and length-to-beam ratio of 8.3:1. The Minoan ships had the added advantage of a top speed of 33 knots, achieved by four 16-cylinder Wärtsilä Sulzer diesels.

The *Olympia Palace* and the *Europa Palace* followed in 2001-02 for competition on the Ancona-Patras route, modifications including a full-length upper trailer deck with internal ramp access from below, and cabins replacing the large airline-style seating halls. The result was a 25% increase in trailer deck capacity and a 15% reduction in passenger capacity. Fincantieri subsequently used its Minoan Lines ro-pax design as a template for a new class of five ferries for the Italian state-owned Tirrenia di Navigazione – the *Bithia*, the *Janas*, the *Athara*, the *Sharden* and the *Nuraghes*, built at Castellammare di Stabia between 2001 and 2005.

Not satisfied with seven newbuilds in as many years, Minoan ordered three more ro-paxes from the Samsung shipyard in South Korea for delivery in 2001-02. The 26,995-ton *Oceanus*, *Prometheus* and *Ariadne* were however short-lived members of the fleet, all sold for a profit within four years.

A fourth Greek operator to build anew in the late 1990s was Strintzis Lines, which rebranded itself Blue Star Ferries, the

Top: CTN's Norwegian-built *Carthage* links Tunis with Marseille and Genoa. Here she is berthed in the italian port in July 2004. *(Bruce Peter)*

Above left: Tirrenia's *Sharden* approaches Olbia, Sardinia's main ferry port, in June 2010. *(Bruce Peter)*

Above right: Blue Star Ferries' *Blue Star 1* leaves Rosyth during her brief spell operating as a Superfast vessel to Zeebrugge in the summer of 2007. *(Bruce Peter)*

Right: Hellenic Seaways' *Nissos Chios* gathers speed as she leaves Piraeus in July 2009. *(Bruce Peter)*

The *Star*'s relatively sophisticated gourmet restaurant, designed by the Finnish interior design firm Aprocos. *(Bruce Peter)*

In contrast, the pub on the *Star* has a slightly more folksy atmosphere better to appeal to a diverse clientele. *(Bruce Peter)*

identity applied to its two new ro-pax vessels – the 29,415-ton *Blue Star I* and *II* for the Ancona-Brindisi-Patras route – built in the Netherlands by van der Giessen-de Noord. It simultaneously introduced the much smaller 10,193-ton *Blue Star Ithaki* (built by Daewoo in South Korea) on domestic Aegean routes from Piraeus and Rafina to Santorini.

Two other new domestic ferries, the *Blue Star Paros* and the *Blue Star Naxos*, followed in 2002 for the longer Piraeus-Paros-Naxos-Santorini-Ios-Amargos service and were modified to provide more overnight berths. Two further ships in the series were locally sourced from the Hellenic Shipyards at Skaramanga, but building delays saw them purchased instead by Hellenic Seaways and completed in 2005 as the *Nissos Mykonos* and the *Nissos Chios*. Together, these five vessels helped to transform the Greek domestic ferry scene, and their 27-knot service speed effectively 'shrank' the Aegean, bringing the furthest islands to within a half-day's sailing time from Piraeus.

NEW-GENERATION DAY FERRIES

In northern Europe, the EU's single market was having similarly positive effects on hitherto less prosperous member states, most notably Ireland. Investment in new ferry tonnage on the principal Irish Sea routes saw Irish Ferries become a major player, thanks firstly to a pair of new ro-pax vessels built by van der Giessen-de Noord for the Dublin-Holyhead route – the 22,365-ton, 21-knot *Isle of Innisfree* (1995) and the 34,031-ton *Isle of Inishmore* (1997). These were followed by the far more impressive 50,938-ton *Ulysses*, built by Aker Finnyards at Rauma in Finland and, when delivered in February 2001, was the world's largest ferry in terms of hull and superstructure volume. The majority of internal space was dedicated to over four kilometres of car and freight lanes. Nonetheless, Irish Ferries' flagship was an impressive-looking and reliable ship, the hull form optimised to cope with the often turbulent Irish Sea and the superstructure very distinctive in appearance.

On the Dover Strait, SeaFrance (formerly SNCF) ordered a new vessel – the 33,796-ton *Seafrance Rodin* – from Aker Finnyards for delivery towards the end of 2001. The design of the passenger accommodation was influenced by SNCM's Mediterranean overnight ferry the *Napoléon Bonaparte* and featured a similar starboard arcade with double-level expanses of floor-to-ceiling windows. SeaFrance then ordered a near sister, the *Seafrance Berlioz*, built by Chantiers de l'Atlantique at

The bright green Tallink high-speed ro-pax ferry *Star* offers two-hour crossings between Helsinki and Tallinn. *(Bruce Peter)*

Seafrance Rodin leaves Calais on another routine crossing of the Dover Strait. *(Miles Cowsill)*

Saint Nazaire and completed in 2005. These and the *Ulysses* influenced the design of a new fast ro-pax for rapidly-expanding Baltic operator Tallink, which intended to offer two-hour crossings from Tallinn, the Estonian capital, to Helsinki. The 36,250-ton *Star* was delivered in 2007 and is powered by four Caterpillar MaK diesels, easily maintaining the two-hour schedule, although there are 90-minute turnarounds at each end because neither port yet has double-deck loading ramps. So both freight decks must be loaded and unloaded via single sets of bow and stern doors, achieved by large internal ramps which can be hoisted between the upper and lower vehicle decks.

But the *Star*'s most outstanding feature is her passenger accommodation, styled by Finnish interior designers Aprocos. Although essentially a day ferry, she has 520 berths in well-appointed cabins.

The *Star*'s rival between Helsinki and Tallinn is Viking Line's 2008-built 35,778-ton *Viking XPRS* – the first passenger ship with a name chosen because it is easily sent by text message. One of the most pleasingly proportioned ferries of her generation, she lies overnight at Tallin, acting as a floating hotel for Finnish passengers taking mini-cruises there.

Apart from the Swedish and Finnish markets (to which strict regulation of liquor sales ashore apply), the lure of the booze cruise has declined markedly during the past decade. Factors additional to the EU's ending of tax-free sales include the

Viking XPRS, Viking Line's newest vessel, links Helsinki and Tallinn. Careful design and ingenious timetabling allow her to fulfill both transport and minicruise roles. As with Tallink's **Star**, her external design is notably successful. *(Viking Line)*

Rederi AB Gotland's Chinese-built ro-pax ferries *Gotland* and *Visby* rest in Visby in 2003. *(Richard Seville)*

widespread banning of smoking in public places and more general demographic trends towards healthier and more refined lifestyles. Furthermore, the rapid growth of budget airlines has given leisure travellers opportunities to take weekend breaks in any number of European cities.

Even on the ferry routes across the Skagerrak between Denmark and Norway, which is not an EU member, there has been need for change. Norway's largest ferry operator, Color Line, has recently replaced almost all of its entire fleet with impressive new upmarket tonnage built by Aker Finnyards. Color Line has rationalised its network with two new fast and dynamic-looking ro-pax day vessels – the *Superspeed 1* and the *Superspeed 2* – sailing from Hirtshals to Kristiansand and Larvik respectively. Long and sleek 34,231-ton vessels, each is capable of taking large numbers of freight units as well as cars galore during holiday peaks and has a speed of 27 knots. Onboard facilities include dining areas, lounges and shops. With crossing times reduced by up to a third, there is no longer any need for overnight cabins (except a small number for lorry drivers). Instead there are substantial lounges with reclining seats. Both vessels have been outstanding successes, giving the ferry industry in Norway and Denmark a new sense of glamour and modernity lacking in recent years.

There has been similar success on the Dover Strait, where Norfolkline's 'D' class ferries the 35,923-ton *Maersk Dunkerque*, *Maersk Delft* and *Maersk Dover*, delivered in 2005-06 for service between Dover and Dunkerque, have attracted very large numbers of passengers. To offer a relatively luxurious travel experience in comparison with the expanding budget airlines, Norfolkline commissioned Copenhagen architect Steen Friis Hansen to design interiors reflecting the best of modern Danish hospitality design. Truck drivers and passengers alike enjoy high-quality facilities, including a massage room, an Executive Lounge with leather Arne Jacobsen 'Egg' chairs and, throughout, contemporary artworks integrated into the decor. Private cars are parked in a separate garage from lorries. These Norfolkline 'D' class were constructed by Samsung in South Korea – the country of choice for several other significant

Her topsides adorned with Warner Bros' cartoon characters, the *Moby Aki* heads from Olbia to Piombino. *(Bruce Peter)*

Top: The *Maersk Dunkerque* immediately after completion; her light blue livery looked attractive, but was difficult to maintain in Dover strait service. *(Norfolkline)*

Above left: Norfolkline's Korean-built 'D'-class are another notable short-sea ferry design success. This is the *Maersk Dunkerque*'s side lounge, designed by Steen Friis Hansen. *(Norfolkline)*

Above right: The *Superspeed I*'s central atrium space features modern abstract sculptures beneath and backlit blue ceiling. *(Bruce Peter)*

Right: The Bluefins Bar on the *Superspeed I*, giving commanding views over the stern. *(Bruce Peter)*

Seen here leaving Ibiza, Balearia's **SF Alhucemas** is one of a large series of similar ferries built by Astilleros Barreras for Spanish and other owners. *(Bruce Peter)*

One of Balearia's larger Astilleros Barreros-built ferries, **Martin-I-Soler,** arrives in Barcelona from Mallorca in April 2011. *(Bruce Peter)*

newbuilds, including the 36,093-ton *Moby Wonder* and *Moby Freedom* (2001) for Italy's Moby Lines and Stena Line's 43,487-ton *Stena Britannica* and *Stena Adventurer* (2003). The Moby sisters were notable for their combination of ro-pax and cruise ferry design characteristics, a solution that works successfully on the short routes between Italy, Sardinia and Corsica.

Extreme examples of bargain south-east Asian shipbuilding were Rederi AB Gotland's two 28,600-ton ro-pax ferries – the 2003 *Gotland* and the *Visby* – from the Guangzhou Shipyard in China, each costing less than a third of the price of similar ships built in northern Europe. Designed by Knud E. Hansen A/S, these bargain-price state-of-the-art ferries have a speed of 28.5 knots and capacity for 1,500 passengers and 500 cars.

SERIES PRODUCTION

Another way to achieve a lower unit cost is through the series production of a standardised design, as in the case of two large batches of freight-orienatated ro-pax ferries built by Cantieri Navali Visentini at Porto Viro and the Nuovi Cantieri Apuania at Marina di Carrara, the latter ordered by Aldo Grimaldi for charter or sale to other operators. With good turns of speed, substantial deadweight capacities, superior sea-keeping

qualities and reasonable fuel economy, these efficient vessels provide a mediocre travel experience compared with their more expensive predecessors, yet reliably plough back and forth across the North Sea, the Irish Sea and the Mediterranean, efficiently moving lorries and trailers (and some passengers) in considerable numbers. Even Superfast has sold most of its fuel-guzzling 1990s fleet, replacing it with vessels of this type.

Currently, the most up-to-date ferry fleets in Europe belong to Armas (for Canary Islands operation), Balearia (for services in the Balearics) and Transmanche Ferries (for the Channel route between Newhaven and Dieppe). The Armas ships *Volcan de Tamasite*, *Volcan de Timanfaya*, *Volcan de Taburiente*, *Volcan de Tamadaba* and *Volcan de Tijarafe* were followed by the Transmanche Ferries *Cote d'Albatre* and *Seven Sisters*, and Balearia have taken delivery of the *Martin-I-Soler*, *Passio per Formentera*, *SF Alhucemas* and *Abel Matutes*.

THE LATEST GENERATION

Other than building more cheaply, another way to achieve efficiency is by building bigger. Thus the very latest ro-pax vessels are similar in size to the largest cruise ferries of the 1990s. Grimaldi Ferries' 53,360-ton *Cruise Roma* and *Cruise*

Irish Ferries' Finnish-built **Ulysses** makes a bold and futuristic impression, thanks to careful styling by the Danish architect Klaus Horn. *(Miles Cowsill)*

Grimaldi Lines' *Cruise Roma* arrives in Barcelona. She is one of four sisters, two linking Civitavecciha and Barcelona and two others for Minoan Lines' Patras-Ancona service. *(Mike Louagie)*

Barcelona, delivered in 2008-9 to serve the 444-nautical-mile route between Civitavecchia and Barcelona, are primarily carriers of large volumes of freight between two points under the EU's Marco Polo incentive programme to shift road traffic from Europe's highway system to other modes of transport, including rail and sea – but both ferries also include passenger decks and amenities.

While the *Cruise Roma* and the *Cruise Barcelona* were under construction, Grimaldi Ferries acquired a majority stake in Minoan Lines, to which two further sisters were allocated for cross-Adriatic service – the *Cruise Europa* and the *Cruise Olympia*. This gave Grimaldi a ferry network stretching from Finland in the north to Greece in the east, making it a truly pan-

European company. Each of its flagship quartet has over three kilometres of freight lane space – plus room for over 2,100 passengers – yet these freight capacities are moderate in comparison with Stena Line's latest ro-pax ferries, the 63,039-ton *Stena Hollandica* and *Stena Britannica* (delivered in 2010 for the Harwich-Hook of Holland route) which individually can accommodate five-and-a-half linear kilometres of trucks and trailers on four vehicle deck levels, as well as 1,200 passengers.

Whereas Stena's business model is based on achieving substantial economies of scale with bigger ships, in Norwegian domestic traffic the focus has been on developing ferries with environmentally-friendly engines. Hence the use of LNG (liquified natural gas) – a more expensive and volatile fuel but one with far

Brittany Ferries *Pont-Aven* is one of the best-appointed ferries currently in service. Serving northern Spain, she is notable for her spacious teak sun decks and lido. *(Miles Cowsill)*

Top: One of numerous standard ro-pax ferries built by Vinsentini in Italy, the ***Scottish Viking*** was operated briefly by Norfolkline between Rosyth and Zeebrugge. *(Bruce Peter)*

Above: Another successful Italian-built ro-pax design was produced by Nuovi Canterie Apuania for Grimaldi Lines and Superfast. This example is the ***Superfast II***. *(Bruce Peter)*

Right: Grimaldi Ferries' Vinsentini-built ro-pax ***Sorrento*** leaves Tunis in July 2010. *(Bruce Peter)*

A state-of-the-art Dover Strait ferry: P&O's new Finnish-built **Spirit of Britain** is the largest vessel ever to link Britain and France. *(FotoFlite)*

less environmental impact. Fjord 1's prototype LNG ferry was the *Gultra*, built by Aker and introduced successfully in 2000. When the Norwegian government offered other routes to tender, LNG was also specified and further new ferries were built – some by Aker and others by Remontowa in Gdansk, Poland. Now there are nine LNG-powered vessels operating on Norway's western seaboard – though vessels of this type have yet to be ordered for international routes.

As history has demonstrated, the ferry industry has invariably responded positively to new requirements and market conditions, and tomorrow's ferries will be different again from those we see today. Even so, the present era probably counts as a golden age for ferries – and certainly for those interested in ferry design development. While a significant number of vintage ferries, dating from the 1960s-80s period, are still in service, many spectacular new vessels have been built in recent years. Among the most impressive examples of the latter are Brittany Ferries' 39,300-ton cruise ferry the *Pont-Aven*, and Color Line's Finnish-built giants the *Color Fantasy* and the *Color Magic*, delivered in 2004 and 2007 for the Oslo-Kiel route.

Ferry crossings may be short – but on the latest ships, they are very often memorable. No one can deny that since the pioneering *Leviathan* of 1850, ferry design has come a long, long way.

The first of two giant ro-pax ferries for Stena Line's Harwich-Hook of Holland route, the **Stena Hollandica**, is seen approaching Harwich during her inaugural season. *(Miles Cowsill)*

Top: The *Color Magic*, the second of two giant cruise ferries for Color Line's Oslo-Kiel route, in Oslo harbour in January 2010; in terms of size and passenger facilities, these vessels are the ultimate ferries. *(Bruce Peter)*

Above left: The *Color Magic*'s gourmet restaurant faces aft towards the ship's wake. *(Bruce Peter)*

Above right: The internal promenade links most of the *Color Magic*'s main public rooms. *(Bruce Peter)*

Right: The *Color Magic* passes the beach at Laboe at the entrance to the Kiel Fjord in September 2010. *(Bruce Peter)*

Smyril Line's **Norröna** arrives at Esbjerg from the Faroe Islands and Iceland in October 2010. Of especially robust design, this vessel is built to cope with the worst Atlantic storms. *(Bruce Peter)*